THE
ETHICAL
IMPERATIVE

Foreword by **DEBORAH POLLACK-MILGATE**
THE PARITY PODCAST

ANDREW C.M. COOPER

THE
ETHICAL
IMPERATIVE

LEADING *with* CONSCIENCE
TO SHAPE THE FUTURE OF BUSINESS

WILEY

Published by John Wiley & Sons, Inc., Hoboken, New Jersey.
Published simultaneously in Canada.

For general information on our other products and services or for technical support, please contact our Customer Care Department within the United States at (800) 762-2974, outside the United States at (317) 572-3993 or fax (317) 572-4002.

Wiley also publishes its books in a variety of electronic formats. Some content that appears in print may not be available in electronic formats. For more information about Wiley products, visit our web site at www.wiley.com.

Library of Congress Cataloging-in-Publication Data is Available:

Names: Cooper, Andrew C. M., author.
Title: The ethical imperative : leading with conscience to shape the future of business / Andrew C.M. Cooper.
Description: Hoboken, New Jersey : Wiley, [2024] | Includes bibliographical references and index.
Identifiers: LCCN 2024020704 (print) | LCCN 2024020705 (ebook) | ISBN 9781394274833 (hardback) | ISBN 9781394274857 (adobe pdf) | ISBN 9781394274840 (epub)
Subjects: LCSH: Business ethics. | Social responsibility of business. Leadership.
Classification: LCC HF5387 .C6666 2024 (print) | LCC HF5387 (ebook) | DDC 174/.4–dc23/eng/20240601
LC record available at https://lccn.loc.gov/2024020704
LC ebook record available at https://lccn.loc.gov/2024020705

Cover Design: Wiley
Cover Image: © steheap/Adobe Stock
Author Photo: Courtesy of the Author

SKY10078067_062424

To my mother, Beatrice Devean Cooper. You are my guiding light and the embodiment of leadership in its purest form.

And to the late Dinisa Folmar and Wilhelmina Nesbitt. Never forgotten.

Contents

Foreword

It is fitting that *The Ethical Imperative* begins by describing a conflagration, a burning house in which a family member dies. The burning house was a predictable consequence of years of neglect. One might say we find ourselves today in the moment just before the house catches fire. If we do not act at once, there will be demise. The conflagration is predictable. One might argue convincingly that portions of our house are already smoldering.

Yet Andy Cooper comes from a place of hope. While this hope may be naïve, my urgent wish is that it is not. We only know one thing for certain: the need for hope is profound. Andy's *Ethical Imperative* cannot guarantee success, but we know without the strategic vision he offers, we are stuck biding our time. Living in the moment, we are hopeful only that the next disaster—COVID, wildfires, gun violence—at least leaves our immediate family and friends unharmed. The instability and constant worry encourage us to retreat to our corners and hoard our resources for ourselves.

A corporation may choose to do the same, and lawfully so. We are stuck urging, but not compelling a company to care about community interests. Andy notes that a corporation's relentless pursuit of profits at the expense of the greater good may result in it collapsing in on itself. I couldn't agree more. The wish to avoid collapse may be what we need.

Thankfully, Andy also understands nuance. While Bernie Sanders rails on about "corporate greed," Andy knows that the picture is more complex. Corporations do not have one essence, and they are, importantly, made up of human beings. Andy reminds us of the enormous treasures that are today's companies, and he knows that chastising companies into submission isn't productive.

Andy's approach is pragmatic, especially in the context of these United States. We may wish to solve our problems at the government level—one would have hoped that better building codes would have saved his cousin—and yet our anti-government strain runs deep and gets in the way of our ability to solve problems quickly. It is fitting that Andy would look to an entrepreneurial, corporate-led effort. It is not clear companies will take up this challenge, but we have seen increasing efforts.

Andy offers a path for those who are ready to act. The strength in his approach is its focus on both the corporate institution and the human beings that make up the institution. *Growing relational assets* is groundbreaking in its recognition that relational growth must be nurtured throughout the corporate institution and its lifecycle. The path does not end at promotion. *Human capital investment* is necessary to maximize corporate value. Employees are invested in their companies when they are themselves valued and challenged to grow and contribute according to their unique talents. Importantly, nurturing relationships and freeing up employees to contribute to the institution does not overlook *Strengthening on a program*, which ensures that feedback is routine and built into all levels of the organization. *Corporate dynamism* may be Andy's most significant contribution yet because "malleability" in a world where the challenges appear different every day is critical.

Lastly, as an IP attorney myself, I hold in my heart a special affinity for *Brand Integrity*. To me, a company's identity as an organization must permeate at every level within, to stream outward to consumers. It's the glue of the organization that keeps everyone moving toward a common goal. The *Ethical Imperative* is well-advised to be cognizant of the power of this glue.

I have known Andy for more than a few years now, and know him to be engaged, thoughtful, hopeful, forward-looking, and never at rest. I share his confidence in Gen X, Millennials, and Gen Z. Thank you, Andy, for giving us a much-needed framework just when we need it.

—Deborah Pollack-Milgate
The Parity Podcast

". . . America has lost the moral vision she may have had, and I'm afraid that even as we integrate, we are walking into a place that does not understand that this nation needs to be deeply concerned with the plight of the poor and disenfranchised . . . I fear I am integrating my people into a burning house."

— Martin Luther King Jr., *a conversation with Harry Belafonte*

Introduction:
The Conflagration

The structure, they say, went up like a match. It had been grandfathered through generations of building codes, and on February 9, 2021, at 4:30 a.m., it became a mushroom cloud above the small neighborhood of Sandhill in Walterboro, South Carolina. The smoke coming from the 100 block of Ann Court could be seen for miles.[1]

Its occupant was nowhere to be found.

The Colleton County fire department later discovered that my cousin Meme was inside. Her government name was Wilhelmina Young Nesbitt.[2] Meme had naturally long and silken black hair that hung low down her back. Her piercing hazel eyes were deep and inviting, and her cheekbones were raised and proud such that she appeared to be smiling even when she was not. But from what I can remember, she was almost always sad.

At only 53 years old, Meme became the first fire fatality of the year in the small town of Walterboro—population 5,400. Perhaps it was failing infrastructure. They say the roof of the home, an ugly umber color that stood out from its neighbors, had already collapsed in the rear of the building before the firefighters arrived. Or, perhaps, it was something else.

Officially, the death was an accident, but the truth is that Meme died from a maelstrom of failures. The community she grew up in, my community, offered few opportunities for her. Few jobs with health benefits, poor mental health services, and a virtually nonexistent state social safety net that created a void that nearby relatives could not fill.

1

When I was a boy, Meme came to church dressed from head to toe in black. In our small, Free Will Baptist Church, her attire was somewhat unusual for a "regular" service. There, in my grandfather's church, she veiled herself, walked to the pulpit, and kneeled in front of the congregation while chanting gibberish just as Pastor Gregory Clayton (also my cousin) reached a crescendo in his preaching. My father, Reverend A. L. Cooper, who then went by his initials to avoid confusion with me, sat on the rostrum with other clergy offering a searing gaze of concern.

Pastor Clayton stopped cold in the middle of his sermon. I can't remember the topic, but I was about nine years old then, and probably wasn't listening anyway. What subsequently ensued was over an hour of direct, corporate prayer and "laying of hands" for Meme—the entire church together. One minister suggested we "cast out the demon within her." I can remember thinking, even at a young age, that the thing Meme actually needed in addition to prayer was serious mental health intervention, the kind that was not available in Walterboro.

The episode, and Meme's untimely demise, is emblematic of systemic failure. She came from a poor community. Local services were inadequate and even her home buckled under the neglect of resources. She and I were both products of the same, undervalued social construct. We were America's working poor and therefore unseen. But, as Michael Caine's character says in the movie *The Dark Knight Rises*, "Sometimes the pit sends something back." Unlike Meme, I made it out. And, three decades later it occurred to me that, in the panoply of preventable deaths, I have a real opportunity to save people like Meme.

Since the day I left my family's single-wide trailer on Viola Court, I could not stop thinking about my reasons for leaving. All that I loved was in Walterboro, but all that I needed was not. So, I left for Washington DC; then to Atlanta, Georgia; then to Kansas City, Missouri; and on to Louisville, Kentucky—each place yielding a credential and a host of life lessons. But Walterboro was never far from my thoughts. At 32, I became the youngest general counsel of an American airline, and subsequently a senior lawyer for the world's largest social media company. Each turn focused my heart on the important role corporations can, and do, play in our daily lives.

In 2018, when I joined the corporate leadership team of United Parcel Service Airlines, I had no clue that pandemic, social unrest, and even political turmoil would be immense challenges to navigate during my tenure. But there, in the thick Kentucky bluegrass—through lockdowns, social anxiety stoked by the killing of Breonna Taylor, and political unrest emanating from Washington DC—I cut my teeth on leadership. First, I had no employees to supervise, then

I had three, then eight, then 30, and then I joined a leadership team of 20,000. And each day I saw a little bit of Wilhelmina in each of my employees. Some worked mightily to make ends meet, others to get an education or health coverage, and still others to secure a promotion to buy a modest home and achieve the proverbial American dream. Each relied on the possibility borne out of work, and it was my job to lead *for* them.

America's Millennial generation, my generation, are often maligned as entitled and whiny, but in 2020 we became the largest generation in the U.S. workforce, and I believe we have an urgent message for America's corporate leaders. The message is clear to me because I have been on the messaging apps, received the direct messages on social media, and engaged on a consistent basis with my contemporaries, many of whom are inclined to burn down the edifice of America's free enterprise system as swiftly as Meme's house. If we want to preserve the very best of American enterprise, then corporate America must become better, and soon.

There is no shortage of critics who would prefer to see the enormous wealth of private firms diminished. To be sure, they point to valid examples of greed and excess. But they overlook the enormous social good and social mobility enabled by enterprise. I have a front-row seat to the good companies *can* do, if only they will. For example, during the 2019–2021 COVID-19 pandemic, I worked with thousands of UPS workers around the globe to deliver over 1 billion vaccines during the unprecedented global health crisis.[3] It was a feat no government could accomplish alone. More catastrophes like COVID are on the horizon as climate change, natural habitat destruction, and ecological disasters present challenges that only large and competent organizations will have the capacity to solve.

On July 19, 2022, the United Kingdom recorded a temperature of 40.3°C (104.5°F). At the time, it was the highest ever recorded temperature in UK history.[4] But it was foretold. Five years earlier, the International Monetary Fund urgently reported that domestic policies alone cannot fully insulate countries from the consequences of climate change. "Higher temperatures," the IMF stated, "will push the biophysical limits of ecosystems, potentially triggering more frequent natural disasters, fueling migration pressures and conflict risk."[5] Today, western governments appear impotent, and the "hope and change" of the fleeting Obama years have lost their luster, leaving young people to turn to extreme economic ideas. This is the environment in which I assumed corporate leadership, and the need to level up could not be clearer.

Millennials, like me, have come of age in a conflagration of crises—not unlike Meme. In this environment, profits and positive earnings raise more questions about how results were achieved, rather than the results themselves.

Organizations that navigate what authors William Strauss and Neil Howe call the next generational "turning" will either have a thriving business or go up in flames like 100 Ann Court. It is an existential challenge, and the solutions require a new breed of leader willing to look *inside* the besieged homes of consumers to see, as Jack Swigert famously said on the *Apollo 13* mission, "Houston we have a problem." Today, we need corporate leaders to make decisions with greater appreciation of impact, and I need you to be one of them—a conscientious leader who appreciates the human element in a total cost equation.

When I was younger, my father and I were on a long drive together. We were leaving our home in coastal South Carolina, to a town in the interior; one of those places where there was only one church and a gas station. We would often get into philosophical debates on the road.

My dad was a cynic. He contended that young people would end up just like the generations before them. Millennials, in his view, would not change much about the world. Of course, I couldn't let that go. An acolyte of Gene Roddenberry's work (the maker of *Star Trek*), I was programmed from a young age to be hopeful.

I responded with visceral anger that Millennials would change all of the things that were wrong with the world: racism, hate, inequality. My dad just smiled at me and shook his head disapprovingly. "You'll see," he said. "You'll be just like all the other generations before you. Just keep living."

Time will tell who is right—my dad or me. Or, perhaps, neither of us is right. A split decision is a possible outcome as well. Still, the weight of this question hangs over the entirety of society as we approach a generational junction. The direction we turn will have major implications for America's corporations and free enterprise as we know it.

In the American economy, the start of the twenty-first century can be characterized as a time of rising inequality, where those living in the Walterboros of the world struggle to maintain their financial footing. Social mobility is giving way to a permanent underclass. Corporate leaders seemingly abandon any pretense of responsibility to society in favor of shareholder value at any cost. This has led to a series of corporate scandals and an accelerating decline in public trust. Change is urgently needed, but it will only come about if corporate leaders are willing to, as Millennials say, level up.

The remainder of the twenty-first century will be critical for the future of capitalism in America as generational divides widen over the appropriate role of corporations in society, and government's oversight of them. It remains to be seen whether corporate leaders are up to the challenge.

Something must change but this much is clear: the answer does not lie in abandoning our free enterprise system, but rather improving it so that all members of society have an opportunity to benefit. This will require corporate leaders to listen to the concerns of younger generations and implement solutions that help our businesses improve in the face of rapid generational and social change. If you want your business to thrive through this tumultuous period of change, then this book is for you. The preservation of capitalism depends on mitigating the outcomes that have left small towns and rural communities reeling from underinvestment, lack of education, and poor job opportunities. This whirlwind of issues seeds many untenable social outcomes like isolation, resentment, and depression that have huge implications for domestic tranquility, health, labor movements, and population growth.

This book continues a 20-year conversation with my father. It is also written for those, like him, who I've met in corporate leadership through the years and who understandably have genuine skepticism about the imminent and fundamental change upon our society, and the dangers that it could pose if we do not respond appropriately to the challenges. Like Meme, there were breadcrumbs along the path of life that signaled a need for help, but few listened, and the result was tragic.

So, I have two objectives for this book. First, to influence new generations to view business as a transformative force for positive change rather than an immovable obstruction to progress. And, second, to influence business leaders to think conscientiously about a corporation's role in local communities and our broader society.

The book is divided into three parts. The first part, Chapters 1–3, explores the conditions fueling a sociological fire spreading across American society, and the urgent need for corporate leaders to respond. Part II, Chapters 4–9, outlines who the conscientious executive is, and what qualities will be needed to address the challenges detailed in Part I. Finally, Part III, Chapters 10–15, discusses five crucial moves for a leader to level up, and how to strengthen the qualities enumerated in Part II for effectively responding to the urgency of the moment described in Part I.

The hostility felt by those shut out of the American dream is like faulty electrical wiring inside an old wooden house. But the house need not be demolished. Capitalism need not be supplanted wholesale. Free markets need not be subsumed by planned economies. With proper care and attention, investment and compromise, even old things can be made anew. This book explores ways to rewire outdated and perilous corporate behaviors and how we may reinvigorate the moral leadership that the future demands of its leaders.

PART I

The Burning House

"The world we know is gone. But keeping our humanity? That's a choice."

— Dale, *The Walking Dead*, Season 2, Episode 11

1 | Forgotten Towns

A forgotten town—that's how I describe the South Carolina hamlet where I was born. It's so small I usually say Walterboro is a stone's throw from Charleston rather than pinpoint its location. Even so, it used to be a more vibrant setting in the countryside. When I drive east from my home in Atlanta, Georgia, I pass through forests, farmland, and tiny towns before reaching the outskirts of Walterboro. Then the scenery starts to deteriorate as I journey past a funeral home, an abandoned gas station, Interstate 95, a Walmart Supercenter, and many fast food restaurants to get downtown. When I finally cross the old railroad tracks, I see shuttered mills sitting in the empty industrial park, a constant reminder that all the good jobs disappeared decades ago.

It wasn't always that way, of course. No town is founded in hopes that one day it will fall into a state of decay and disrepair. Originally known as Walterborough, my hometown sprang up in 1783 as a summer retreat for White farmers trying to put considerable distance between themselves and the threat of malaria that was racing through the countryside unchecked. Like most of the American South, it became better known once a county courthouse was constructed in 1820, a landmark that stands to this very day in Colleton County. The local courthouse still attracts the occasional visitor to town, most recently because of the trial of disgraced attorney Alex Murdaugh, convicted in March 2023 of murdering his wife and son. Netflix made a docuseries about the Murdaugh murders. But the three-part limited series only mentioned the town in passing; alas, that's the kind of place it is.

When the Civil War ended and emancipation came to the South, the Black community built its own traditions and establishments in Walterboro. I was

born in one of those predominantly black communities at what was then a
regional hospital (now essentially a limited-service clinic).

Workers moved to Walterboro when a railroad brought industry to the town.
My grandfather Harvell was one of them. He and my grandmother Viola gained
title to a small patch of unwanted land next to the railroad and built a wood-framed
house that would later anchor the neighborhood called Sandhill, a reference to the
unpaved sand and dirt easements peppering the hilly area. There they raised six
children, including my mother, Beatrice, who attended the same schools during
integration that I would later attend some 30 years later. Harvell built a church on
a small plot and gave the church the land as an offering, and he then divided the rest
amongst his children—each of whom would have two to four children of their
own. My mother, Harvell's middle daughter, placed a single-wide trailer on her
parcel in front of Harvell's house, and that is where I came to know life, in the shad-
ows of a church steeple and my grandmother's front porch.

Walterboro's most notable addition to the twentieth century was the air-
strip built in the 1930s that made the town home to the Walterboro Army
Airfield, one of a vast network of army air training facilities during World War II.

Even the big city feel came to Walterboro for a time when Interstate 95 was
built through the town in the 1960s, making it a resting place for those living
on the East Coast in big cities like New York, Philadelphia, and Washington
DC headed to Florida and back up again.

To be sure, Walterboro is not forgotten by those of us who love the people
and the place. But for corporate America, my hometown offers few incentives
for investment beyond fast food for interstate travelers. To really thrive, in most
cases you must leave—and so I did. I aspired to have more.

Many towns like Walterboro dot the landscape of the Deep South: Yemas-
see, St. George, Cottageville, Smoaks, Ehrhardt—towns seemingly forgotten.
But for a poor boy like me, growing up between the Spanish moss and sweet-
gum trees of the low country, the existence of these places was both an inconvenient truth and an invaluable reality.

The railways that ran through town in the early 1900s served the corporate
interests of Rockland Bleach and Dye Works, as well as other construction,
lumber, and turpentine businesses. Because these industries needed manual
laborers, working class folks of all races were able to find some work in Walterboro for a time. Grandpa Harvell spent some time dipping turpentine, which
ultimately helped him buy a few acres of land near the railroad. It wasn't the
best land. The harsh sand and poor earth made better sandbags than turnips.
And the presence of pollution from nearby factories made the surrounding area
prime real estate for dumping waste of all kinds.

In addition, the existence of the railway meant the ever-present potential of disaster—a fact that became all too real for the people of East Palestine, Ohio, on February 3, 2023, which saw one of the worst train derailment disasters in U.S. history. East Palestine, population 4,700, is another Walterboro. A place so often forgotten and frequently home to the poorest Americans. But, despite the risk of disaster, the exploitative use of the area by corporate interests, and marginally good earth, it was still home. It was what we could afford to call home.

In many ways, an early alignment of corporate interests was integral to my family story. The capital from the rail industry led to a meaningful opportunity for a poor family to acquire a homestead, though by the time I was born in the 1980s, Rockland and subsequent businesses had faltered, their discarded industrial complexes and mills arrayed the main arteries of Walterboro like dinosaur bones jutting from the sand.

My cousins and I would run up and down the now long-abandoned rails, playing and laughing as we tried not to fall. But as an adult, I saw them as a testament to how the capital project's failure had sapped Walterboro's economic development, making it even more improbable for White and Black families alike to climb out of poverty.

As a corporate lawyer who has worked in and for some of the world's largest companies and law firms, I am captivated by the coexisting life and death of Walterboro's economy, having seen this story repeated in towns and cities across the nation. Corporate success fosters a mosaic of prosperity across the towns it touches, while its failure leaves a concomitant trail of dying communities. Walterboro is an exemplar of this unbroken story that plays on repeat across the decades of American history.

In some ways, the Walterboro railroad could be analogized to the Tennessee Gas Pipeline, a massive project that started in 1943. The project was a set of natural gas pipelines that ran through Texas, Louisiana, Arkansas, Mississippi, Alabama, Tennessee, Kentucky, Ohio, and Pennsylvania, and all the way to New England, New York, New Jersey, and even West Virginia.

The biggest sections of the pipeline couldn't go through the big cities because they had too much sewage and subway infrastructure below ground. So, the backwoods towns played host to these massive industrial efforts. For brief periods of time, those little boroughs became boomtowns full of men needing places to live, food to eat, clothes, entertainment, company, everything that a small traveling army requires. Depending on the work conditions and the weather, sometimes workers would stay for six weeks, other times for half a year, but the boom always ended, and they moved on to the next staging point, leaving behind the people who had come to know prosperity for just a short while before it was snatched back from their grasp.

The breakdown between mighty corporate interests and regular folks who can barely be seen from corporate towers is a painful disparity to witness from both sides of the playing field. The clearer my view became of life when peering through a corporate lens, the more I felt like my own version of what sociologist Arlie Russell Hochschild would call a stranger in a strange land. Was this the same America I was brought up in? Like many corporate leaders who hail from America's rural communities, I sense a cognitive dissonance; there is a constant tension between making quantitative decisions against those decisions' qualitative impact on real people. The notions of loyalty, of homecoming, of giving back to the town that raised you, the idea that "it takes a village"—they all seemed to vanish into thin air the farther I moved away from the place I called home. It irked me at first, then it began to fester as my scope of responsibility grew. And I wasn't alone in my discontent: my generational peers took to the streets in protest in 2020 and began to target not only social injustice, but the American free enterprise system as an organizing principle.

Despite my degree in economics, I would never consider myself an economist like Joseph Stiglitz, Thomas Piketty, or Michael Hudson. They have written extensively on free-market economies and ways to make them work for everyone. I approach the topic, however, like Wilhelmina Nesbitt, as an observer and a subject of the system constructed for me. But, also, as a daily participant in a small part of the economic machine. With each passing day it becomes clearer—pressing even—that we embrace a new business model to win the future.

Increasingly common, widespread economic hardship and substantial inequality presage the demise of our current version of free enterprise. Like the burning of a house, it is a gradual process marked by several warning signs— precursor embers if you will. Capitalism has been a lynchpin of western economics for centuries, but its stability is by no means assured. The forces of political unrest, deep inequality, and economic collapse might be the harbingers of capitalism's undoing—small fires that may grow until everything is engulfed in flames. It may start with indicators such as decelerating financial mobility for young people and widespread scarcity among those living near the poverty line forcing abhorrent choices between food and medicine; while power is consolidated in tiny, insular groups of people and elite institutions. This process could even culminate in an outright rejection of today's economic orthodoxy—a revolt against the status quo fueled by disillusionment—and an embrace of alternative economics like central planning, which professes to redistribute wealth more fairly.

The first sign of a burning house is usually smoke. In terms of the worldwide economic system, the smoke is manifested in increasingly frequent financial crises and recessions. For example, between March 10, 2023, and May 1, 2023, a mere 52 days, the U.S. financial system experienced two seismic bank failures. First, Silicon Valley Bank failed after a bank run, marking the third-largest failure of a financial institution in U.S. history, and certainly the largest since the 2007–2008 financial crisis. Then, First Republic Bank was shuttered by the California Department of Financial Protection and Innovation, and subsequently the Federal Deposit Insurance Corporation was appointed receiver. True, the economy has always experienced cycles of growth and decline, but in recent decades these cycles have steadily become more intense and frequent. Millennials, particularly, have experienced three recessions by the time we entered adulthood. We were often graduating, finding a job, and attempting to raise a family through economic hardship and uncertainty. Ours is a generation defined by instability at almost every critical life moment. Consider this: roughly 30% of all economic recessions in the last 70 years have occurred during our generation.

In contrast, there have been roughly 11 recessions since 1948, each impacting generations at different developmental stages. For example, the 2008 financial crisis, dubbed the Great Recession, occurred around the time Millennials were graduating high school or college. While the recession was hard on the 401(k) retirement portfolios of Generation X, who at the time were around 35, it was devastating for Millennials who were attempting to enter their first employment market. To many young people, these frequent sputters of the free market were an indicator of capitalism's fragile edifice.

The Great Recession sent shockwaves around the world as governments from all countries scrambled to address the economic catastrophe. Jobs for the working class evaporated, and faith in markets plummeted. Some governments surprisingly stepped up to the challenge with forward-thinking regulations and a little economic stimulus, which provided stability, until the 2020 pandemic. To be sure, there were calamities like the European debt crisis beginning in 2009, the Chinese stock market crash in 2015, Brexit between 2016–2020, and the U.S. trade war with China in 2018. Had effective political will and leadership prevailed, these challenges could have been overcome.

As proverbial flames grow around this metaphorical house, ordinary people begin to feel the heat. Those without means will inevitably face difficulties due to widespread poverty and inequality in a society characterized by a yawning gap between the rich and poor. Labor markets stand to cause some of the most substantial problems as labor exploitation, unemployment, underemployment, low wages, and limited access to health care and education create a cascading problem for working people.

Eventually, the house catches fire. The smoke and heat now betray the existence of a raging inferno. The danger becomes easy to spot and manifests as a declining faith in institutions. This sobering tumult of disillusionment escalates into an explosive uproar for reform seen best expressed by public protests, insurrections, general strikes, and demands for change that seriously threaten social stability.

As the house fire reaches its climax, so too does the pressure for systemic change. For some, this could lead to a shift away from free enterprise toward various systems designed to enact crushing regulation and predictable outcomes as people seek more equitable and resource-efficient ways to organize society. In making this transformation, alternative economic models would undoubtedly arise. These systems could range from new modalities of ownership to novel democratic governance styles—empowered by advances in technology such as artificial intelligence—and further efforts to incentivize sustainable production practices. There is no guarantee that any of these changes will resolve the immense challenges that we face, but they may be seen as the only pathway to put out the fire and improve people's lives.

Prolonged economic distress is a perilous situation as it pushes society away from what exists into the arms of something more desperate. We may soon embark upon a voyage into the unknown if we allow this economic fire to rage on unchecked.

Shadows of Dutch Tulip Bulbs

If you were into computer games in the 2000s like I was, then you undoubtedly knew about The Sims. This incredibly successful game series has a wonderful backstory. A game designer named Will Wright struck inspiration for the game in 1991 when his home was destroyed by a terrible string of fires that struck Oakland, California. The fires claimed 25 lives and destroyed approximately 3,000 homes. When a dwelling is destroyed, the owner must replace everything that made the house a home, and Wright envisioned all that as a game experience. While The Sims is now a part of our collective cultural lexicon, Wright had a hard time selling the fact that the game was just a simulation of people experiencing real life. Wright was turned down a few times before Electronic Arts took a gamble on him and released the first game in 2000. By making the game like real life, casual gamers, and particularly female gamers, were attracted in numbers never seen before in the industry.

I spent hours in The Sims where my character could live in a mansion and go from one economic success to another. Back then I was far less certain about the course my life would take, thus gaming was a great escape. Inadvertently, the game enshrined the concept of leveling up in my mind. In gaming, "leveling up" is the process for gaining experience, skills, and abilities, or better tools to progress to more difficult challenges or to access previously unreachable places.

Who would have thought that a now ancient games series would reflect so remarkably on today's real-world corporate life? A career in the trenches of any major corporation is not unlike an avatar grinding out a daily task in a virtual world with the hopes of one day unlocking the ability to hire and fire other avatars! Seriously, though, today's corporate decision-makers also need to level up because yesterday's standard business paradigm is now obsolete.

Our behaviors have been exposed, for good and bad, by the vast means of information sharing now easily accessible from our cell phones. Corporate decisions that lack regard for the potentially exploitative nature of business operations, and its impacts on communities, are now a rallying cry for an entire generation of consumers. While some organizations are making great strides toward aligning their business models with community needs, too many are still using old strategies in a rapidly changing world.

META is gamer-speak for Most Effective Tactic Available. The term was first coined by military strategists, but it can be applied to any situation where the goal is to achieve the maximum possible effect with the limited resources available. In its simplest form, "meta" means using whatever works best, regardless of whether it is conventional or not. For example, in business, a meta approach might involve investing in a start-up that is using cutting-edge technology to enter or disrupt an established market. Crucially, meta practices are not about slavishly following established rules or doing things the way they have always been done. Instead, they are about finding the most effective way to achieve a goal, even if that means breaking the mold.

Today, I see corporate leaders forgetting that a meta approach is supposed to be agnostic of convention. For example, for decades a meta network planning strategy often involved bypassing small markets and towns in lieu of big cities, further reinforcing historical disparities between resource-rich metropolises, and often starved small towns looking for access to amenities and opportunities. That old approach succeeded in routinely pitting local populations against each other within the same state or region. Slowly, political disagreements emerged between rural and urban population centers. This phenomenon explains why towns in the Atlanta metropolitan area where I live (like Roswell and Tucker), are so fundamentally different socially and economically than the town of Brunswick, where Ahmaud Arbery was murdered, and even Waycross, Georgia, the nearby town where my dad was born. Slavishly following a conventional meta in an updated game is a surefire way to lose. In business, it can reinforce undesirable results in broader society, results that fester and radicalize future consumers.

But why should I care about little towns where people dream to leave? Because a conscientious executive—that is a decision-maker committed to doing what's right—calculates value in view of social cost as well as economic costs. This will be discussed later in more detail but doing what is right is as simple as considering all known variables and outcomes with special attention to human impact. The result is a more durable business to navigate tomorrow's sociological fire.

Most of America's Walterboros are in the Midwest or South. There are several reasons why everyone should care about these little forgotten towns. First, they are a vital part of America's history and heritage. Second, they represent an important part of the country's economic diversity. Third, they offer a unique and valuable perspective on the American experience. And fourth, they engender a strong sense of community that is sometimes lacking in metropolises, and in the aggregate, have outsized influence on the narrative shaping the view of corporations. This translates into political power in a republican form of government. These overlooked places shape public policy with their electoral influence and thus their inclusion in corporate investment is good business.

Consider the development of blockchain and the resulting problem-solving industry driving its expansion, also known as "mining." While the internet endlessly debates whether cryptocurrency is an economic evolution or a passing fad that may be the twenty-first-century version of the Dutch tulip bulb market, crypto mining has become something far more serious of a topic in recent years to central banks. Our free-market system, and the lack of regulation, has given rise to companies purely focused on the creation of cryptocurrency.

Today, crypto mining requires large amounts of computer processing power as users take part in what amounts to a virtual race to solve a math problem first. The winner of said race gets to add the transactions taking place to the blockchain and is rewarded with cryptocurrency of their own. If this was a game being played by 50 people around the world, nobody would care much, which was the case in Bitcoin's nascent days of the late 2000s and early 2010s. But the race to win the right to alter the blockchain and get that episodically valuable cryptocurrency has become a global phenomenon. There are more than

100,000 computer groups all over the planet trying to win the race and solve the problem first. That means every time it starts, there are going to be about 100,000 losers who have revved up those processors for absolutely zero net gain. Still, the bigger problem is the staggering amount of electricity being used to power the great race.

Immense fossil fuel energy is often required to mine cryptocurrencies and makes their minting impractical when accounting for the environmental impact. According to the Center for Global Development, the mining of a single Bitcoin consumes as much energy as 18 American adults do in an entire year.[1] Not exactly a realistic place to invest your money when you already fall well short of the poverty line. Thus, the very nature of that potentially lucrative venture not only creates environmental challenges, but also keeps digital currency in the hands of the already well-to-do. What's more, investors can now take stakes in crypto mining ventures. These ventures added corporate leadership teams to the race, and they want to be the biggest and the fastest to win the prize. In this environment, being conscientious about environmental impact could wind up feeling like entering LeMans in a push-pedal eco-car while everyone else has 440 hp engines in their Ferraris.

When you're trying to stretch your weekly paycheck and whatever benefits a modest wage might afford, the last thing on your mind is getting on the internet to charge up a $500 electric bill chasing something you can't see, smell, or hold in the palm of your hand. For sure, some in the crypto community are trying to develop solutions that use less energy, but accessing digital currency remains elusive for people in forgotten places.

Whether or not the crypto boom continues, its early implementations were a resource drain and skewed heavily in favor of an unrepresentative population sample of early adopters. This led to initial skepticism by those left behind by the trend and is an example of a "negative externality." Negative externalities are the mostly unintended, yet harmful impacts caused by commercial actions. They often fuel political disagreements because there are always two groups: one party interested in the activity and positively engaged as a beneficiary, and another negatively impacted and wholly disengaged or adjacent to the foregoing.

In a perfect world, no corporate leader wants to deal with politics. But in the real world, neither the conservative market philosophy of nonregulation nor the liberal vision of strong government control wholly answers the question of how to create sustained growth and prosperity without horrendous externalities in general, and specifically within America's forgotten towns.

Today's executives are hyper-focused on profit rather than on value. I recall an old boss who was fond of saying, "I'm focused on issues that involve a B" (referring to "billions" in value to shareowners). But the old "META" that so many corporate decision-makers still cling to—and its negative externalities—impede that focus on value. In other words, social and political problems are distracting from our core mission to build values-oriented businesses. Both businesses and communities must level up together and mediate solutions between them or the gap will continue to widen, and things will become even more polarized than we already feel they are. In a worst-case scenario, the free enterprise system that enables the wealth of so many could be fundamentally replaced by younger generations who experience only the bad aspects of a market economy seemingly rigged against them.

Enter the conscientious executive.

Today's market corrections are driven as much by consumers expecting corporations to be outlets for change as by the market conditions themselves. We now operate in an emotive market—one still controlled by supply, demand, and price, but also by esoteric notions, like the environment, social justice, and other personal passions and evolving norms.

In 2016, Deloitte conducted a survey entitled "Capitalizing on the Shifting Consumer Food Value Equation," and found that half the consumers in the survey claimed they chose foods and beverages based on health and wellness, safety, social impact, and experience more than price, taste, and convenience. Deloitte concluded that "consumer-led disruptions represent an opportunity, even an imperative, for manufacturers and retailers to reset and reposition themselves with consumers and shoppers."[2]

One would think corporate decision-makers would take advantage of those new opportunities. But instead, the 25 biggest U.S. food and beverage manufacturers dismissed them as fads—and experienced disrupted sales. What a huge miss! Misalignment with a market of that magnitude makes it harder to grow and serve places like Walterboro, where the median income for a family sat at $32,549 in the 2020 Census and 30.1% of the population is below the poverty line.

As a capitalist, I am forced to acknowledge that this extreme stridency—that is, our refusal to endure short-term pain for long-term change—is causing the very foundation of our free-market structure to collapse on itself. The truth is that corporate leaders often resist investment and transformation even when change would serve long-term interests because of fears driven by quarterly earnings and Wall Street analysts.

The market does not self-regulate as well as it could because firms are increasingly unresponsive to the desires of consumers. Our communities, our societies—our environment—cannot survive the unsustainable and often detrimental nature of the old meta.

We must recognize that ramifications no longer take years but mere minutes—a 280-character post is enough. Time and effort are no longer excuses that we can hide behind like a shield. Consumers have the power at their fingertips to spread messages in a matter of seconds. We have seen social media induce change across the world, toppling dictatorships, and exposing corruption internationally. We've gone beyond the tipping point of only worrying about "getting ours" at the expense of the rest of society. We must align with our consumers, and in doing so, we must revitalize our forgotten towns.

We.

Must.

Level up.

2 | Forgotten People

My phone rang out with an unfamiliar alacrity. I knew something was amiss. I reached for the nightstand next to my bed on the thirty-second floor of the old Mandarin Oriental in Atlanta. The normally unremarkable ring tone sounded ominous. "Hello," I answered. "Bring your people back to the office," the voice on the other end demanded. It was my boss. A towering figure with an unmistakable radio–like voice, he was a good-natured man with whom I occasionally disagreed.

"I heard about your decision to let your team work from home, and I want you to reverse yourself," he said. I looked at my wife who could hear the deep and bellicose voice on the other end of the line. I began to argue with one of the best bosses I've ever worked for.

"Bring your people back to the office or you will no longer be on my staff," he instructed and then ended the call.

I've never been the guy to mindlessly follow orders, but my daughter Claudia had just been born and I needed a job. So, I began to ideate. What I needed was time; time for leaders in my centenarian organization to see what I saw, which was a fundamental shift in how the world would work in the face of the growing pandemic. I walked to a corner of the hotel room and sat down. The television was on a cable news channel, and it was coverage of a political rally. Scrolling along the chyron at the bottom of the screen read the words ". . . be conscientious." I hadn't a clue about the story it referenced. But the words jumped off the television screen and parked in my brain for hours.

My mind wandered to Lee, a young employee whose elderly mother recently moved in, and instantly made Lee a pandemic caregiver. Lee's mom was especially at-risk and needed to avoid exposure at all costs. Then I thought about Jon, a young man whose recent disability after a car accident made remote work the best option for his circumstances. He, too, would have to find a way back to the old meta. Then I thought about my cousin Wilhelmina—a specter who often materialized just when I needed to make a hard decision. She reminded me to think about those whose voices are not in the room. She represents the forgotten.

I see forgotten people everywhere. They are not ghosts but flesh and blood like you and me. They are often building porters, Walmart greeters, and grounds-keepers. They are like Ms. Carol, who would always stop by to "check on me" when I worked late as a young associate at the law firm.

Every morning, before the sun is up, they rise to face yet another long day. They do yeoman's work with essential skills. They clean or toil on assembly lines trapped in a seemingly endless cycle of work hours. To some, these forgotten people are invisible in plain sight. They carry a heavy burden of enduring exhaustion, financial stress, and difficult decisions. Every day is an uphill battle to make ends meet, often choosing between paying rent or feeding themselves and dependents.

The word "conscientious" comes from the Latin *conscientia*, which means awareness of right and wrong. The word was first used in English writing around the mid-1600s to describe someone who is guided by a strong sense of morality and a desire to do what is right. Psychologists today use the term "conscientiousness" to describe a personality trait that is characterized by a sense of responsibility, dependability, and a strong work ethic. People who score high on conscientiousness are often described as being organized, responsible, and reliable. A modern understanding of the word "conscientious" preserves some bits of the moral definition in its earlier Latin use. After all, having a strong sense of responsibility is impossible without an understanding of the duty owed to oneself or others, and a motivation to carry out that duty faithfully.

When I refer to conscientiousness throughout this book, I am generally referring to the word's classical Latin roots highlighting an awareness of right and wrong and its associated moral context, rather than the modern definition. Although, even within the modern definition there are trace amounts of moral obligation.

Conscientiousness is a well-studied concept in the sciences. In 1987, Paul Costa and Robert McCrae developed the Five Factor Model of Personality (FFM). The model comprises five major dimensions—openness, extraversion, agreeableness, neuroticism, and conscientiousness—that together make up an individual's distinct personality type. Unlike mental disorders defined in other classifications such as the oft cited *Diagnostic and Statistical Manual of Mental*

Disorders (Fifth Edition), conscientiousness is considered a "normal" trait by scientists. A normal trait is one that is considered within the typical range of human behavior and does not meet the criteria for a mental disorder. Conscientiousness has been shown to greatly impact behavior across different scenarios from everyday interactions to determining future success or failure. People who are high in conscientiousness tend to be reliable, efficient, and self-disciplined. They set goals for themselves and make plans to achieve them, and they can stick to those plans even when faced with obstacles or distractions. They tend to be ethical and show a high degree of integrity and honesty in their actions. Conscientious people are often respected and valued in their workplaces and communities.

Generally, it is considered the most potent noncognitive predictor of occupational performance. In a 2019 study by Dr. Michael Wilmot of the University of Toronto and Professor Denize Ones at the University of Minnesota, conscientiousness was remarkable among personality traits. The team quantitatively analyzed 92 meta-analyses reporting relations to 175 occupational variables. They found that, of the 1.1 million participants across nearly 2,500 studies, conscientiousness showed strong and "generalizable effects for performance across available occupations." They further note that "[c]onscientiousness is much more than being orderly and neat," rather it "reflects motivational tendencies—tendencies to set goals, work towards them, in a consistent, reliable manner;" and that "[o]rganizations would do well if they measure conscientiousness in hiring and talent management decisions."[1]

Whereas we inherit many traits from our parents biologically, the big five traits are believed to be a combination of nurture and nature. Michael Pluess, a professor of psychology at Queen Mary University of London, and Professor Robert Power of Oxford University took an interest in the overlap in genetic heritability between personality traits. Uncertain of what they would find, the researchers decided to use genome data on over 18,000 babies to estimate the unique and shared heritability of the Big Five personality traits to further understand personality overlap in twins. Regarding conscientiousness, the researchers noted that "conscientiousness is a trait defined by high levels of thoughtfulness, good impulse control, and goal-directed behaviors. Highly conscientious people tend to be organized and mindful of details. They plan ahead, think about how their behavior affects others, and are mindful of deadlines."[2] Hypothetically, they contemplated, twins may share a similar disposition if traits like conscientiousness are moored to genetics.

However, Power and Pluess discovered that conscientiousness, had "nonsignificant heritability results." In other words, conscientiousness is a uniquely personal trait not always genetically associated, but rather remarkably specific to each person. Accordingly, when building a team, organizations that use nepotism as a guideline, may find that certain qualities rarely transfer from generation to generation. Growing up, the young men in my neighborhood would often talk glowingly of the exploits and accomplishments of our elders and wonder why the eldest children of those same men failed to achieve similar greatness. It turns out that, sometimes, the apple *does* fall far from the tree.

We can draw a couple of conclusions regarding the importance of conscientiousness from these studies. First, high levels of conscientiousness drive us to achieve our objectives and cultivate a strong sense of responsibility for group goals. It also fosters a dedicated work ethic, unwavering commitment to organization, and exceptional job performance. Simultaneously, it helps us avoid harmful and disruptive conduct that can sidetrack our progress.

Second, pedigree provides no information about an individual's conscientiousness. Thus, large organizations will have teams with an array of traits (openness, extraversion, agreeableness, neuroticism, and conscientiousness) that combine to create a composite corporate identity.

There are personal benefits, too, for those who are highly conscientious. In an oft replicated study, Patrick Hill of the University of Illinois and a team of researchers published a paper on the connection between conscientiousness and longevity. In the 2013 paper, the researchers found that conscientious individuals tend to lead longer lives. Moreover, conscientiousness can be a predictor of career success.[3] A 2020 longitudinal study spanning 12 years published by Kevin Hoff of the University of Houston found that personality growth materially predicted career outcomes better than "adolescent trait levels and crystallized ability."[4] In all cases, the researchers found that conscientiousness, along with extroversion and emotional stability, had the strongest effects on career success. And conscientiousness specifically was strongly tied to career satisfaction.

Armed with this scientific understanding of conscientiousness, and after more than a decade of studying the inner workings of major corporations ethnographically, my thesis is simple. Any process, thought, experience, or emotion that *can* manifest at an individual level, *may* manifest at an organizational level given the right conditions. This means that corporations can perpetrate acts that are hateful and loving, experience stages of life like growth and death; demonstrate vindictiveness as well as generosity; be innovative and stagnate; sick and healthy; uncaring and conscientious. All these expressions result from the composite personality that emerges as a distinct corporate reputation and is driven by individuals within the organization. The conditions for these manifestations are a function of constantly changing variables like the age of the

workforce and leadership team, the training of the average worker, the experience of junior executives and directors, and the judgments made about where
to invest and who to promote. The logical conclusion is that when we hire,
promote, and retain conscientious leaders, companies act conscientiously—but
the opposite is also true.

The conscientious executive stands in contrast to the archetypal traditionalist executive. Throughout this book I will refer to the traditionalist as a corporate leader who exemplifies stereotypical traits such as timidity, resistance,
arrogance, dogmatism, inflexibility, tunnel vision, intolerance, outmoded
conduct, narrow mindedness, authoritarian tendencies, and loophole-
seeking behavior. For context, these characteristics follow the acronym
T.R.A.D.I.T.I.O.N.A.L. and roughly track the various negative attributes articulated by *Forbes* writer Meagan Casserly in her September 2010 article "Ten
Archetypes of a Terrible Boss."[5]

Traditional leaders often occupy positions of great power and influence.
But it's no secret that they can be timid in their actions and decision-making.
Whether it's a fear of upsetting the status quo or a lack of confidence in their
own abilities, traditional leaders frequently struggle to assert themselves in
politically difficult situations. They may resist change, often preferring the status
quo over any shifts in power or societal norms. This resistance can stem from a
desire to protect their own positions of authority, or from a fear of losing the
stability and predictability that traditional constructs provide. However, this
resistance can also be a hindrance to progress and innovation, missing opportunities to take full advantage of new technologies, ideas, and cultural practices
that could be a benefit over the long run.

Their actions and words may often come off as dismissive and arrogant,
leading to a lack of openness and trust. Particularly when ascending to leadership through selection rather than merit, their actions and words may often
come off as egotistical because of self-consciousness. They are often deeply
entrenched in their beliefs and ways of doing things, and they can cling dog-
matically to ritual and oppose change and progress. This can be frustrating for
those who are looking to break free from traditional ways of thinking and make
real change.

Long-serving leaders are often deeply rooted in their customs and beliefs.
I've worked for many chief executives, including some of whom worked for a
company for over 40 years before ascending to the top job. While this can be
seen as a strength in some cases, it can also be a weakness. In today's rapidly
changing world, inflexibility can lead to missed opportunities and an inability
to adapt to shifting circumstances. While they may have a deep understanding

of institutional traditions and values, they can also become overly focused on accomplishing narrow goals and objectives "in the way things have always been done" without considering the bigger picture today. This can lead to decisions that overlook broader contemporary social and economic factors.

Occasionally, a leader may ascend precisely because they paid homage to old institutional beliefs and practices. This can be a hindrance to corporate progress, particularly regarding issues such as gender and racial equality and LGBTQ+ rights. Past success can often be an albatross to leaders who look back on old victories as the present rapidly evolves. It is important to question and reevaluate traditional practices that may no longer serve us. This includes our perceptions of leadership and how it is manifested in our communities.

Traditionalists are not always bad. They are often known to be strong in their leadership style, often relying on respect, tradition, and hierarchical structures to maintain order. However, this type of leadership can also be seen as authoritarian, hindering innovation and progress. Traditional leaders often have a reputation for being shrewd when it comes to finding loopholes. These leaders can be cunning negotiators, able to navigate complex legal systems and work around obstacles that would stump others. Some may view their maneuvering as evidence of a lack of ethics, but others argue that it is simply a benefit of having a deep knowledge of an organization.

Despite these negative stereotypes, traditional executives are often referred to in glowing terms in some circles. In Hollywood lore, they are analogized to a shark or tiger. Indeed, two of the most watched television shows on air today are *Shark Tank* and *Hell's Kitchen*, each paying homage to the manifestly cutthroat nature of "the boss" persona and highlighting the aggressive and confrontational nature of business. Here, we will refer to the behaviors of traditionalist executives with the shorthand "Tiger": tenaciously inconsiderate, greedy, egotistical, and ruthless.

The Tiger manifests stereotypical behaviors like seeking personal success at all costs—even if it means sacrificing the well-being of others—like the board of Globodyne in Jim Carrey's side-splitting yet sobering movie *Fun with Dick and Jane*. For example, the Tiger may work long hours and expect their employees to do the same, without considering the impact on employee work-life balance. They may make decisions without seeking input from others or considering the impact on employees and stakeholders. For example, they may also implement cost-cutting measures that result in layoffs or reduced benefits without considering the impact on employee morale or well-being.

In contrast, the conscientious executive employs sober and measured thinking about the many repercussions from an action. Tim Cook, for example, was interviewed by CNBC during major tech layoffs in the opening months of 2023. When asked whether Apple would follow the likes of Microsoft, Alphabet, and Amazon in making dramatic cuts to human capital, Cook noted, "Apple doesn't have plans for big layoffs." Pausing for a moment Cook continued, "I view that as a last resort and, so, mass layoffs is not something that we're talking about at this moment."[6] To lower costs, and in full view of the personal pain that comes to families when job cuts are broad and deep, Cook demonstrates the conscientious path, opting for a measured approach to slow the rate of new hires instead of laying off existing staff. Apple's stock, in contrast to other companies, soared through a volatile period for Silicon Valley.

Traditionalists prioritize short-term profits over long-term sustainability or may ignore ethical considerations in pursuit of financial gain. For example, they may push for aggressive sales targets or cut corners on product quality to maximize profits, without regard for the impact on customers or employees. They may seek out attention and accolades while disregarding the contributions of others or taking credit for the work of their team. They may insist on leading all important meetings or making all final decisions without considering who made the slides and did the leg work. They prioritize their own success over the well-being of others or the organization. For example, they may engage in aggressive litigation, or use fear and intimidation to silence dissenting voices; and when the consequences arrive, they jump out of the plane with a golden parachute.

In contrast, the conscientious leader incorporates stakeholders in decisions and considers impacts that are often overlooked by the traditionalist. They seek to bridge good reasoning and sound judgment. Accordingly, the conscientious executive asks normative questions like *whether* a thing should be done despite an ability to do it; *whether* there are the social implications to a course of action; *how* contemplated actions align with core values; and considers if there are social risks to a proposal, including impacts on marginalized communities, workers' rights, and environmental sustainability.

Jonathan Haidt, author of *The Righteous Mind: Why Good People Are Divided by Politics and Religion* makes a compelling argument that reasoning and judgment are separate processes. Jonathan points out that "we do moral reasoning not to reconstruct the actual reasons why we ourselves came to a judgment. We reason to find the best possible reasons why somebody else ought to join us in our judgment."[7] In other words, we often think through decisions about a course of action, not to better understand our own decisions, but rather in search of the best arguments we can present so that others may join us in agreement. This is why your marketing team goes through bouts of idea retread; why your legal team continues to point out obstacles rather than paths forward; and why your sales team's conversion rate oscillates wildly. The "right" course of action is more often the consensus rather than the unilaterally designated solution. To level up, then, means bringing nuanced judgment and reasoning to bear, and building stakeholder consensus into that decision-making.

If being conscientious is a typical trait, then we can expect that data for employees in successful companies, like those in the Fortune 500, will show higher levels of thoughtfulness, integrity, and ethical behavior, right?

It does not.

The Edelman Trust Barometer (ETB) is an annual survey of public trust in institutions and organizations, including businesses. The methodology of the survey involves interviewing a representative sample of the general public in various countries around the world, including the United States. For businesses, the survey asks respondents about their trust in the leadership of companies, as well as the companies themselves. In 2020, the survey noted a trend that has generally continued every year since. It found that trust in businesses, as well as in other institutions, has been declining worldwide. In the United States, the survey found that only about 50% of respondents reported that they trust the leadership of companies to do what is right. This is a significant decrease from previous years and suggests that employees are becoming more skeptical of the intentions and actions of company leaders. CEOs, journalists, and government officials consistently rank among the least trustworthy leaders and a whopping 52% of respondents indicated that capitalism as an organizing principle does more harm than good.[8] We will refer to the Edelman barometer occasionally as it consistently produces clear and reliable data.

Conscientiousness, this supposedly normal human behavior, seems to break down at an organizational level. Perhaps it is a victim of expectations in corporate leaders? The idea of a "conscientious" executive in modern times is almost oxymoronic. But the tides are turning. With greater awareness of environmental sustainability and ethical considerations in business decisions, a conscientious executive is increasingly necessary; one who can balance sound economic strategy with qualities such as empathy for those affected by their choices. The challenge ahead lies in finding leaders who break from this old stereotype and approach decisions with putting people first.

★★★

The chyron vanished a second time as I surfaced from deep thought.

I pondered my hotel telephone call with my boss. He must be seeing the same data as me regarding COVID infections and death. To me, the data was clear.

But then it dawned on me that we each may be placing emphasis on different data. We were, after all, a data-driven company. Whereas I was focused on local infection rates, he was focused on employee no-shows, sick call outs, and building production. His data indicated that we had to get people back in the office and soon. Mine said that we needed to prioritize safety. Either way, we needed to find a way to be productive in this new environment. But all data has limitations. Erika James, dean of the Wharton School at the University of Pennsylvania, notably takes exception to the phrase "data-driven" because "it assumes that data alone points you in the right direction." Instead, James encourages her teams to "be 'data-informed'—using data as one decision-making factor alongside personal judgment, relationships, culture, etc."[9]

Together, my boss and I had to get on the same page regarding the data to move in the right direction.

I specifically pursued corporate law to avoid emotionally charged issues like death. I chose to service clients in the telecom and high-tech industries for more than a decade, resolving matters that at their most fundamental level relate to money. Meanwhile, I've watched my wife, Amy, work heart-wrenching family and medical malpractice cases that have kept her up at night, further validating my decision.

But the COVID-19 pandemic brought death to my doorstep.

Close friends died. Others reached out to me for advice and referrals on final arrangements and estate planning. Employees all over the world had to juggle quarantines with local and international legal implications. In one day, I handled urgent tasks like helping essential aviators navigate international quarantine laws, then discussed information sharing with the COO of a major hotel chain, and finally, assisted state and local governments with requests related to overwhelmed morgues and funeral homes.

Avoiding weighty issues became a fool's errand.

I was 31 years old, leading a big department of one of the largest cargo airlines in the world. Most folks don't think twice about how Mediterranean-sourced seafood winds up on the menu in a Utah grille, but from 2018–2021, it was my job to know. With nearly 300 aircraft servicing 800 destinations in more than 220 countries, UPS operates one of the safest and most efficient cargo operations in the world.

I never imagined guiding a team through a generation-defining challenge like a global pandemic, but there I was, locking horns with colleagues, wrestling over data, and analyzing employee safety options in the middle of a global health emergency. Like most executives, the opportunity was positioned to me as a stepping-stone for promotion to senior executive. The opportunity to make history at the company as a barrier-breaking first to lead the airline's combined legal, regulatory, and communications teams was also a bonus. So, I uprooted my pregnant wife in her third trimester from our home in metropolitan Atlanta and moved across the country to the decidedly less metropolitan Bluegrass state, Kentucky.

A deep and abiding sense of responsibility fell upon me in March 2020 when we finally had a name for the "mysterious" illness allegedly from the Far East. I was not only concerned for the safety of my teams, but also the 20,000 employees and their families in my business unit. I also couldn't stop thinking about my newborn daughter. Amid the airline industry's plea for government support and optimism for a COVID cure, leaders debated, evaluated, and occasionally disagreed as information from the Centers for Disease Control evolved.

The pandemic was a sociological inflection point, leaving an indelible mark on every aspect of life. Its reach transcended borders and impacted individuals regardless of background or privilege. For the first time in a century, we were all experiencing the same thing, at the same time, everywhere; and it exposed so many social problems. From December 30, 2019, to July 31, 2021, the World Health Organization reports that there were approximately 200 million cases of COVID infection and more than 4 million deaths. In the United States alone, there were over 34 million cases and more than 600,000 deaths during the same period. The pandemic also disrupted every aspect of daily life. It laid bare deep structural inequities in society, disproportionately affecting those on the margins: minority groups, seniors, and individuals living in economic hardship. It was also a dramatic demonstration of the vulnerability of health care systems as hospitals scrambled to cope with an avalanche of patients. Its impact resonated far beyond the realm of public health, with its repercussions felt across much of the economy. From job losses to business closures and financial insecurity, no segment was spared from challenges posed by lockdowns and travel restrictions. In the logistics industry, though, we experienced a boom as everyone began shipping more to socially distance themselves.

It wasn't all bad. As a society, we learned to rapidly develop new medicine and scale distribution networks worldwide. In aviation, we certainly learned to adapt networks to dynamic circumstances across national airspace. Moreover, we explored new potential for international collaboration between countries; people came together globally like never before despite physical limitations caused by social distancing measures. Communities came together to support one another particularly to alleviate food insecurity and, uniquely, Millennials gained an appreciation for the small things in life, such as spending time with loved ones, enjoying the outdoors, and simply being able to leave the house without fear. Crucially, Millennials learned to value life over work.

The corporate capacity to change became evident during the COVID pandemic. Most companies evolved to offer remote work and delivery options. Other institutions were not as resilient. In the United States, some politicians kept to old-world metas, ignoring the constant uptick in dying countrymen. I was particularly astounded when Dr. Deborah Birx said in a March 29, 2021, CNN interview that all but the first 100,000 deaths were "avoidable"[10]—a devastating example of how failing to adapt can have horrific consequences. The price of social division was high.

Searching for Light

Matlin and Stang, two researchers studying happiness and positivity in the 1970s, identified the "Psychology of Pollyannaism." This cognitive process selectively favors pleasant information over unpleasant information, leading us to remember positive memories more easily.[11] The term "Pollyanna" is often used to describe an excessively optimistic person who can make it difficult for others to express negative emotions. A decade later, psychologist William Dember and Larry Penwell conducted a study that showed depression scores were not significantly correlated with scores on "Pollyanna" measures, indicating our positivity bias is separate from mood disorders like depression.[12] Further research over the decades suggests there is a universal positivity bias across culture and language. And as we age, we tend to remember more positive than negative information due to cognitive decline or healthy cognitive processing. Generally, older adults are better at focusing on the positive attributes or consequences of their choices compared to younger people.

As the heavy cloud of COVID hung over everything I did—regardless of how difficult and emotionally charged my job was—I searched for the positive. Perhaps it was a bit of Pollyanna in me. I decided to celebrate inspiring examples of leadership through the pandemic with a series of posts on LinkedIn. I didn't expect much response, but soon my few hundred followers grew to 10,000, then 15,000, and then more than 40,000. Clearly, I had tapped into a burning desire for light while we were collectively in a dark place.

I was particularly drawn to the example of New Zealand Prime Minister Jacinda Ardern, an "almost" Millennial, born about five months prior to the 1981 starting point for that generation, who proved that some of the best leaders are born early or late in their generation cohort and are better able to communicate cross-generationally. In February 2020—before any other country took similar action and with zero COVID cases in New Zealand—Ardern limited foreign entry from known hotspots. Rather than apologize for what others called a drastic move, she later closed the borders completely and mandated quarantine for all returning "Kiwis."

Ardern's decisiveness addressed one of the greatest challenges to civil society in modern times. She was not only strong, but also *compassionate*—which is her trademark. She and her party were reelected in a landslide victory—a sign that after years of a take-no-prisoners approach in politics and business, most people found strength *with* compassion a welcomed change.

Being bold is never a bad thing if you have the conviction to stick to your guns and the steadfastness to go the distance. New Zealand's prime minister wasn't content to be part of the "wait and see" crowd so she took matters into her own hands and saved countless lives by refusing to be a passive observer in the fight against COVID-19.

It's hard to be the first to act, however. Recall when Will Smith slapped Chris Rock at the 2022 Academy Awards; the assembled Hollywood glitterati in attendance did absolutely nothing in the moment. (Although, many expressed outrage hours after the event once they had gotten the pulse of the situation from their agents and their Twitter accounts.) It's like no one wants to be the first to move, the first to take a stand. The same is true in business.

No one expects corporate leaders to be right all the time, but they do expect us to find a hill to stand on. Jacinda Ardern did that and the clarity of her leadership became a beacon of light for others to follow. I would have to follow her example. I was the first VP at the airline to instruct their teams to work from home during the pandemic.

The Upward Pressure of Stakeholders

The 2020 U.S. election was especially polarized—a situation made worse by corporate leaders' collective worry of governmental retribution if they criticized the winning party or its agenda. While nothing strikes fear into the C-Suite like being on the wrong side of a political election, this paralyzing atmosphere silenced corporate voices at a time when they were needed most. I felt the polarization palpably as each leadership decision triggered careful scrutiny and committees of review in virtually each organization I supported, from nonprofits to corporate boards.

Indecisiveness was the wrong answer; it almost always is. Business, as my instructors at McKinsey would say, is about making bold and strategic choices. As the social expectations of consumers increase, they want (and expect) corporations to take a conscientious—and dare I say moral—stand. The pandemic triggered a broad psychological reorientation that caused people to see things through a different lens—a more basic lens where right and wrong, good and bad, life and death became fundamental filters to sift information. When a business occupies a position counter to this new lens and the public good, consumers may choose to spend their money elsewhere. COVID-19 amplified this.

Corporate leaders playing by a twentieth-century meta often refer to this as being "canceled," but the pejorative term "cancel culture" is really nothing new; it has historical roots in all free-market systems. When England refused to abolish slavery in 1791, a sugar-industry boycott led to such a huge decline in sales that shops began advertising their sugar as processed by "free men" to gain back customers.

In the 1920s, famous auto industry pioneer Ford ran an anti-Semitic weekly newspaper. His company pressured car dealers across the country to buy multiple subscriptions to the paper and hand them out to customers in the stores, explaining why the newspaper's circulation topped 900,000 by 1926. Beginning on May 22, 1920, and lasting for several years after, the newspaper's front page ran a story with the headline "The International Jew: The World's Problem."

The outrage was immediate and angry. Ford fought back, wielding his wealth as a cudgel, and targeted prominent Jews. In response, Fox Film Corporation threatened to show newsreel footage of wrecked Ford vehicles before all its films. When car sales plummeted, Ford apologized and shut down the newspaper.

Despite political efforts to color cancel culture as anti-American, it is just a market-based response by consumers who are affected by negative externalities. They are making their voices heard using the tool of business: money. If we, as business leaders, don't heed their voices, those very consumers may force us to reverse course with their money. They will not only become politically active; they'll become radicalized to the point that they threaten not just our business but the *way* we conduct business. Gen X, Millennials, and Gen Z entrepreneurs are already laser-focused on supporting institutions that are a net positive for local communities, and they're prepared to gank old-meta business.

Adrian Wooldridge, a business columnist for Bloomberg noted that nearly 40% of young Americans prefer socialism to capitalism.[13] But there is hope. A study by Wake Forest University found that about 68% of younger Millennials agree that "competition is good" and "stimulates people to work hard and develop new ideas," while only 9% disagree. About 73% of younger Millennials agree with or are neutral about the idea that "people should be allowed to keep what they produce, even if there are others with greater needs."[14] In short, tomorrow's consumers may be less capitalistic, but they are no less entrepreneurial. They reject current notions of self-interest as motivating principles in lieu of considering the total impact of their economic decisions. They may even go so far as to actively boycott firms that they view as harmful. But they still believe in competition and keeping that which is hard earned. Thus, navigating tomorrow's consumers could be as simple as knowing what they care about and acting accordingly. This is the essence of capitalism: give the people what they ask for.

In short, we have arrived at a generational intersection with a small window of opportunity to course correct.

Traditionalists often address (or dismiss) cancel culture in three ways: (1) they openly refuse to align with community needs, hoping the issue will go away over time; (2) they miscalculate community needs, either in a faux show of effort or simply because they do not take time to fully understand the actual needs; or (3) they intentionally address only select issues (the easy ones) while ignoring others (the hard ones).

But those attitudes cannot stand in an era when social media has created such a close connection between consumers and companies. Customers, especially Millennials and Gen Z, understand the power of the dollar—with some even analogizing it to casting a ballot. The logic goes, when I decide to spend my dollar at a company aligned with my values, and when I boycott companies that don't share my values, my money impacts my community's future as much as voting in an actual election.

The Power of Corporate Money

Growing up working class taught me that corporate money translates into power, actual and perceived. My mother, after all, worked for Wachovia Bank, and gave us daily reminders that taking care of our money was important just like caring for our mind, body, and soul. My experience working for multiple Fortune 500 companies has confirmed that truth. With money, corporations gain access to key stakeholders in various power centers, from legislative to regulatory. Because great power comes with great responsibility, this disproportionate access yields an unequal responsibility to ensure that whatever policies are advanced by unequal access do not harm consumers. After all, the private sector employs more than 80% of America's over 200 million workers according to the Bureau of Labor Statistics.[15] How we deploy our vast resources has a wide and deep impact on our employees and their families.

The Edelman Trust Barometer is not the only sensor registering broad-based discontent with corporate America. The iconic Gallup Group, in February 2023, released data indicating that Americans are least satisfied with the nation's moral and ethical climate (20%), the way income and wealth are distributed (24%), and the size and influence of major corporations (27%). This trio of ratings is one of the lowest ever registered since Gallup began recording in 1935.[16]

Episodic social unrest suggests that Gallup's polling is correct. The general public appears to be getting desperate enough to take action beyond the ballot box. From the events at the U.S. Capitol on January 6, 2021, the seizure of the Supreme Court, National Congress, and the Planalto Palace in Brazil on January 8, 2023, nationwide strikes in France throughout January 2023, and even a general strike in the United Kingdom around the same time, social angst resulting from nonresponsive leaders creates negative conditions for business. Even the tenor of the stories we consume has taken an ominous turn. In 2023, Sam Esmail's Netflix film *Leave the World Behind* spent several weeks as a top-viewing experience on the platform, and in 2024, Alex Garland's dystopian film about a second American civil war raked in more than $10 million in its debut. Obviously, stable and positive conditions for business growth is our ultimate goal. And stunningly, when corporate leaders decide to positively influence and align with communities, amazing things happen.

For example, new Amazon employee Carla Johnson learned she had brain cancer only a few months after starting work at an Amazon warehouse in Bessemer, Alabama. Bessemer has an average median income about $3,000 less than Walterboro—a low-income town with few opportunities. The typical cost of brain-tumor treatment ranges from $50,000 for a small benign tumor to more than $700,000 to treat and remove a malignant tumor.

Fortunately, Carla didn't have to worry about her medical expenses. By making the decision to provide health insurance from day one, Amazon essentially saved Carla's life. Perhaps that's why the workers at her warehouse voted against unionization when a vote was called. The *New York Times* called the vote "a runaway victory" for the company,[17] as many workers simply felt the pay and benefits were already good. When it came time for the union vote, the employees decided that their voices were already being heard and they didn't need an outside organization to lobby for what the company would do on its own.

A crisis like the COVID pandemic acts as a culling event separating companies that were more like the capricious grasshopper rather than the disciplined ant in Aesop's fable. Seemingly successful businesses across the country fell into bankruptcy within weeks of having to close their doors for safety precautions, sending all their employees out onto the unemployment line in a most frightening affair. Thousands of others, like JCPenney, guaranteed their employees security for a short window of time, but then folded up shop to ensure that C-Suite year-end bonuses were delivered. Despite filing for bankruptcy in May 2020, JCPenney still paid its CEO an eye-popping $3.5 million bonus—a decision that drew criticism from industry stakeholders who believed those funds should have gone to supporting employees instead.

Amazon, despite often (and unfairly) being the favorite whipping boy of opportunistic detractors, was ironically one of those companies that stepped up during the pandemic. Amazon raised its minimum wage, allowed for unlimited paid time off, pumped up overtime pay, and gave two weeks of sick pay to anyone diagnosed with COVID-19. Within 11 days of the shutdowns happening across the country, Amazon posted a message on its site that still stands today and reads in part, "Amazon has zero tolerance for price gouging and longstanding policies and system to prevent this harmful practice . . . Amazon is and will remain a customer-obsessed company . . . [and we are] humbled by the trust our customers have placed in us during this difficult time."[18]

Amazon's profitability was secure during the pandemic because its e-commerce business model was well adapted for such an event, making it even more notable that the company promptly posted a message about the value of community synergy, while other companies hesitated on decisions regarding pandemic accommodations such as remote or hybrid work.

Drug store CVS similarly made big, bold moves during COVID, including bonuses and sick leave for part-time workers and up to 25 days of backup child or elder care for every single employee. Even more impressively, the company waived its traditional delivery fees for all prescription medications, knowing that there were plenty of population segments that would be at tremendous risk leaving home, even to go pick up a prescription. The cherry on top was CEO Larry Merlo's announcement that the company would start the greatest hiring assignment in company history, adding 50,000 new workers, and specifically targeting workers displaced from the Hilton and Marriott Hotel chains.

Target also went an extra mile with its workers, allowing high-risk employees defined as those who were pregnant, nursing, senior citizens, or had immuno-deficiency disorders to stay home for 30 days of paid leave. That was on top of increases in hourly wages, paid leave for COVID-19 patients, and elder/childcare for all employees. It wasn't just the additional benefits, but the idea that Target and the other companies believed that this too shall pass, and were guiding their workers toward that better tomorrow, confident it was on the way.

But despite pandemic efforts made by some businesses, trust in corporate America continues to sag. The lack of trust and confidence demonstrated by the Edelman and Gallup surveys are glaring red flags for businesses. Society relies on business leaders to create an environment that empowers employees to thrive. This means supporting access to fair pay, affordable housing, and health care—even for life-changing illnesses like brain cancer. By striving to achieve these fundamental elements of life security, the tension between disparate groups dissipates and creates greater opportunities for profit and stronger business conditions for growth. Coca-Cola understood this in the 1950s and 1960s during Jim Crow and segregation. Coca-Cola was one of the few corporations at the time to actively support the cause of racial equality, hired African American sales representatives, and ran advertisements promoting racial unity. It's been printing money ever since and often evades the social uproar that impacts other beverage companies because it has long taken a conscientious stand.

The Edelman Barometer contains a silver lining. Despite the abysmal numbers regarding trust, overall the public still believes that the business community is one of the only trusted institutions today.[19] In other words, the government fared far worse. This fact places a heavy burden at the feet of every corporate leader. As business leaders, it is up to us to help create real and lasting social stability because it connects to our core profit goals. While politicians often prioritize victory over negotiation and leave society waiting for needed change that seemingly never arrives, genuine strides can be accomplished when businesses lead the way toward community betterment.

The Corporation Next Door

In the oft-maligned *Citizens United v. Federal Elections Commission* (2010) Supreme Court decision, the Court held that the First Amendment prohibits the government from restricting independent expenditures for political campaigns by corporations, and noted that "[b]ecause speech is an essential mechanism of democracy—it is the means to hold officials accountable to the people."[20] This ruling not only set off a wave of activism against dark money in politics but also questions about the nature of corporate existence: Are corporations really people?

I've never thought corporations were people. But they certainly are made up of people who combine their efforts to animate a corporate personality. This is why our working thesis is that any process, thought, experience, or emotion that *can* manifest at an individual level, *may* manifest at an organizational level given the right conditions.

Let's assume for the sake of argument that corporations are people. They have an address, they pay taxes, they need to use roads and bridges, they need local utilities like water and electricity, and by virtually every legal metric of personhood they have an existence that operates like any household. They can even be your neighbor with the rights and obligations that come from being a good (or bad) one. It follows that if businesses are our neighbors, then they should have the same responsibilities and expectations to our mutual community as every other neighbor. They are obliged to become positive contributors to the community, to keep the shared neighborhood unpolluted, adding value rather than degrading or taking away, following the law, and even voicing concerns when matters affect the community. From this perspective, the community is every bit an interested stakeholder in the corporate existence as an employee stakeholder, a corporate shareowner, or even a retail investor.

For the conscientious executive, the universe of corporate stakeholders includes every person who buys the enterprise's goods and services, is impacted by its commercial activity, and holds a share of the business. In other words, conscientious leaders recognize the nexus between corporate actions and the local communities we serve and are especially attuned to that relationship.

That's why social media campaigns, technology-enabled dissemination of information, and the so-called "cancel culture" movements aren't necessarily negative developments for the free market. They are data signals that have to be interpreted correctly. They push corporations to deliver products and services consumers want to see—while also pushing business to bring any negative community impact in line with positive community benefit.

The result? We level up to stronger corporate growth and profit, and communities, simultaneously.

It's not ideal that our public sector leaders are so distrusted. You have to go back to the end of Richard Nixon's days in the White House to find a time when fewer people turned toward the government in search of hope, leadership, and reassurance. That leaves a significant leadership gap that corporate leaders must fill out of necessity. Why? Because our organizations are capable of effecting change; real change, like with Amazon worker Carla Johnson's brain cancer. While individual politicians might have good intentions on climate control, equality, racial justice, and a hundred other topics, those good intentions typically fall by the wayside when they are forced to navigate one subcommittee after another.

Corporate decision-makers need to be better than our contemporaries in the nation's capital and from state to state. We have to be, because we aren't getting paid simply to keep greasing the wheels of a donor class that lines our pockets with financial contributions every two to six years. Businesses, on the other hand, don't have to languish through all those layers of bureaucratic muck and mud to get something done. With the right leadership in place, we can see an issue, determine the change that is necessary, and breathe life into a solution. Our consumers understand that strong corporate leadership can do just the opposite of what we see in Washington. It doesn't have to worry about the next election. Its constituents can speak directly to the people in charge, and they in turn can wield power and influence to right wrongs, shine disinfecting light in dark places, and act as a beacon of all things good to those near and far. This is the reality of what a great corporation can do.

Conscientious leaders are needed more than ever. We must lead with sound moral character and vision because we can move faster than governments to create meaningful change and bring value to our communities. Business remains a key institution in which society places trust and business leaders must make moral calls that can have a tremendous impact. These moral decision nodes may be all that stands between today's free enterprise system and its demise. It is the challenge of each generation to level up our ability to lead with conscientiousness, purpose, and vision; and to remember the forgotten people and places along the journey toward a better tomorrow.

3 | Adapt Today, Thrive Tomorrow

In the 1980s, the Winans were an American gospel quartet from Detroit, Michigan, consisting of brothers Marvin, Carvin, Michael, and Ronald. Deborah Kerr Winans, then wife of Carvin, wrote a song called "Tomorrow," which ended up being one of my father's favorite songs. The essence of the song is that it's okay to give in to the urgency of important things. In the final lines, Deborah notes, "tomorrow is not promised; don't let this moment slip away; your tomorrow could very well begin today."

The urgency of tomorrow's challenge for business is always on my mind today. While patience is certainly a virtue, it is sometimes necessary to act quickly for important matters. Delayed action can lead to undesirable or even irreversible consequences. Recognizing when a situation calls for expediency over patience is key—one must weigh the relative significance and time sensitivity of the issue against available resources for action. Today's forward-thinking leaders recognize that progress cannot be delayed until some future date. Speed is required to stay ahead of increasingly breakneck change.

Entrepreneur Azeem Azhar calls today's business environment "the exponential age," a topic on which he has also penned a great book by the same title.[1] Only by acting with urgency will we be able to seize opportunities and navigate challenges emerging at an exponential pace. Waiting for a more convenient season is an old-meta luxury unavailable to us post-pandemic.

Teleportative Solutioning

Conscientious executives recognize the importance of speed in decision-making. Traditionally, speed is key in beating competitors to market. However, the conscientious executive views speed through a moral prism. Recall, etymologically, *conscientious* is a word with a foundation in doing what is right.

Why, then, is it right to move fast? We all understand, at a fundamental level, that time is of the essence in an emergency. You wouldn't calmly stroll to the shore to save a drowning friend. But the same principle holds true in business today. Livelihoods, families, and careers are not toys to be played with by executives.

In an economy where developments, trends, and changes occur in rapid succession, being at the vanguard of changes demonstrates both a concern for and alignment with the needs of consumers and employees who drive the business. It can save lives or a downstream dependent business, and even feed a family. The faster, more agile executive has therefore become paradigmatic among today's leading, moral players. Indeed, speed has become part and parcel of the characteristics needed for success in a world where shifts happen near instantaneously and understanding the value of speed will be fundamental on our journey to level up.

Leaders in Australia showed the price of slower action during its worst bushfire crisis in recorded history. The fires spanned from June 2019 to May 2020, peaking in January 2020. Over 18 million hectares of land were burned (a little more than 69,000 square miles), and more than 1 billion animals were estimated to have died. A significant, regrettable, foreseeable, and potentially preventable mass extinction event. When it was all over, an area larger than the entire state of Georgia in the United States had gone up in flames. The bushfire crisis was a defining moment for the Australian government, revealing serious flaws in its response and sparking widespread criticism for its handling of the disaster.

Jonathan Vea, a worker in Australia's Darwin, Northern Territory recounts, "[w]e waited on the water's edge all night. The smoke was dense. Even though we were wearing swimming goggles, our eyes stung. Our throats were raw. To help us breathe, we used medical masks and a torn-up sarong wrapped around our faces." Peter Papathanasiou, the author of *Little One* and *Son of Mine*, who lives in Canberra, Australia's capital city, remembers the stress of the moment noting that the fires "[. . .] put a strain on our small city. The streets are deserted . . . [t]he national airline stopped all flights. The postal service halted all deliveries. Petrol stations sold out of fuel, supermarkets sold out of bottled water, and bank ATMs were emptied of cash. It's the stuff of the apocalypse. Only time will tell how our long-term health is impacted [from the smoke]."[2]

So, what went wrong?

Australia's governmental response was roundly criticized for being too slow. Many communities were left without adequate support and resources, such as water and food, for days or even weeks after the fires started. The government's failure to respond quickly missed an opportunity to prevent further spread and damage. Also, political leaders used the crisis as an opportunity to score points and place blame rather than working together to find solutions. For example, Prime Minister Scott Morrison was criticized for taking a holiday in Hawaii during the height of the crisis, while Deputy Prime Minister Michael McCormack dismissed the link between the bushfires and lack of preparation for changing climate conditions, calling it "inner-city raving by people who have probably never held a hose." (McCormack would later be removed as a leader by his political party.)

Australia's approach to tackling wildfires was uncoordinated, with the government's preparedness contribution falling from 2003 continuously through 2018 when only 23% of funding came from federal sources. In response, Prime Minister Morrison provided a "one-off" injection of funds in 2018 and again in 2019. Yet, on both occasions, flames had already taken hold across the eastern coast. The fragmented system mired national disaster planning where multiple portfolios controlled resources like defense and health while external agencies such as the Bureau of Meteorology also influenced operations and disaster response.

In the case of the bushfire, speed and coordination from Australia's leadership team could have literally saved lives.

No one knows whether tomorrow's next social fire will begin, spreading as one incident, say an allegedly stolen election ignites a successful capitol riot. Or, whether the flashpoint will be a radioactive one that permeates white hot for years until finally igniting mass demonstrations. It could present as growing inequality sparking general strikes similar to those in the United Kingdom and France in the early winter of 2023. Still, the spark could start an event that rapidly spreads from a known flashpoint to an unrelated matter, like aggressive policing leading to civil unrest. What we do know is that swift action could make the difference between dramatic economic loss and a short-lived, contained unrest that is both bad for business and society.

The 2020 pandemic was a noteworthy flashpoint for business. Among other things, it heightened social activism by consumers. A 2020 Tufts University Tisch College poll published by Gallup noted that young people were more politically engaged than ever before because of the pandemic. Approximately

79% said they realized how much politics impacts their lives, and 60% felt inspired by a movement to voice their views at the ballot box. And, even before Australia burned that same year, the proliferation of extreme weather events was top of mind generationally as the effects of a changing climate became more and more evident.[3] Millennials have lived through "once in a lifetime" economic recessions, catastrophes, and pandemics before entering their prime. My wife, for example, was a Katrina evacuee and the event still resonates for her in a profound way. These conditions lay the perfect groundwork to ignite a social fire. It was not long until activism found its way to the corporate door-step. By 2022, journalist Chris Taylor noted in his article "Boycott Nation" that fully 37% of six-figure earners, 32% of Gen Z, 28% of Millennials, 28% of those whose political affiliation is Democratic, and 24% of Republicans are engaged in some form of company or product boycott.[4]

Even amongst heavily unionized work forces like at UPS Airlines, there were additional attempts to organize in a reaction to growing corporate profits. This endured unabated until the summer of 2023 when UPS and the Teamsters reached a last-minute deal to avert a general strike.

In 2019, I was serving as the executive sponsor for the airline's Young Professionals Business Resource Group. As the broad political and social malaise deepened, I penned "Adapting for The Future: Five Strategies for Successfully Incorporating Millennials" for our company newsletter. At the time, UPS had nearly 500,000 employees around the world, and like most companies, our generational trend accelerated toward young workers. "Today's workers," I pointed out, "value purpose, collaboration, inclusivity, challenging engagement, and flexible working conditions (including working from home) over fancy titles, and [. . .] we must move fast to align with those needs."[5]

Barely a year later, when the pandemic hit, that opinion became reality. As if playing oracle to my own career narrative, we were having animated conversations about speed and alignment amongst the airline leadership team. Strategies for adapting over time to a Millennial workforce became immediate tactics for surviving the pandemic. For the airline, a large portion of our 20,000-strong workforce were college students, a result of the Metropolitan College program, which is a partnership between UPS and the University of Louisville. Still, I advocated, we *could* move faster because conscientious leadership demands that crisis not set the pace of change alone.

The concept of "fast" is relative. Today's leaders must adopt what I call teleportative solutioning, leveraging recommendations and data to act near instantaneously. This is necessary as we enter a new era defined almost exclusively by the relationship between corporation and worker.

As the term suggests, "teleportative solutioning" requires that decisions be made, and actions taken, with little time between the two. To that end, there are two ways to view a team's speed: internal and external.

Internally, speed requires removing layers of bureaucracy and ensuring visionary ideas are embraced, not merely analyzed. It requires the removal of multiple approval signatures and allows portfolio managers to make big decisions on their own. Retooling spans of authority and eliminating unnecessary layers of review, when done correctly, can keep transformative projects from stalling and provide greater agility in the organization. Externally, speed requires aligning with the changing needs of the communities served by the business. Operationally, this means giving local and regional community operations teams the dispensation to do what works best in their locality.

Flexibility is the key, which enables the business to take advantage of its greatest asset—its people. But above all, it is the ability for any single leader to clearly understand how their action impacts the whole that will define success in this new environment. This approach to management shifts the dynamic between employee and employer—one that prizes each for the capability to make swift decisions without relying too heavily on committees and approvals. The true test of teleportative solutioning lies in its deployment—specifically, allowing those closest to the work to act with wider discretion to maximize their effectiveness. Only conscientious leaders capable of building trusting teams can be effective here.

An *employee* begins to operate within a teleportative environment when they can answer the following statement in the affirmative. *I know with complete certainty that I possess the authority to make this decision, or I know the full name and phone number of the exact person who can give me approval to move forward with a course of action today.* When more than two levels of review are necessary, conversations become less about action and more about marketing skills and personal relationships. It allows managers to impose an "ask-me-first" hegemony, over innovation, that is stifling and decelerates productivity.

A *manager* operates within a teleportative environment when they can answer the following statement in the affirmative. *I can respond to any request to do [X] within five minutes of seeing the request. Any authorization requiring more authority can be escalated and resolved within 24 hours.*

Of course, teleportative solutioning does not require the removal of all internal checks and balances for compliance and accounting purposes. It does, however, demand clear guidance on what authority is delegated within the organization and ensuring those delegations are not abused through the normal audit and compliance mechanisms. I instituted these reforms within my own teams and productivity increased dramatically. My deputies at the time, Stephanie, Jeff, Bob, and Mike, met often to review and calibrate authorization guidance for the department to ensure that, for appropriate tasks, I could be almost entirely removed from approval decisions. Tomorrow's leadership frontier will be as simple as an employee messaging a leader for permission to buy the team coffee and receiving both the authorization and capability to act on it within minutes—a concept not as crazy as it used to be given the explosion in instant global communication. Or, even better, empowering team leads with appropriate authority upfront, without the need for further deliberation.

Electronics and tech giant Best Buy is a good example of this. Corie Barry was appointed CEO (the company's first woman in the role) in 2019 and was almost immediately faced with steering Best Buy through the pandemic.

Some businesses waited to see if the pandemic would end quickly, hoping they would not have to make any drastic changes. While businesses shuttered their doors and laid off employees, Corie Barry immediately reoriented the business to the new environment by implementing contactless curbside pickup and free digital consultations with tech experts, moves that normally would have taken months or years to roll out. She empowered local store managers to make a wide range of decisions best suited for each local area.

Barry instinctively knew people suddenly stuck inside would need the company's technology to work from home along with home improvements for lockdown entertainment. By speedily prioritizing customer and employee safety over profit and eschewing the traditional "we've always done it this way" corporate attitude, Best Buy *increased* sales and patron loyalty during a crisis that devastated so many other businesses. Not only did Best Buy find a way to boost sales during the pandemic, but it strengthened customer relations and loyalty as well.

Best Buy's first-quarter sales soared 37.2% in 2021. That wasn't just a glitch caused by COVID shutdowns a year earlier; the company was up 27.2% in revenue paired against its numbers from 2019. Best Buy helped people realize that there was immense value inside their own four walls to be used doing simple, valuable pastimes like learning, cooking, remodeling, and redecorating. The good times kept rolling for Best Buy, which jumped another 20% in Q2 2021 to $11.85 billion, blowing the doors off industry predictions.[6]

That kind of instantaneous attitude adjustment is—and will continue to be—necessary beyond the pandemic as more and more consumers refuse to accept old-school leadership styles and meta practices. Barry's deftness was a far cry from the cultural genuflection around remote work (and other topics) that most executives navigated during and after the pandemic. As a society, for example, we used to culturally tolerate abrasive, even abusive leaders because they "got results." Even in my own career, I have had no shortage of run-ins with "old school" managers who thought busting skulls was the way to increase production. But try doing that to a Millennial or Gen Z employee today. Cultural evolution has raised "mutual respect" to the same level of importance as equal pay for equal work regardless of race or gender.

In the past, employees wishing to speak out often found themselves deterred by the perceived futility of their efforts. The likelihood of being ignored, censored, disparaged, or terminated created an atmosphere of discouragement and fear. But social media offers a platform for dissension to attract the attention of the masses. It takes less than five minutes for a bureaucratic delay in response to a trivial request (say, for office coffee) to end up virally shared on the "For You" page of social media platforms for the consumption of millions of customers. Instantaneous modes of communication necessitate teleportative solutioning.

What Innovation Says About Your Speed

The rate of innovation is a good barometer for a leadership team's responsiveness for a few reasons. First, it reflects their ability to foresee and adapt to changing market conditions, customer needs, and emerging trends. Second, it reflects a culture of innovation, encouraging employees to think creatively, propose novel ideas, and develop innovative strategies to tackle obstacles. Finally, it indicates a commitment to maintaining market relevance. Ideally, all leaders would participate in innovation and support various avenues to facilitate, ideate, capture, and execute ideas.

Technology leaders, such as Apple, Google, and Microsoft, use regional whiteboarding and collaborative virtual "innovation sessions" to capture ideas and opinions, which are then shared with their legal departments for evaluation and patent filing in short order.

For example, Meta Platforms, the world's largest social media company and parent company of Facebook, Instagram, and WhatsApp, has pioneered a global patent program designed to drive inclusive innovation from historically underrepresented innovation centers like women engineers. My colleagues Jeremiah Chan, Shayne O'Reilly, and Allen Lo represent the industry vanguard of this unique approach to increasing innovation in one of the most forward-leaning companies on earth.

3M, another innovation-focused company, steadily builds on its 100,000 patents worldwide and, even in a pandemic, filed an additional 668 patents in

2020 alone. Perhaps that is not surprising for the company that created Post-it Notes, the elegant (and now ubiquitous) thought-capturing tool. At 3M, "dog-fooding," a tech industry term for using your own products or services internally before commercial launch, is standard fare along with group idea sessions.

Using a somewhat different approach, UPS's Upstarts (a program like *Shark Tank*) gathered teams from different departments internationally to create and pitch ideas directly to the C-Suite, bypassing middle management. This program was the brainchild of my friend David Lee, VP of Innovation at UPS, who later joined Cox Communications and the board of Fast Radius. I was fortunate to lead a team in David's program and pitched a concept reinventing how we think about physical location in parcel delivery. Theoretically, a phone location could be used in place of a physical address for dynamic delivery. We made it to the finals but weren't selected, so no, UPS will not deliver your volleyball to you on the beach—at least not yet. But it was exciting to innovate with a group of strangers—an opportunity more old-fashioned companies may not have given to an employee like me who was not in operations or sales. These are the kinds of solutioning modalities that become culturally entrenched in tomorrow's most successful companies.

To Beard or Not to Beard

For more than 100 years, UPS required drivers and other frontline employees to be clean-shaven. But we eventually began encountering fierce competition for talent. Prospective employees weighed whether such a clean-shaven requirement was worth the effort when compared to other employers with less restrictive policies. Then in 2020, 113 years into UPS's operation, it dawned on a forward-thinking leader in HR that perhaps facial hair wasn't as important as having enough people to deliver packages. I was happy with the change and chose to don a beard myself. More importantly, I felt we moved quickly to implement the change in our operations. But the social media reaction was less enthusiastic than mine, as people responded to the announcement with comments like, "Facial hair is still a thing at that company?!" The internet's collective guffaw at the pace of change was notable to internal stakeholders who, for the most part, were elated with the change and perhaps spent more time discussing the newfound freedom than Media Take Out.

Going through the experience of changing the facial hair policy at UPS Airlines underscored a story that a colleague shared with me from his early career. Mike was taking a class in business school and a corporate executive was invited to discuss interviewing at local firms.

The guest speaker was from a major U.S. corporation and mentioned two candidates he'd recently interviewed. The first interviewee was a decent candidate. He had a good background, good degree, decent experience, was dressed immaculately, and he even got to the interview 15 minutes early. He shook hands, said thanks, the whole nine yards. The second finalist did a spectacular job during the interview. But he arrived at the interview barely a minute before it started, and as the recruiter rose to shake hands, noticed the candidate was wearing neither socks nor a belt. When the hiring team met that afternoon to compare notes, he brought up the missing socks and belt, eventually bending the ear of the other decision-makers to go with the better-dressed, less impressive candidate over the guy who killed it despite not wearing a belt.

The recruiter ended on that note, convinced he had just persuaded the class about the value of the little things. Mike raised his hand and said, "That's the stupidest thing I've ever heard of." He pointed out how ridiculous it was to value someone wearing a belt and socks over someone with qualifications that clearly would help the company grow immediately. By the time his rant was over, even the professor was convinced.

Conscientious executives embrace a simple truth: in life some things are worth holding on to tightly while other things are dispensable. The distinction lies in our ability to embrace the vital while releasing the trivial. Imagine how much better off fossil fuel corporations would be if they had implemented their own sustainable-energy strategies in the mid-1990s instead of dragging their heels for a half-century, anchored to decades of tradition and convention. Imagine the kinds of renewable energy that could be on the market today. Tesla may never have been conceived.

An unmistakable duality characterizes business today: those who recognize the need to move faster versus those who resist swift transition in lieu of the slower pace of tradition. But increasing our speed of decision-making can accelerate the path to community alignment and highlights a core value for next generation leaders. Community is our why. Here we unlock an important characteristic of the conscientious leader, namely, to do what is right, each decision is centered first on values. Let's consider two examples of organizations leading with values.

To Kneel or to Stand

On September 4, 2018, Nike endorsed Colin Kaepernick, the first NFL player to kneel during the national anthem in protest of police brutality and racial inequality. While old-school analysts predicted Nike would experience at least a temporary revenue decline, four days following the announcement, the company's stock rose several points on both the Dow Jones and the S&P 500, sales grew 31% (more than double the same period in the previous year), and Nike received an estimated $43 million worth of media exposure in less than 24 hours.[7]

To traditionalists, that provocative marketing tactic had been a wild gamble, but Nike had done its research and knew that those who would get upset were outside its target market, and it didn't care. Nike took a political stand that resonated with its customer community. But, above all, it was a moral decision first. Consequently, at little economic cost, the company captured an entire generation of brand-loyal consumers.

This wasn't just a gut reaction by Nike, either. It didn't splash Kaepernick's face on TV the week after the controversy began. The truth is that although he had played in a Super Bowl during the 2012 season and then in the NFC Championship game the following year, Kaepernick might have been one of the less notable athletes that Nike has ever endorsed. Kaepernick just missed leading his team to the Super Bowl title. The team lost 34–31 to Baltimore in Super Bowl XLVII, despite him throwing a touchdown and rushing for another, and a terrific sophomore year in the NFL as well. He did go on to sign a six-year contract worth as much as $126 million, with $54 million guaranteed money. But Kaepernick was fined twice—once for bad language on the field that was picked up by a microphone on TV and a second time for wearing headphones to a press conference (Beats by Dre) instead of the league's headphone sponsor (Bose). The San Francisco 49ers missed the playoffs entirely and their head coach split for his college alma mater.

The next year Kaepernick's star lost even more luster as he lost his starting job midway through the season and wound up getting hurt, missing the rest of the year, and requiring three separate surgeries to get in shape for the 2016 season. He had lost a step off his quickness and struggled in training camp. In the 49ers' third preseason game, he did not stand during the national anthem, and the following week, knelt on the sideline while it played, to protest racial injustice and police brutality in the United States. His protests came barely a month after a highly polarized case of a police officer, Jeronimo Yanez, shooting and killing Philando Castile during a routine traffic stop.

Tempers flared, and Kaepernick continued to kneel, drawing support and criticism from all corners. He lost and regained his starting job, restructured his contract, and eventually became a free agent to look for a new team. Imagine his surprise when Kaepernick wasn't offered a single contract throughout the off-season and into the 2017 training camps. The NFL had forgiven Michael

Vick for running an illegal dogfighting ring and Ray Lewis for obstruction of justice in a murder case. The league brings back over-the-hill quarterbacks all the time. But Kaepernick, somehow, was shut out. In 2017, Kaepernick continued to make the rounds as an activist, but also filed a grievance against the NFL, citing owner collusion to ban him. In 2018, despite having not played a game in two seasons, Nike launched the campaign with Kaepernick, raising awareness about social issues and weathering the inevitable backlash to do the right thing.

Nowadays, some consumers will buy Nike shoes no matter the price.

GOOD CHICKEN

Now, consider Chick-fil-A, a strong example of cross-community relevance. In a landscape of burger joints and tacos, Chick-fil-A stands alone. Originally found in shopping mall food courts, Chick-fil-A eventually opened an independent, freestanding location in Atlanta in the mid-1980s. It spread quickly across the South, but never was trying to "out-grease" McDonald's or Burger King for the quick buck. It stayed true to its foundational beliefs of good food, good service, and Southern Baptist values.

Its founder, Samuel Truett Cathy, expressed his religious beliefs through the company's literature from day one, and although he passed away in 2014, the company remains committed to his original idea of what the franchise should look like. When he penned his business plan, Cathy wrote, "I was not so committed to financial success that I was willing to abandon my principles and priorities. One of the most visible examples of this is our decision to close on Sunday. Our decision to close on Sunday was our way of honoring God and of directing our attention to things that mattered more than our business."[8]

It's a bold step because many people go out to eat on Sunday and imagine how many people would like a nice family meal after church at a place like Chick-fil-A. But Cathy's family has never wavered from his intent. Even the restaurant's locations in shopping mall food courts and at Mercedes-Benz Stadium in Atlanta are closed on Sundays. The latter case is remarkable when you consider that the stadium's primary tenant is the Atlanta Falcons, who play 95% of their games on Sundays! The revenue loss is massive, but Chick-fil-A continues to adhere to its values.

Chick-fil-A came under fire in 2012 when Dan T. Cathy criticized same-sex marriage and it was revealed the company had donated more than $5 million to the WinShape Foundation, an organization founded by Samuel Truett Cathy and which opposes same-sex marriages. Politicians representing several large cities were critical of the viewpoint, students tried to block the restaurant on their campus, and it cost Chick-fil-A partnerships and advertising dollars as well.

But while some people disdain Chick-fil-A for its apparent social positions, others love the company fiercely and not just for the delectability of its fried chicken patties or its great customer service. That loyalty is also due to Chick-fil-A's four principal service programs:

- Chick-fil-A Shared Table, which has served more than 8 million meals in local soup kitchens, shelters, and nonprofits;
- True Inspiration Awards, which provides hundreds of thousands of dollars in annual grants to dozens of education, hunger, or homelessness nonprofits that are "Black-led or serve communities of color";
- Remarkable Futures Scholarships, which helps "team members" pursue a higher education; and
- Chick-fil-A Leader Academy, a national high school leadership program focused on "impact through action."

These programs both engage and align Chick-fil-A with communities in Atlanta and across North America. In fact, the combination of quality products and outcome-focused philanthropy is so powerful that, like Nike, it has inoculated the franchise from those who have tried to boycott it.

Although some hope that Chick-fil-A leaders will feel pressured to disavow their conservative Christian positions and donations to organizations supporting the same, the company listens to its consumer base in the same way progressive organizations do. The company knows it can weather some bad press because its customers are loyal to its brand, products, and services—just as Nike's are. In 2018, Chick-fil-A's revenue grew 16.7% to reach $10.5 billion. Over the past 10 years, its annual sales have tripled. Currently, it is the number three fast food restaurant in the United States in terms of revenue, trailing only McDonald's and Starbucks. Remarkably, it has done so with far fewer locations. The average Chick-fil-A location makes $4.6 million in revenue per year, far ahead of second-place McDonald's at $2.8 million.[9]

One of my colleagues moved to Chick-fil-A in 2022 as a corporate employee in Atlanta, Georgia. She explained to me that the company's conservative culture is authentic and extends to how employees engage with one another in social environments. I am told Chick-fil-A executives engage in acts of service to one another including, in one example, the complete resodding of an administrative assistant's yard when they could not find help to do the work.

The company will also pay venues to *not* serve alcohol during Chick-fil-A events in consideration of the premium the company places on soberness and fidelity of its executives to family. The point is, Chick-fil-A is authentic in its values-based service, which generates strong support and detraction, but never questions about where the company stands.

Chick-fil-A and Nike stand as two examples of companies that have achieved extraordinary alignment in their respective lanes despite making different choices. They "stand on their convictions" and are rewarded for it by the communities that know them best.

There's no time to waste for businesses today to do the same. Really there never was, but in decades past, business moved slower. Today, there is a palpable fear that any change could presage a reputational decline. Why champion an athlete who is also a social justice advocate? Why stick to our religious beliefs when it might cost us a certain customer base? It took the reckoning of digital technology and social media to finally start unhinging the old meta. Today, not making a swift authentic decision often brings about the worst outcomes. Conscientious leaders appreciate the urgency of the moment and act quickly to adapt, innovate, and earn the loyalty of customers. Don't let a single moment slip away to make authentic decisions. Your tomorrow could very well begin today.

The Conscientious Executive

"When a milestone is conquered, the subtle erosion called entitlement begins its consuming grind. The team regards its greatness as a trait and a right. Halfhearted effort becomes habit and saps a champion."

— Pat Riley, Rule of Entitlement, *The Winner Within*

4

Move Beyond
Comfort

Tomorrow's leaders cannot be afraid of the heat. In fact, they must be driven by a burning desire to fix broken things, and a passion to preserve the best of business—making products and services that change the world and improve humanity. So, what kind of person is this conscientious executive and what qualities will they need to address tomorrow's inferno? Let's begin with courage.

Take the example of Chick-fil-A from the last chapter. The company provokes such strong emotions that even a beta reader of this book's manuscript read the portions about Chick-fil-A and remarked: "I do have to say, the only example I was not a fan of was Chick-fil-A. They have homophobic leadership, but they make damn good chicken [. . .] I'd be careful that your views don't align to the homophobic ones. I get what you're saying with Chick-fil-A . . . but it rubbed me the wrong way and left a bad taste in my mouth. I'm sure you wouldn't like a company that touted racist rhetoric but gave back to low-income white communities."

While I agree that homophobic views are certainly not ones I would align with, in an interesting way, the critic validated the need to include Chick-fil-A as an example here. The journey to creating better organizations begins with conscientious leaders willing to do what's right and evolve in that direction authentically. Growth is, among other things, a function of time and speed. The way CEO Andrew Truett Cathy (the son of Dan T. Cathy and grandson of Samuel Truett Cathy, the company's founder) is influencing growth and change at Chick-fil-A, while holding true to the values that make the company great, is, in a word, courageous. There will always be detractors. Courage, for the conscientious executive, is demonstrated by hearing the criticism and being thoughtful about which changes are necessary and what traditions demand protection. And in fact, Andrew Cathy has moved Chick-fil-A in a more inclusive direction by ceasing donations to anti-LGBTQ+ organizations.

Nike, an unabashedly liberal company, has also faced criticisms over the years. These criticisms include labor practices such as low wages and long working hours in contracted factories; environmental impact from production processes; and marketing practices promoting controversial themes or sometimes unrealistic beauty standards. It, too, demonstrated courage by reversing course on some practices.

In 1991, Jeff Ballinger published a report on Nike that shook the athletic shoe industry. An activist and labor rights defender, he uncovered alarming conditions in Asia-based factories contracted by Nike through interviews with workers and factory audits he conducted himself as well as his analysis of those provided by the company. His findings stirred intense critique from activists, consumer groups and governments around the world. Ballinger's report included details about worker pay and conditions that were shocking. One of those workers detailed in the report was a woman named Sadisah. Ballinger noted, "Sadisah's net earnings [show that] . . . [s]he put in six days a week, ten and a half hours per day, for a paycheck equivalent to $37.46—about half the retail price of one pair of the sneakers she makes . . . Sadisah worked 63 hours of overtime during this pay period, for which she received an extra 2 cents per hour. At this factory, which makes mid-priced Nikes, each pair of shoes requires 84 man hours to produce; working on an assembly line, Sadisah assembled the equivalent of 13.9 pairs every day. The profit margin on each pair is enormous. The labor costs to manufacture a pair of Nikes that sells for $80 in the United States is approximately 12 cents."[1]

Ballinger's report spurred aggressive efforts by Nike to address these labor concerns, such as increasing transparency around its labor practices and working to reduce its environmental impact. To Nike, exploitative labor practices did not fit with the values it sought to live as a company. Nike began pushing the entire apparel industry on fair wage standards. Notably, the effort not only influenced Nike internally but others in the industry as well.

Both Chick-fil-A and Nike demonstrate remarkable courage in standing up for their values despite opposition but also changing in ways that make them more accessible and mainstream. Criticism only emboldened the leadership of each company to move forward with passion and purpose. In those areas where valid criticism is levied, each organization meaningfully considers the critique and adjusts when appropriate. Each company demonstrates that they are not afraid to stand for what they believe in. This shows that they are not just businesses, but organizations with a purpose and a set of values that they are willing to fight for.

In Part I of this book, we defined a conscientious executive and explored the principal way they behave differently from traditionalists, namely, they move fast. We also learned that they behave in this way because they are earnestly trying to do what's right. Speed, for example, is driven by a desire to preserve jobs and create maximum synergies between the corporate interest and the communities they serve. The type of courage expressed by Nike and Chick-fil-A, too, exemplifies another core value: honesty. In the context of conscientious leadership, honesty is not only about behavior habits; it's about authenticity. Consumers pay attention to how consistently a company's behaviors match their stated values.

Conscientious leaders understand the importance of disclosing who the organization is truly, which is a bit like exposing who we are as a group of people. It can be scary, but it is important. Chick-fil-A is authentically a Southern, Christian company. Nike is authentically a West Coast, progressive company. In each organization, leaders seek to project the most positive and truthful identity to consumers. Where organizations routinely fail in the market today is by obscuring the truth of the corporate identity. Saying you care about the environment or inclusivity when you are frequently cited by regulators for environmental infractions, when you retreat from diversity goals out of fear that activist lawyers will call, or when you promote a leadership team that doesn't reflect society, creates a cognitive dissonance between words and actions. The mismatch is easily detected by today's consumers and employees alike and will immediately result in a loss of credibility.

So, who are you, really? Organizations that struggle with defining an authentic brand narrative often find it hard to resolve the image they want to project with the culture that exists in their company.

UPS has a delightfully odd ritual among Fortune 500 companies. During the holidays, UPS senior managers, office staff, and even corporate lawyers stand shoulder-to-shoulder sorting, loading, and delivering packages. Leaders are expected to be hands-on operators as the company strives to deliver what was promised. Knowledge of conditions on the front lines is invaluable in making better decisions. It shows employees that every leader in the company can empathize with the front line, and it is a nice cultural relic of an earlier time.

That might be why sending my department staff to work from home when the COVID pandemic began in March 2020 was such a difficult decision. It felt incompatible with the blue collar, rolled sleeves, shoulder-to-shoulder culture of the operation.

The "Air Group" as we called it, referenced a combination of operational districts known as the Flight, Hub, and Maintenance Districts. The various operations were arrayed on a fragmented campus around the city of Louisville and culminated in the crown jewel of the operations network, the Air Hub. Worldport, as we called the Air Hub, is a monstrous 5-plus-million-square-feet facility with a perimeter spanning over seven miles co-located with Louisville's commercial airport.

Worldport is truly a modern marvel in both its design and operation. The facility is packed with logistics technology, conveyors, lifts, tilt tray sorters, and other machinery designed to limit the number of times a human touches a package. My office in this bureaucratic web was an unassuming 10-by-10 room in the Air Group Building with faded carpet flooring and 1970s furniture. The blinds were dark and metallic because why wouldn't they be? And my file cabinets were filled to the brim by a predecessor who relied primarily on printing and filing physical documents. (I was the first Millennial to occupy the post, and it showed as my first order of business was to digitize and get rid of as much paper as humanly possible.)

Recall my early morning phone call about remote work in the last chapter? When I returned to Louisville from my vacation at the Mandarin, I had to address the differing views with my boss. He continued to oppose the notion of remote work for our white-collar teams for well-founded reasons.

On one hand, we received frequent reports on COVID infection rates and fatalities, although we didn't know exactly how it spread at the time. I believed transitioning to remote work would not show a lack of respect for frontline workers but, rather, would demonstrate concern for the safety of all our teams. Reducing exposure for as many as possible was good for everyone.

On the other hand, the prevailing sentiment was: *if our drivers are out on the roads, then we will be in the office.* And we clung to the hope that COVID was "just a flu." With our limited knowledge of the disease at the time, both of our points of view could have been right. But for me, it wasn't a hard choice. Employee safety would always win against optics and other considerations. In the end, I had to muster up my courage to do what I thought was right. A shoulder-to-shoulder frontline culture is a great waypoint, but we must be willing to quickly adjust when the terrain changes and in a way that preserves our authentic corporate identity.

I slow walked my team's return to the office, giving as much flexibility to individuals to call out of work for any reason. Turns out, I made the right call.

It wasn't long before our new CEO, Carol Tomé, validated the commonsense notion that department leaders could individually designate their teams for remote work as appropriate for the business. Carol understood the potential incongruity of telling employees on the one hand that you care about their safety while on the other hand requiring nonessential personnel to be in an office during the height of a communicable disease outbreak. The corporate office provided guidance that aligned our practices with our identity as a service organization that cared about safety first. The result was one of the safest, most efficient air operations in the world through the "once in a generation" pandemic event.

Few relish the opportunity to mediate differing views with an organizational superior on an important issue. But we'll never evolve our corporate culture if we don't have the audacity to challenge the ideas of others, and the courage to deviate from convention at times. It is the obligation of the conscientious leader to tilt against decisions that do not reflect the shared, authentic values of the organization. Tilting can be hard especially within the constraints of tradition and history. But it is no less necessary, and probably more courageous, to do so in those circumstances. Taking decisive action early ensured our legal team remained COVID-free, at least until the omicron variant in December 2021.

Lip Service Versus Real Alignment

Brown Grove, Virginia, is a community awash in heavy industry. It was founded in 1870 but was cut in half by Interstate 95 in the late 1950s, and then became a neighbor to the Hanover County Municipal Airport, two concrete plants, and a commercial landfill. The local community in Brown Grove came together to file a lawsuit against a planned Wegmans corporate distribution center that, according to the townsfolk, would bring more trucks and pollution to the neighborhood, whose infrastructure had long been ignored by local and state officials, and where roads often flood. The site is a wetland that provides well water for many residents who have yet to gain access to municipal water. It's also the final resting place of many town founders.

A similar lawsuit was filed in the Brentwood neighborhood of Washington DC. Brentwood was originally a White neighborhood protected by the now obsolete Home Owners' Loan Corporation in the 1930s and 1940s until racial covenants were outlawed and minorities began to move in. Today, Brentwood is mostly Black and home to an Amtrak maintenance facility, a construction corporation with two locations, a road-paving company, a city garbage truck fleet, a recycling center, and several auto repair shops. The city of

Washington DC also planned an additional bus terminal for 230 school buses. Notably, studies show that school bus exhaust is even more carcinogenic to humans than commercial-truck exhaust.

In both cases, decision-makers for the proposed projects claimed they were committed to being "good neighbors," a phrase *The Washington Post* quoted multiple times. But Brentwood denied its community's request for an environmental impact assessment because its "promise" of an electric bus fleet by 2050 made it "unnecessary." And in the Brown Grove case, Wegmans said that it changed its development plan based on residents' concerns, that the company it hired to search for unmarked graves failed to find any human remains, and that its distribution center would add jobs and tax revenue to the county. But residents countered that they were never consulted directly by Wegmans on any occasion, the updated plans still failed to address their concerns, and they could show Wegmans authorities themselves where many of their ancestors were buried.

When consumers talk about corporate lip service, they raise examples like these. How can one be a "good neighbor" when the community is ignored?

Meaningful engagement at the corporate level is a personal affair and it didn't take me long to realize this in dealing with the Pleasantdale community in Doraville, Georgia. For years, UPS has operated a package operation there and specifically in the Pleasantdale community. The operation became known as "P-dale" amongst employees. Anyone who has seen a logistics operation in full swing understands the amount of noise and light emanating from the operation can be disruptive. "Yard birds" (our slang term for a designated short-hauling vehicle), forklifts, and tractor trailers all elevate the natural ambient decibel of the local area, but if you add to that the sound of people, the whirring of conveyors, and the beeping of OSHA mandated alarms, it can be too much to bear for residential communities.

Decades ago, when UPS opened the P-dale facility, it was a sleepy part of North Atlanta with little traffic and only a few residential communities. Today, as the population of Atlanta and its suburbs continues to explode, Doraville has shared in the growth and expansion. Communities have popped up around industrial operations, including P-dale.

As neighbors moved in, so too did the complaints about noise and light. Threats of lawsuits were soon to follow, and our leadership team had to decide how we would respond to the new challenges from the community to our operation.

It would have been easy for a multi-billion-dollar behemoth to swat away local community concerns like Wegmans did, but it would not have been *right* to me. After some back and forth, we agreed on steps that could be taken to reduce the impact of sound and noise through barriers and other measures at a modest outlay for the company. Moreover, we did what we said we would do without delay. It's not perfect; solutions rarely are, but the method of community outreach was effective. And all it took was a little courage and authentic outreach.

All too often, parties undertake negotiation with local organizations to resolve differences only to walk away because the discussions get tough at times. But saying one thing and doing the other is the opposite of courage. If you promise to engage, then fully engage—this is what conscientious leaders do.

Courage seldom makes the news, and if it does, it doesn't have much of a shelf life. That's not what thrills most people and gets them clicking, tweeting, and resharing. The stories about the guy who saved three kids out of floodwaters or the woman who donated a kidney to save her own sister's life are relegated to sixth or seventh on the list of top headlines, and that's on a slow news day. Doing great things doesn't get you noticed by pop culture anymore. But doing what's right buys goodwill and peace, which is worth its weight in gold.

The Brown Grove community and Wegmans locked horns in court. Wegmans bristled at the complaints raised by the community and zealously litigated the matter all the way up to the Virginia Supreme Court. I'm sure the lawyers representing Wegmans received a handsome sum as they, quite advantageously to their firm, provided effective "scorched earth" counsel to Wegmans at every stage of the case. Then, in February 2023, the Virginia high court declined to rule on the merits but handed a tactical victory to the local community. The court held that the "allegations of particularized harm made by the homeowners are fairly traceable to the [zoning] Board's 2020 decision to approve Wegmans's conceptional development plan" and, in ruling for the petitioners, concluded that the lower court "erred in finding that the homeowners' pleadings did not allege a sufficient factual basis for standing."[2] The Wegmans fight continues, and in like fashion, the Brentwood neighbors continue to fight their case in Washington DC as of the date of this writing.

It's not hard to see that the approach taken in my negotiations with the Pleasantdale neighborhood offers a better path than the often uncertain and costly alternative of litigating against future neighbors. In the end, Wegmans and Washington DC may win their disputes with Brown Grove and Brentwood, but at a cost. Moral obligations that encourage compromise have not historically been celebrated in the business world. It takes tremendous strength for individuals today to be brave in the face of possible criticism rather than taking the easy road and seeking praise or admiration for being a tiger.

Conscientious leaders, in contrast, are courageous because they resolve to do what is right despite the difficulty or lack of praise from Wall Street analysts.

Leveling the Paying Field

Business leaders were thought to be bold and clever when they generated profit by any means necessary. Executives who displayed that kind of cutthroat "courage" were often rewarded by seeing their shares and stock prices shoot through the roof on Wall Street. Not today.

Enter Dan Price.

As Gravity Payments CEO, Dan was ridiculed when he decided to be compassionate instead of ruthless. It started in 2015, the day he saw one of his workers with a fast food training manual on her desk and discovered she worked a second full-time job—yet still wasn't making ends meet. After talking to other employees, he realized his company had a salary problem, so he did the unthinkable: he raised the minimum yearly pay to $70,000 for all employees—and lowered his own pay from $1.1 million to the same amount—a 14,729% pay cut.

Pundits and financial experts called him a "socialist." They predicted the company would fail and his employees would soon be in bread lines. Gravity Payments, they assured the public, was the perfect case study on what not to do.

Gravity Payments did, indeed, become a case study at Harvard Business School—on success. Six years after Price's "socialist" move, the company's revenue had tripled. It had added 70% more employees while turnover dropped by half, which supports the notion that retention is a result not a goal. Its customer base had doubled, and its payment processing had increased from $3.8 billion to $10.2 billion a year.

But the effect on Price's staff was even more telling. Employees had 10 times more babies, purchased 10 times more homes, paid down 70% of their debt, and raised their 401(k) contributions by 155%.[3]

By having the courage to ignore the culture that insisted paying employees well is not only bad for business but anti-American, Dan Price aligned Gravity Payments with its community, which opened the door to unimaginable success.

Thump Your Tail

Courageous leaders like Dan Price broke through their traditionalist culture in the face of open hostility, just as we did with remote work and facial hair at UPS Airlines. We often associate that kind of courage as a natural and static trait, but researchers at Stanford University School of Medicine think they have identified the fear and courage regions of the brain and have further demonstrated that they can be influenced.

In the study examining fear and courage reported by Stanford Medicine, researchers Lindsey Salay, Nao Ishiko, and Andrew Huberman selectively modified specific sets of nerve cells in mice's brains to stimulate either a fear or an active-courage response. The mice were then put in a large chamber with a video-screen ceiling. When a bird-shaped symbol appeared on the video, the unaltered control mice would freeze to avoid further detection, hide under shelter, or run as fast as possible. The mice whose brains were altered to prefer the fear region tended to freeze in place.

But the mice whose brains were altered to prefer the courage region stood in the open and rattled their tails as though ready to fight, a behavior seldom seen in nature against a flying predator. The scientists could even hear their tails thumping with vigor.[4]

This discovery may help people overcome phobias, posttraumatic stress disorder, and chronic anxiety. If nothing else, the study demonstrated that we can all leverage our inherent courage with the right stimuli. In other words, you can learn to be courageous!

Conscientious executives can confront the worst impulses of an organization by first understanding its baseline behaviors. Because any process, thought, experience, or emotion that *can* manifest at an individual level *may* manifest at an organizational level given the right conditions, the best leaders are constantly learning what triggers a fearful response in an organization's key decision-makers. Like Huberman's mice, identifying the circuits that determine reactions, such as whose ego may be triggered by an opposing view or whose yearly incentive will be impacted by a decision, can inform how to best steer the company toward a Pleasantdale resolution and away from a Wegmans quagmire.

When confronted with a crisis or questions, do we typically flee? Hide or go silent? Or do we stand in the open, thump our tails, and get ready to fight? The answer is organization specific. For example, when economic headwinds rattle profitability, often the first reaction from C-Suite leaders is to become more "efficient," which could be code for layoffs. It's not a bold or courageous response to challenges, rather it is a response founded on concern about future assumptions and projections. Look to Apple as a contrast. Understanding Apple's historical and often stimulated response of fearlessness in the face of headwinds explains why the iPhone maker's CEO appeared unflagged by questions about layoffs in his 2023 CNBC interview. Of course, Apple's balance sheet is a fortress unlike most companies, thus making it better able to navigate economic uncertainty. But it is also true that Apple behaves like Huberman's mice.

Costco similarly experienced the pressures to drastically raise prices like most companies did during the hyper-inflationary, post-COVID era. It responded, however, with a courageously different approach. It made only modest price increases, and retained all employees. Notably, it continued to preserve its traditional hotdog-drink combo for $1.50. In its third quarter earnings report, Financial Planning and Investor Relations SVP Rob Nelson said "[w]hile we continue to mitigate the impact of price increases as best as we can, we remain comfortable in our ability to pass through higher costs while providing great value to our members."[5] The company went on to implement only modest membership rate increases and be the warehouse of choice for families earning $100,000. Why? Because Costco's leadership team is trained to be fearless in fighting for member value.

In a noted TEDxSydney talk titled "We are gamblers at heart, but there is still hope," researcher Elise Payzan-Le Nestour pointed out that we often make bad decisions because we are hardwired to be greedy and lack self-control, even when we know the right action to take.[6] To avoid these pitfalls, therefore, we must change our reflexes with training and discipline or through a process that forces us (or our organization) to *think through* challenges rather than succumb to them.

I once worked for a boss who was obsessed with moving as fast as possible. Generally, speed is desirable when purposeful. But speed for the sake of speed can be improvident. His was the latter. To be sure, he likely intended to motivate everyone to be their best, but the imperative left little to no room for questions or rethinking. In contrast, his immediate successor believed we should be better, not necessarily bigger, and thoughtful, not necessarily quicker. That meant looking at what the organization did, how we did it, whether we were doing everything to our best ability, and, if not, figuring out a better way to serve our customers. She scrapped the unfocused speed thing and encouraged the leadership team to be courageous in pointing out past practices that needed reconsideration.

The corporate environment is often so pressurized that reaction eclipses rethinking. Traditionalists reflexively push against anything that questions their cultures or doctrines—as if adapting to new terrain isn't fundamental to generating new revenue. Locked in a pattern of behavior, these are the leaders who careen their organizations into head-on collisions with local neighbors. As Adam Grant says in his book *Think Again*, "[r]ethinking is not just an individual skill, it's a collective capability, and it depends heavily on an organization's culture."[7] That's why those who have the fortitude to listen and include diverse voices (including criticism) in their decision-making stand out as courageous leaders. They recognize short-term pain and sacrifice are worth the risk in the long run, not just for themselves and their businesses but for their communities' present and futures as well.

Meet the Tough Standard

My dear friend Deborah Pollack-Milgate is an accomplished patent lawyer in whom I have entrusted the most sensitive patent matters over the years. She's based in Indianapolis, and often disarms the most egocentric east coast litigators. On several occasions I've watched her sweep the floor with Ivy League lawyers who are aghast with surprise after discovering how much their rear end hurts following a deposition with Deb.

In her spare time, Deborah is engaged in a passion project known as the Parity Podcast. The show is a woman-owned enterprise focused on partnering with male allies to accelerate gender parity with their signature Parity Prescription. I was honored when Deborah asked me to cohost an episode of the show with her. And that's when I met Dr. Ronald Levant, the father of modern-day masculinity studies.

Ron is an author of 19 books, and author, coauthor, and editor or coeditor of over 250 articles. His most recent book, *The Tough Standard*, with Shana Pryor, examines the connection between masculinity and violence.[8] He has been one of the leading pioneers of the field of the psychology of men and masculinities and played a leading role in developing this new field in the late 1980s and 1990s.

Interviewing Ron was as exhilarating as it was insightful as the discussion of masculinity in corporate settings had unique relevance given the often lopsided and unnecessary tilt toward men in executive roles. Particularly, our discussion about boyhood made a lasting impression on me. In discussing his career path, Ron noted that he became increasingly aware of the role that shame plays in most men's lives. He notes that boys tend to be "locked into their hearts by the harsh injunctions of the male code." Courage is one of those characteristics we teach young boys, and it is often conflated with toughness. Often these false notions describe how a "man" should act in a circumstance, which largely colors corporate business. They may cause us to be recalcitrant when we should be accommodating. They may cause us to walk away from a negotiation when we should stay and talk.

There are also cultural components to how men see courage. As a boy, I remember being taught that I needed to have courage and be "tough." This toughness was largely to prepare me to be a dark-skinned minority child in a largely White South Carolina classroom. I was told not to care what others think about me. To some extent, the programming worked, but I had to balance it later in life with grace and understanding. After all, we are social creatures, and so we're always concerned on some level about how others perceive us.

New generations in the workplace increasingly expect leaders to know when they need to listen and to not use the status quo as an excuse to avoid doing the right thing. This is the hallmark of courage for today's workers.

And while being courageous is risky, by being a coward, we pay an even higher price.

Courage is influencing peers and senior leaders that your team's safety demands a new way of working remotely despite default cultural norms.

It is telling corporate leaders that it will take longer to build a Wegmans distribution center because you want to involve the community.

It is accelerating your promise to replace Washington DC school bus fleets with electric vehicles instead of doing the minimum required.

It is making a deal with community neighbors about light and sound pollution in the absence of a legal obligation because there is value in being a good neighbor.

Today's leadership imperative is to level up by listening to *all* our stakeholders— our employees, our consumers, and our communities—and ignoring the voices outside that group, even when those voices are louder, harsher, or more threatening. This takes courage.

Today's consumers have an inherent understanding of adversity. We all face it. We all risk offending someone when we tell the truth. We all face challenges in our lives, be it from external forces outside of our control like inflation or government regulation, and also from internal pressures like a work issue or a personal situation. This context is implicitly understood by Millennials and Generation Z by virtue of their lived experience. Accordingly, very little quarter is given to corporations that refuse to have a backbone when episodic, economic hardships arise.

The most successful leaders and organizations will encounter difficulties along the path to business success as well. Here's the lesson: responsible leaders make tough decisions that align with the best interests of the organization and *all* its stakeholders. While Wall Street may not always be in favor of such choices, the courageous move is to navigate past the temporary headwinds. Rather than catering solely to institutional shareholders, we need to consider the bigger picture. Though short-term setbacks such as stock price fluctuations are possible, the long-term benefits of conscientious leadership far outweigh any immediate pains. By prioritizing the welfare of often overlooked stakeholders like employees and customers, we can create positive ripple effects that will validate our decisions far into the future.

5 | Good Habits and the Price of Renewal

At UPS, Peak Season is generally the period beginning around Thanksgiving and ending just after Valentine's Day. During this annual period of extraordinary activity, it is not uncommon for the logistics network to operate at or above anticipated capacity in most operated facilities.

Peak Season 2017 was unlike any other. I had been working in our Pleasantdale Hub on the manual sortation line since about 2 a.m. one morning. "This one goes on the green belt. That one goes on the brown," I intoned mentally. Muscle memory overtook brain power as I picked up another package from the endless stream of boxes sliding down the primary conveyor belt. Robotically, I assessed its condition and sorted the package. Instinctively, I looked up toward the roof where a small window served as my clock, and I saw the first sliver of daylight, which meant it was about 6 a.m. For unionized shift workers, the glint of dawn meant a well-deserved break. For white collar "office" workers like me, it meant saddling up for phase two of our workday. With hardy reminders of the value of partnership in the business, and *sometimes* free donuts or pizza, we sauntered off to a holding area to be assigned new tasks. The days stretched for 12 and sometimes 18 hours. My task was to get in my personal delivery vehicle (PVD) and start delivering packages. My PVD at the time happened to be my beloved, midnight black Infiniti g37 S drop-top convertible that required premium gasoline. I wasn't thrilled to fill its custom leather seats to the brim with heavy boxes. But the price of partnership required sacrifice, and so I did.

Later that evening, I completed my deliveries in the small town of Powder Springs, Georgia, a little more than 30 miles from my home then in Sandy Springs (a suburb north of Atlanta). As you drive through Georgia's countryside around dusk, you see the sun's generous orange and yellow hues wash tall buildings in a glow. By the time you leave the city skyline, everything opens into vast fields and forests. At night, the drive becomes daunting once in Powder Springs as navigating the byways of the town reminded me of how cow paths dominated the road systems of old Georgia. It was not the safest job for a 30-year-old Black man, in a blacked-out Infiniti, making stops at random houses in a rural North Georgia town. So, I made my final delivery and quickly turned toward home.

Upon my arrival home, I relished the thought of cracking open a cold brew. I pulled into the garage, exited my vehicle, and noticed as I went to close the car door that I had somehow missed a package next to the front passenger door wedged between the seat and safety belt.

Staring at the small package with great indignation, I faced a moment of truth: I could choose not to see it, I could mark it as lost on my phone, or I could wait until tomorrow and sort it back on a belt to be delivered again. The latter option would result in a failed service commitment, unfortunately.

It was in that moment I understood my dad's admonition that our values become evident when no one is looking. I was really, really tempted to walk inside and crack open that beer. Instead, I took the long, hard road back to Powder Springs to make that final delivery—not because I received any extra penny to do so but because it's who I am, and it's who I want my team members to be.

If we want our teams to be at their best, then they have to trust we are doing the hard work. Doing our best even when no one is looking become the unconscious habit of conscientious leaders.

Similarly, in the absence of regulations and public scrutiny, organizations that do more than the minimum for people have stronger outcomes. Remember that our working thesis is that any process, thought, experience, or emotion that *can* manifest at an individual level, *may* manifest at an organizational level given the right conditions. So, the muscles we build as individual leaders become the muscles we build as organizations.

Habits are powerful tools that shape our lives. They form gradually. Habits formed at the individual and organizational levels can be powerful forces of productivity. The more times we repeat a behavior in particular situations, the stronger those habits become. Research shows us why and how these habits stick with us, allowing them to influence daily decisions without conscious thought.

On an individual level, we might create daily routines for optimizing a workspace or dedicating set times to checking emails; collectively, organizations may form shared habits that guide problem-solving, methods for efficient production, or promote healthy stakeholder relationships. Good habits can create efficiencies, foster collaboration, and encourage creativity—but bad ones can cause stagnation, inhibit growth, and make changes difficult to execute. For any enterprise to thrive, periodic scrutiny of organizational habits helps to discern and rectify activities that either bolster or degrade performance.

Psychologists Wendy Wood, Jeffry Quinn, and Deborah Kashy spent years researching the formation of habits. In a study, they used self-report questionnaires to gather information from participants about their habits and the context in which they engage in those habits. Participants were asked to describe their habits in various domains of life, such as work, leisure, and relationships, and to rate the strength of their habits.

The survey data was analyzed to identify patterns in habit formation and to explore the relationship between habits and other psychological variables such as personality and motivation. Participants were signaled by a watch alarm each hour to report their behaviors, thoughts, and emotions in a diary—a stable context. To ensure accuracy in completing the diary, participants were instructed to make their hourly entries while the events occurred. Participants reported their thoughts by answering the open-ended question, "What were you thinking about during this activity?" Participants would write a short description of a single thought.

In a second study, which included more participants and a longer reporting period, the researchers allowed reports of multiple thoughts and behaviors. Participants carried the diary forms with them, recording their behaviors, thoughts, and emotions and rating them on a scale from very easy to very difficult, and from almost no attention required to constant attention required.

The researchers found that, in a stable context, aspects of the cognitive process controlling performance become automatic and relatively easy to execute. In other words, it literally becomes easier to do tasks like lifting weights, doing laundry, or studying when those behaviors become habitual. Their performance demands less from their cognitive processes and ultimately strengthens responses over time.[1]

I knew this from experience. After nearly seven years of rolling up my sleeves for Peak Season, the task became less painful, and even enjoyable at times. I think most UPS executives share that sentiment. The habit, however, was a shared bond between every UPSer from the highest station to the lowest and tied the organization together in a cultural experience. Service, after all, was our core business.

Another endearing eccentricity at UPS was to require leaders to maintain a clean desk. At the end of the day, when you leave your office, the desk should be clear of papers and forms. The clean desk rule was not just a security objective, it was a cultural relic designed to encourage orderliness. The clean desk became an organizational habit. Each desk became a reflection of the person and thus the organization. The logic is simple. If you start and end the day with a clean desk, you reinforce the value of accomplishing tasks more efficiently. By ending each day with the act of organizing and returning things to their appropriate place, the operation for the subsequent day is set up for success. Like the no beard policy, the clean desk rule was ingrained like so many traditions in mature organizations. Some traditions have enduring relevance others become stale; this is why it is so important to reexamine organizational habits often.

Unlike the no beard policy, however, this kind of organizational habit is impactful in any logistics environment because each person relies on another to complete an objective. Resources must be in their proper place for the operation to move in an efficient manner. Like any cooperative game, the players have a common objective that they must work together to achieve; they must communicate regarding this common objective; they must often share information, coordinate their actions, and support each other; they must make decisions together and thus listen to each other, compromise, and find solutions that benefit the group as a whole; they must depend on each other's actions and, ultimately, each contribute to the outcome meaningfully.

The U.S. military has long recognized that individual habits create and support the conditions for organizational achievement. U.S. Navy Admiral William H. McRaven explained to the University of Texas in a 2014 graduation speech, "[i]f you make your bed every morning you will have accomplished the first task of the day. It will give you a small sense of pride, and it will encourage you to do one task and another and another. By the end of the day, that one task completed will have turned into many tasks completed. Making your bed will also reinforce the fact that little things in life matter. If you can't do the little things right, you will never do the big things right."[2] A habit as simple as cleaning your desk or making your bed creates powerful psychological connections between individual leaders and organizational performance. Imagine how equally powerful bad habits can be.

A meaningful habit is not surplusage, but rather an important tendency acquired through prior success, and thus encouraged to be repeated. According to the *American Journal of Psychology*, a habit is a fixed way of thinking or feeling that occurs subconsciously. Because positive and negative habits can be formed, they must be subject to periodic evaluation by organizations. By consistently evaluating and improving upon our habits, we can create positive cycles that reinforce good behaviors and ultimately lead to greater success in various aspects of life.

Rooted by Legacy

James Casey, born in 1883, founded UPS in 1907 at the young age of 19. Originally named the American Messenger Company, it became UPS in 1919. By the time I joined UPS in 2015, the company had collected Casey's sayings, values, and the policies developed from them into a formal policy book. It is customary to start meetings by discussing a value from the policy book. These are frequent and deep conversations about company policies and values before every meeting regardless of topic. I would often explain how whatever policy is discussed aligns with my own values and invite my team to discuss how and if the policy aligns with their own values as well. Over time, I've seen members of my team incorporate UPS's values, and some of my own, into their own lives.

As we discussed the company's core beliefs, our conversations would often turn from the timelessness of the enumerated values to the way new ones align with them. In turn, these new shared values bring us together. And as a result, our team grew closer. The actual legal issue to be discussed at the meeting always seemed to have greater clarity and the solution gained more perspective following policy book discussions. I witnessed how honest conversations about company policy forged stronger bonds and appreciation of core values, resulting in greater synergy. When we were challenged by COVID, I had complete confidence that any member of my team could guess my decisions without asking because they understood the values upon which my leadership rested.

And so, Daniel Abraham's famous prose in *The Prince of Spring* is true. Every new season is a result of sacrifice.[3] To paraphrase Abraham, flowers don't return every spring. That's a lie. The world is renewed. The renewal comes at a price, even if the flower grows from an ancient vine. The flowers of spring are themselves new to the world, untried and untested. The flower that wilted last year is gone. Petals once fallen are fallen forever. Flowers do not return in the spring; rather they are replaced. It is in this difference between *returned* and *replaced* that the price of renewal is paid. The renewal of our organizations is a matter of relentlessly evaluating and improving our habits. In this process, we have to accept some things will wither away, while stronger, refined values will take root. These new values will grow from the same ancient vine, but they will be better suited for the challenges of the present and future.

In a conscientious organization, the rank-and-file and directors are part of an ongoing continuum of moral principles that guide how we do business when things are difficult and confusing. Every action we take must be aligned with core values, and in this way, it becomes much easier to incorporate divergent voices, contemplate difficult questions, and make courageous decisions.

Loyalty Dividends

Costco wasn't always Costco. In fact, it got its start as Price Club in 1976 in sunny San Diego, California. That wasn't just a catchy title either, but the brainchild of founder Sol Price and his son Robert. It was one of the first retail warehouse clubs in America and was headquartered inside an old airplane hangar that had once belonged to the eccentric, legendary Howard Hughes, which is still open today. Price Club targeted small business owners who would buy in bulk after paying an annual membership fee. The store had its IPO (initial public offering) in 1980 and by 1986 had over 1.1 million members. The company merged with Costco, a warehouse market based in the Pacific Northwest, in 1993 after turning down an offer from the mighty Walmart spinoff Sam's Club. By 2014, Costco was the third largest retailer in the United States; today it boasts almost 300,000 employees and in 2020 exceeded 100 million members.

Costco cofounder and CEO James Sinegal was there from the beginning, a son of working-class Catholic parents in Pittsburgh; he became a billionaire, in part, through an unceasing work ethic and core values. At age 19, he started as a bagger at FedMart and started moving his way up the chain. By the mid-1970s, he was executive vice president in charge of merchandising and operations and used that springboard to take on similar roles at other big chain companies.

James was famous in the Costco family for traveling to every store location every year to inspect them personally for cleanliness, service, friendly employees, stocked shelves, and every other tiny detail. He was one of the first pioneers to realize that a warehouse store like his shouldn't just be a place to shop, but a place to get a myriad of needs satisfied, almost like a miniature mall of goods and services without all the glitz and sparkly lights of a shopping complex. So, he created Costco with fresh food, an eye-care clinic, a pharmacy, a gas station, and a place to rotate, repair, and replace car tires. He was known for a benevolent style of management and customer service that made him plenty of friends in the customer base and fans in his employee ranks.

Importantly, he offered higher compensation than the industry standard. Costco provides health care benefits to more than 90% of its employees, compared to the average 60% in the U.S. retail industry. Not surprisingly, Costco is reported to have the lowest employee turnover rate in all of retail. From Price to Sinegal, Costco has created a culture around being obsessed with value and passing it on to customers, of treating employees well, and delivering what customers need and want. It is a habit upon which all executives agree and animates every action taken by every employee.

Even though Sinegal retired in 2011, Costco continues to uphold his values of passion, integrity, ownership, and motivation. As a result, Costco's customers and employees are some of the most loyal in all of retail. My own family remains loyal, long-time Costco members because James Sinegal's core values are evident in every Costco store we enter. Values beget loyalty, and that loyalty pays dividends in challenging times as indicated by Costco's SVP of Investor Relations Rob Nelson. In the same quarterly earnings report discussed in Chapter 4, Nelson noted that despite recent inflationary pressures that Costco would not be raising membership fees, and among other things noted "[w]e're not seeing a lot of change in our throughput [foot traffic] in the buildings. . . . We're not seeing trade down really. We're seeing a little bit of shift in where people are spending their money."[4] Translation: their customers are really loyal. Good corporate habits can make any organization successful.

On My Airplanes

Delta Airlines is one of many, large, Atlanta-based corporations. Founded in 1928, the airline has many hubs, but none more prominent than Atlanta Hartsfield-Jackson Airport, which has been among the busiest airport in the world since 1988. In fact, nearly every American east of the Mississippi has transited the airport at some point. After teetering on the edge of bankruptcy due to high fuel costs and barely avoiding a hostile takeover by U.S. Airways in the mid-2000s, Delta built itself back up to be one of the most successful airlines in the country, if not the world. The company generated $16.4 billion in revenue in 2005, and by 2015 was back up above $40 billion per year.

State and city governments love having a major corporation as a resident and do as much as possible to ensure they are happy and they don't consider leaving for greener pastures. The city of Atlanta and the state of Georgia are no exceptions to that rule.

Delta employs roughly 33,000 people in Georgia, and in 2018, the corporation was set to benefit from a renewal of tax law legislation that would give it a whopping $40 million tax break from the state. But a tragic thing happened on the way to the tax break, and it showed just how nasty things could get in a hurry.

On Valentine's Day, 2018, 19-year-old Nikolas Cruz entered Marjory Stoneman Douglas High School in Parkland, Florida, and murdered 17 people, and injured 17 others. It was the deadliest U.S. school shooting ever at a high school, surpassing the dark days at Columbine High School in Colorado in 1999. Cruz used an AR-15–style semi-automatic rifle, a weapon that has unfortunately become synonymous with school shootings. The National Rifle Association (NRA), one of the most powerful influencing bodies in the country, hails the weapon as "America's rifle," which has drawn the NRA considerable criticism because of its use in several of the most gruesome mass shootings in American history.

After the Stoneman Douglas High School mass shooting, Delta announced it would end airfare discounts to members of the National Rifle Association. The NRA consistently opposes regulations on assault rifles and other firearms. Delta was hardly the only company to take action like this, but it was the one that conservative Georgia politicians could most easily punish for its stance.

As a result, Georgia politicians cut Delta out of the tax-break renewal for what they felt was an attack on conservatives. The state's then Lieutenant Governor Casey Caigle, went as far as to tweet that he would personally "kill any tax legislation that benefits @Delta" until the airline backed off its ban on NRA discounts. As an executive across the street, I watched the back and forth in horror.

Delta CEO Ed Bastain punched back hard after the bill was passed, writing in a company-wide memo that, "Our decision was not made for economic gain and our values are not for sale. We are in the process of a review to end group discounts for any group of a politically divisive nature."[5] The gesture turned the company's controversial move quickly into a positive one, as New York Governor Andrew Cuomo tweeted the next day, "@Delta, if Georgia politicians disagree with your stand against gun violence, we invite you to move your headquarters to New York." The governor of Virginia made a similar offer later that day.

Delta convinced those lawmakers to reinstate the tax break with one of the most impressive and least-used political strategies by a corporation—it did nothing and said nothing and sat around taking care of its own for nearly six months.

During that time, Lieutenant Governor Cagle, who was running for the GOP nomination for governor, lost the primary, effectively ending his involvement in the whole deal. Then, the state's governor, Nathan Deal, who was ineligible to run for reelection because of term limits, suspended the fuel tax that would have decimated Delta because he didn't have to worry about what his party would think of him.

Yet the Republican state legislature voted to revoke the tax credits again when the CEO publicly announced that Georgia's 2021 voting bill, SB202, did not match Delta's values. At this time, the issue was almost as controversial as automatic weapons. Critics took a dim view of ballot access restrictions championed by the Georgia House of Representative. After the 2020 presidential election, President Donald Trump claimed rampant voter fraud took place in Georgia, which voted for a Democrat for the first time since 1992. A recount showed that President-elect Biden won the state's tally by over 12,000 votes. In response, the legislature spent the next several months formulating plans to make voting far more restrictive. This led Delta's CEO to release another memo to employees on April 1, 2021, stating that "the entire rationale for this bill was based on a lie: that there was widespread voter fraud in Georgia in the 2020 elections. This is simply not true. Unfortunately, that excuse is being used in states across the nation that are attempting to pass similar legislation to restrict voting rights."[6]

Delta stood its ground and again came out ahead. Sure, there is some pain associated with losing tax credits, but the pain is short-lived. The success of being on the right side with consumers is invaluable. Today's consumers react to clear and definite statements of values. And react to Delta they did. Bastian explained: "Delta believes that full and equal access to voting is a fundamental right for all citizens. . . . We are committed to continuing to listen to our people and our communities and engage with leaders from both parties to ensure every eligible employee and Georgia voter can exercise their right to vote." Notably, the loyalty customers have to this premium airline endures. In July 2023, Ed Bastian was interviewed by Liz Hoffman and was asked about remote work. Ed smartly noted, "[w]hen I talk to CEOs and they moan about how they're having a hard time getting their employees in, I say 'I know where they are—they're on my airplanes.'"[7]

Today, Delta continues to thrive and offers a cautionary tale for other politicos looking to do battle with principled organizations. And the company remains one of America's safest and most profitable airlines despite the political blowback.

Values, when taken seriously, are a core strength, and I proudly fly as a medallion member on Delta exclusively because of them. But corporate values not only shape behavior of consumers like my own loyalty to Delta. It also influences employee performance.

Values Drive Results

A study, published in *Frontiers in Psychology*, outlines in detail the fact that ethical leadership increases employee satisfaction, productivity, and willingness to rethink and transform.[8, 9] While leaders use norms and procedures to shape the work environment, it's our informal behaviors and habits that shape it most. When we live by our values, we automatically encourage ethical behavior while reinforcing our own credibility. The more ethical a company's leadership, the more it produces positive outcomes.

The researchers sought to test the hypothesis that ethical leadership has a positive correlation to employees' readiness to change. To do this, they evaluated three of the largest public foreign trade organizations in the country by taking a random sampling of over 350 employees who directly reported to middle and lower-level managers in each organization.

A robust 38-item scale was used to measure the ethical leadership of middle and lower-level managers, specifically the various ethical leader behaviors that comprise this scale, namely, people orientation, power sharing, fairness, concern for sustainability, ethical guidance, role clarification, and integrity. The scale used a Likert response format (1 = "strongly disagree," 5 = "strongly agree"). Sample items used included statements like: "can be trusted to do the thing(s) he/she say(s) he will do" and "shows concern for sustainability issues." The responses were averaged for each respondent such that higher scores indicated a stronger ethical leadership.

The study found that ethical leaders are superior to transformational leaders when operating within defined organizational culture. While change leaders effectively communicate their visions and facilitate organizational transformation, ethical leaders do so with a higher degree of trust and empowerment, especially because they are more likely to include their employees in the change process.

When employees have faith in their leaders' intentions, they feel a stronger sense of control and self-confidence and are therefore better able to face the unknown. In other words, conscientious leaders navigate their teams through uncertainty better. And because the ebbs and flows of business are always uncertain, conscientious leadership is a differentiator between those companies that navigate change well and those that fail.

Recession-Proof Relationships

Conscientious leaders have a habit of self-critique—one that I became well-acquainted with during my first job out of law school. The 2008 Great Recession was like the opening line of Charles Dickens's *A Tale of Two Cities*—"It was the best of times, it was the worst of times." Without question, it was a time of great economic hardship, but it was also a time of great innovation. With traditional jobs in manufacturing and construction hard to come by, many people turned to entrepreneurship and found new ways to make a living. The sharing economy, for example, took off during the recession, with companies like Airbnb and Uber providing new opportunities for people to earn money. At the same time, the recession also spurred a wave of creativity, as people looked for ways to stretch their limited resources. From community gardens to DIY websites, the Great Recession gave rise to several trends that are still with us today. In many ways, then, the Great Recession was not simply a time of misfortune, but also a time of opportunity.

Officially, the Great Recession lasted 18 months from 2007 to the middle of 2009. It took six years from the end of the Great Recession to recover to the pre-recession rate of long-term unemployment, which didn't reset to normality until June 2015. That's the environment into which I graduated from law school.

Emory University is well-respected, and my legal education more than prepared me for a first-year apprenticeship at a reputable firm, but the combination of high unemployment and a dearth of job openings made it extremely difficult to find employment, even for highly educated professionals. Like most, I found myself sending out hundreds of applications without so much as a response, let alone an interview. For my peers who did land interviews, the competition was stiff. Even low-level openings that would not typically be considered by an Emory graduate began receiving applications. It was a discouraging time for many people, and it took a toll on both their mental and physical health. Luckily, I eventually landed a job at a good firm. The catch? I had to move to Kansas City, Missouri.

Shook, Hardy & Bacon was one of the country's top law firms. At the time, it was paying entry-level associates a whopping $110,000 a year. That was an eye-popping number for a 24-year-old law school graduate and certainly one from Walterboro, South Carolina. My parents told me to pack my bags. I was in no position to say no to an offer like that. I didn't realize how much my world would change with that offer.

Before the offer, I was jobless, and my only savings was leftover student loan money. So, to have a roof over my head while I frantically searched for work to avoid going back to Walterboro, I stayed at a roach motel on Memorial Drive in Atlanta.

The motel must have been nice once, but time had not been kind to it. The paint was peeling, the windows were cracked, and the roof was leaking. Pimps and sex workers turned adjacent rooms into brothels, and needles were strewn about the property. Shirtless voyeurs hung out on balconies overlooking the parking lot, and gunshots occasionally went off on the weekends. The lobby reeked of cigarettes and urine, and the walls were stained with God knows what. I was in a place of despair but not without determination to find a way out.

One morning, I was awakened by a phone call and the powerful voice of my mentor Dinisa Folmar, an attorney at Coca-Cola. "What are you doing, Andrew?" It was around 7:30 a.m., and I could sense Dinisa had just finished Bootcamp workout class. I lied. "I'm up and working on a project," I said with as much force as I could to avoid sounding as if I'd just been roused from sleep. "Well, get dressed and come to the office this afternoon. I have some people I want you to meet." By office, she meant the Coca-Cola Headquarters in Atlanta.

Dinisa was one of America's very best lawyers. She passed away in 2020 leaving an incomparable impact on my life as mentor and friend. She had an extraordinary career as a corporate lawyer in the world's largest and most respected companies, including Coca-Cola, Nike, and Hershey. I met Dinisa in my second year of law school through the Coca-Cola externship program with Emory University. Emory and Coca-Cola have a unique connection through the Goizueta School of Business, which has been a training ground for Coca-Cola's executive ranks for years. That relationship has blossomed since the University's business school adopted the namesake of Coke's former CEO Roberto Goizueta and includes special programs for Emory law school students.

Either during or shortly after the externship, I can't remember, Dinisa became the executive counsel to Coke's then general counsel, Bernhard Goepelt. I'd made an impression on Bernhard unexpectedly one evening when he invited the externs to his home for a wine tasting event in a posh Atlanta neighborhood. Bernhard, a tall and slender German with a penchant for French wine, arranged about a dozen bottles of wine on a table in his dining room with the labels obscured. His senior leadership team along with the interns stood in a circle attempting to match the names of the wines, which were scribbled on little pieces of paper, with the bottles on the table. We were down to the last few bottles of wine, and no one could guess the particular brand.

Bernhard implored the attendees to guess but the room was silent. I don't know what came over me, but I took a stab in the dark and yelled out a brand name with a level of confidence that would have made you blush had you known it was totally a guess. I guessed correctly. Bernhard was pleasantly surprised and asked how I knew the answer, to which I replied, "I have a refined palate." The room broke out in delighted laughter. After the event, Dinisa pulled me aside and asked how I knew the answer. I told her the truth, that it was a complete guess. I figured I'd fake it and win big or go down in flames. The sheer chutzpah of it all was enough to convince her to pour her wisdom into me as a young lawyer. It was the moment that changed my life's course because she committed to being my champion.

Dinisa would go on to mentor and sponsor me for my professional career until her death. She is the reason that I continue to pick up the phone for law students and focus on young lawyer development. I adopted Dinisa's guiding principles to help others whenever possible—not because I feel obligated, but because of how good it makes me feel. You never know when a phone call can be someone's escape from a place of despair.

A Willingness to Change

I interviewed in Kansas City not long after Dinisa rescued me from that roach motel. Imagine, a poor boy from rural South Carolina walking into a marble and glass Amlaw 100 firm in a city he's never been to before. It began like a bad joke. My first interview was with a partner named Bill Sampson, author of the novel *Wheat Fields*, and former Navy judge advocate.

I walked into Bill's office, sat down, and braced myself for what was sure to be the most difficult interview of my life. He came from behind his desk and sat next to me in a mahogany chair. And what happened next was life changing for me. Bill didn't ask the normal interview questions like "Why do you want to work here?" or "Tell me about your patent law experience." He inquired about my life. Seared in my memory is the most thoughtful and gracious man who was willing to give me a shot. When we talk about making social progress, the most impactful outcomes happen when people like Bill extend an opportunity to people like me. And as I look back over the years, it was his decision to give me an equal chance that changed the course of my career.

Bill was not an archetypal law firm partner. He was introspective, thoughtful, and deliberate in his actions—a leader who considered how he could help shape lawyers for generations to come. The quintessential Kansan, Bill carried an approachable air about him, and was as plain spoken as if he had once been Dorothy's uncle from *The Wizard of Oz*. Unfortunately, not all the partners shared such traits; one partner, who I'll call Mitchell, was a difficult manager to work with during my time there.

As any new law firm associate working on high-profile cases does, I did my best to please Mitchell, but nothing seemed sufficient. My writing was never good enough, ideas never creative enough, and despite an earnest desire to learn his style, I always seemed to come up short. He gave me a scathing review. So bad, in fact, that my moderator exclaimed it was "the worst review she had ever seen completed for an associate." It was, however, an outlier.

The signals I received from working with Mitchell, while helpful in some regard, also conflicted with the signals I received from others like Bill. Mitchell gave me negative feedback while others gave me positive feedback. I will never forget Mitchell penning the words "he can't write" on my evaluation, which happens to be a common trope about young Black lawyers. It became a zero-sum proposition: Was I doing a good job or not?

Mitchell truly believed I would not cut it in the profession. Perhaps I was actually a terrible writer at the time. After all, I was a first-generation college graduate and first-generation lawyer. No roadmap or template was given to me. But, rather than allowing one partner's perspective to discourage me and to avoid engaging in unproductive conflict, I opted to proactively pursue the truth. So, I reached out to multiple mentors and partners and pursued additional work opportunities, questioning everything along the way. Bart Eppenauer, a partner and previously Microsoft's chief patent counsel, was one of those mentors. He was effusively complimentary of my writing. Together we authored amicus curiae before the U.S. Supreme Court. So, I was confused by conflicting data. But, I knew one thing to be true, that a price would be paid to overcome Mitchell's criticism. I would tease through it and improve myself by first mastering Mitchell's style.

A strong desire to self-assess pushed me to understand the purported deficiencies. By learning Mitchell's way, even when I occasionally disagreed, I realized that improvement is principally about the willingness to change. Like the flowers of spring, some of my own habits fell away and were replaced. For example, some diction, vernacular, sentence structure, and syntax were supplanted with a new approach, and accomplishing this grew a new ability from an old vine.

Because I sought out so many other opinions, I was able to counter the one critical opinion and ensure my career wasn't prematurely derailed. At the same time, I demonstrated my willingness to confront my shortcomings and make appropriate changes to help all my partners as much as possible.

When pitched in a difficult situation, either professionally or personally, I have found that looking inward is the most beneficial way of addressing the challenge. Undoubtedly, external feedback can give insights into a situation, but self-assessment is equally important. Grounding myself in this knowledge has enabled me to confidently face every challenge head-on.

As conscientious leaders, it is our duty to attentively consider harsh truths and to perform honest evaluations of ourselves. We can't let criticism stop our momentum and the insights we can gain from unfavorable feedback can be invaluable in making progress. Through introspection and reflection, we can instill a sense of moral conviction in our decision-making, free from the influence of fear. When we pay the price of renewal our organizations flourish in new seasons.

6

Dig Deep
for Inspiration

Walmart Supercenter #1358 is located on Bells Highway, South Carolina, just off Interstate 95. The store is approximately 33,000 square feet and consistently employs between 100 and 200 associates. It first opened in October 1992 and, much to the chagrin of local merchants, is open 24 hours a day, seven days a week. I worked at this Walmart over the summer as a college student, and I can remember what a big deal it was to have a "supercenter" in Walterboro. In the early 1990s Walterboro's 5,600 residents largely depended on agriculture and personal services for jobs. Though a Ford dealership proved lucrative to some extent, other major employers like the Colleton County School District and local hospital were not enough to counterbalance large-scale job losses from the departure of enterprises like the Carolina Freight Company and Stanley Furniture Co., which greatly diminished access to good jobs.

Despite these challenges however, many Walterborlians found economic success through farming and related activities such as tobacco production and selling produce like watermelons and boiled peanuts to travelers stopping along I-95. Unfortunately, the presence of Walmart all but reduced these activities to zero for some—my grandpa among them. The store's presence along the highway also meant that travelers declined to go deeper into Walterboro to purchase food from the local mom-and-pop establishments, or even the more regional offerings like Food Lion, Winn Dixie, or Piggly Wiggly.

Still, despite the downside I was super excited to have a "big town" store in Walterboro. To me, luxury meant having some extra money to buy a VHS tape at the Bells Highway Walmart out of one of the large bins in the store. In those days, an assortment of VHS tapes would be thrown all together and dumped into large containers in front of the electronics department. You had to dig deep into the bins to find good movies at the bottom. On any given weekend, you would see scores of people diving into the bins and sifting through the tapes while tossing ones they'd already seen from one end of the bin to the other. One weekend, my father brought home a bin tape that I have rewatched a hundred times since. *Separate but Equal* starring Sidney Poitier tells the story of Thurgood Marshall, who argued the 1954 case *Brown v. Board of Education* before the U.S. Supreme Court, which ruled that racial segregation in public schools was unconstitutional, and in 1967 became the first Black U.S. Supreme Court justice. I would watch the movie with my sister on repeat along with other hits like John Korty's *Autobiography of Miss Jane Pittman* and August Wilson's *Piano Lesson,* because we both happened to be strikingly nerdy children, and because the acting was so good.

Seeing our fascination with the movie made my parents remark that they would soon have one doctor and one lawyer in the family—a reference to Damien Leake's child psychologist opposite Poitier's Marshall. Angela and I never quite knew who the doctor would be and who would be the lawyer. It turns out, I ended up the lawyer. Angela is still working on being a doctor.

In one scene, Poitier arrives in South Carolina after a long train ride under the cover of darkness. He is driven to a church on a dirt road, not unlike Sandhill, and the congregation can be heard singing "Pass Me Not" from the outside—still a favorite hymn in old Baptist churches. The scene advances into the church where Poitier makes remarks about the challenges of achieving equality in schooling for South Carolina's children. At that time, segregated schools provided substantially different resources for White schools than for Black ones. To improve their chances of success, Poitier recommends to the congregation that they band together to file a complaint against the local school board. After some discussion among the congregants, where opposing views are parried, Tommy Hollis playing Harry Briggs Sr., rises to address the notion that a lawsuit would take anything away from the well-funded White school. He emphatically proposed that all he wanted was an equal education for his children. Briggs was inspired to fight, not for himself but for his children. Upon this conscientious foundation, he rallied other families to fight for their children, and the rest, as they say, is history.

Poitier's historical drama biased me to always wonder about what drives people. What drives people to do courageous things? I could only conclude that, while selfish desires like seeking wealth can be motivating, external factors play a significant role in shaping our actions. For example, love for others can be an incredibly powerful force that inspires us to take brave and selfless actions. Whether it is love for a family member, a friend, a community, or even a cause, the desire to protect and uplift those we care about can lead us to overcome great obstacles and put ourselves in harm's way, like Harry Briggs. And just like the Briggs family, I couldn't resist the legal profession's promise to equip me with the ability to fight for those I care the most about.

What's more, in law school, I learned that I didn't have to be a civil rights lawyer to accomplish this goal. As the world becomes smaller due to globalization, the role of legal advisor has become more important than ever in advancing equity within companies and in broader society. Of course, lawyers play a vital role in ensuring compliance with the ever-changing legal landscape, but we also use our influence to shape decision-making in ways that have a positive impact on communities. Corporate lawyers are at the forefront of initiatives to promote fairness and advance liberty. Our work not only ensures compliance with antidiscrimination laws, but also includes negotiating better pay and working conditions for employees, complying with environmental regulations, and drafting policies that promote more accessible workplaces. Each of these steps can help make a real difference in the lives of individuals and in the culture of a company. And, when more companies adopt these practices, it can have a positive ripple effect on society. In many ways, we are only limited by the extent of our inspiration.

During my tenure with the Coca-Cola Company, I learned that it was more than a beverage company; among other things, it was a research and development company. Particularly, the company's work on food preservation and containerization struck me as game changing for people in remote areas without ubiquitous refrigeration. Novel gas barrier additives, for example, extend the shelf life of carbonated drinks and other food packaging. They were intended to help the distribution and sale of Coke products, but these discoveries can be applied in humanitarian contexts where weather and long transit times make delivery of fresh products and foodstuffs difficult. I even supported pioneering scientists in documenting and protecting their novel developments. This endeavor left a meaningful impression on me, and I left Coca-Cola with a new sense of purpose to serve my community with my newly acquired legal skills. Even ostensibly minor scientific advancements can have far-reaching and significant impacts on society, further highlighting the importance of protecting and preserving scientific progress for all inventors—including those hillbilly inventions that we all have tucked away in our papa's toolshed.

In addition to using its innovation for humanitarian pursuits, Coca-Cola has a long history of community service in Atlanta, Georgia. Coke sponsors the arts, local parks and community spaces, beautification projects, food markets and food banks, and a plethora of other micro-miracles. These efforts have not only helped to improve the quality of life for residents of Atlanta, but they have also helped to put the city on the map as a thriving center of culture and commerce. Indeed, Coca-Cola's dedication to giving back has played an important role in shaping the identity of Atlanta as a city. From technology development to building community parks, the experience at Coca-Cola inspired me to broaden my view of the impact lawyers have, and the abounding opportunities to help others.

Along my career journey, I've sought to champion equality and become a voice for those who are otherwise unheard. Each new role offered a different opportunity to make an impact. I have hired underrepresented employees and women so they could build generational wealth for their families. I've influenced labor and employment issues that dramatically impact work conditions for union workers and their families, and I've helped launch digital-access platforms that helped open China's market to minority- and women-owned businesses. So today, a mom-and-pop shop, like my mom's cake business in Walterboro, can serve clients and customers in new markets. Each decision is calculated to make some small improvement in a small locus of corporate influence. Imagine what we could do if an army of conscientious leaders worked together to the same end!

It's not traditional civil rights work but it is meaningful to the lives of those impacted. Many great organizations struggle to eliminate prejudice and discrimination—but not enough high-octane executives care enough about social justice and the future of our communities to make tough but necessary business decisions. The next frontier for civil rights struggles lies between the cubicles and corner offices of our corporations as much as it does any other arena.

This is what inspires me to get up every morning. And I'm not alone in this. In recent years, there has been a marked shift in the priorities of young workers when it comes to their careers. Gone are the days when a stable job with a good salary was the overriding goal. Instead, millennials are increasingly seeking out jobs that motivate them and align with their values. There are a few reasons for this change. First, they have personally witnessed the damage that can be done when people pursue careers that they are not passionate about. Second, they have grown up in a world where technology has made it easier than ever to find information about different companies and their practices. As a result, they are more likely to research a company before applying for a job, and they are more likely to reject a job if it does not meet their standards (like archaic facial hair rules). Finally, Millennials came of age in an era of great economic uncertainty, which made them more cautious about taking on certain career opportunities.

New Contexts Challenging Old Paradigms

Milton Friedman, one of the most influential economists of the twentieth century, famously said that "there is one and only one social responsibility of business—to use its resources and engage in activities designed to increase its profits." His view was that money was a purely financial instrument, and that its sole purpose was to motivate people to engage in economic activity. This view of money as a motivator has a long history, and it is still prevalent today. The idea is that employees will work harder and be more productive if only they are properly incentivized with cash. This view has, of course, been used to justify high salaries for executives and bonuses.

Milton may have been right to some extent in 1970. At that time, the U.S. Census Bureau pegged median annual income at around $9,870. The Bureau of Labor Statistics, which has been keeping track of family budgets for over a hundred years, notes that the cost of necessities like food, housing, and health care varied depending on the location and specific circumstances, but generally, these costs were significantly lower than they are today. For example, the average cost of a gallon of milk was around 50 cents, a loaf of bread cost approximately 22 cents, and a dozen eggs cost about 62 cents. Housing costs were also relatively affordable, with the median home price in the United States approximately $23,000 according to the National Association of Realtors. This meant that a family of four could potentially afford a home on one salary, depending on the specific circumstances and location.[1]

But we are not in 1970s America. Consider housing. The average sales price of a new home in 2020 was around $391,900 and in 2023, it reached over $410,000 in metro areas like Atlanta. Taelor Candiloro, an analyst for real estate investing firm Anytime Estimate, noted in September 2022 that "if home prices grew at the same rate as inflation since 1970, the median home price today would be just $177,788."[2] Clearly, home prices have outpaced wages, making an essential element of human security nearly unattainable in the United States. At the same time, Pew Research reports that from 1970 to 2018, the share of aggregate income going to middle-class households fell from 62% to 43%.[3] The share held by upper-income households increased from 29% to 48%, and the highest earners, CEOs and the like, had salaries grow by a staggering 1,460%

according to an October 2020 report by MarketWatch.[4] This is largely because between the 1970s and 2020s, worker productivity rose roughly 62% but wages crept up just 17.5%. In other words, even though we are more productive today, we don't realize the benefit of that productivity as much as we did 50 years ago.

Executive compensation over the years is equally concerning. In 1970, the average pay ratio of CEO to median worker was roughly 21 to 1. By 2020, the ratio was roughly 351 to 1.[5] On the high end, CEOs of companies like Google and Walmart often lead the pack. The latter, specifically, earned 933 times the average Walmart worker. (Admittedly, had I known a career at Walmart could be so lucrative, I would have stayed at the register on Bells Highway for more than a summer.) Doug McMillon has been at the helm of the nation's largest private employer since 2014 and has been with the company for more than 32 years. Walmart continues to grow, hire, promote, retain, and serve as an important part of more communities than any other company. So, fair arguments can be made for a hefty compensation. More concerning though, are the instances of exorbitant executive compensation when companies falter and take jobs and opportunity with them in their decline.

Consider Bed Bath & Beyond CEO Steven Temares. His total compensation in 2016 was over $16 million—almost double the next-highest salary in his peer group of CEOs. And Temares would continue to collect increasing compensation awards year over year despite BBB's share price experiencing one of the largest declines in its peer group. In a word, Temares' compensation was unmoored from the company's performance, which is a classic red flag. In February 2023, BBB announced it was closing nearly 150 stores; hardly a surprise as starting in 2017 its stock plummeted from a share price of $80 to under $0.19 cents. Thousands of jobs evaporated because of the company's decline and on April 25, 2023, the NASDAQ formally notified BBB that it would delist the company's common stock from the market. It hardly seems that paying Temares such a high salary was a good decision.

In many cases, economic metrics are unquestionably moving in the wrong direction and the explanations and prescriptions vary. Economists have postulated numerous theories attempting to explain the phenomena of increasing inequality in the modern economy. Oddly, despite ideological variation, there is a fair amount of consensus that extreme inequality is not desirable. And that is the key. The impact of increasing inequality should be as concerning to the conscientious executive operating in the real world as it is to nearly every academic theorist and economists from Robert Reich to Thomas Sowell. Why? Because inequality erodes individual motivation. As necessities become increasingly difficult to obtain through ordinary means, and the factors of production are increasingly concentrated in the hands of a relatively small number of individuals in society, then the ability to drive productivity evaporates as individuals refuse to engage in the futility of work that insufficiently meets their daily needs. Competition wanes when there is nearly total ownership by a few.

Most people understand the dangers of monopoly implicitly, which is the most extreme form of inequality. The less obvious concern, however, is that competition itself, without proper guard rails, creates its own negation.

Motivation and the Hungry Rat

In 1948, researchers Neal Miller and Gardner Hart at Yale University set out to understand the relationship between motivation and reward on learning. Using rats, the researchers hypothesized that there is a connection between greater motivation and greater reward. Their experiment reinforced this view. In one experiment, the researchers caged two rats: one hungry and one sated. A lever designed to release food pellets was introduced. Upon being placed in the cages, the very hungry rat frantically searched the environment for food. The satiated rat goes to sleep after a brief period of exploration. The hungry rat eventually learned that by placing pressure on an affixed lever in the cage, it can gain access to food. During the same time, the satiated rat learned nothing.[6]

In a second experiment, a mild electric shock is used to create discomfort for the rats. The shock arouses the satiated rat to frantic activity searching for a way to stop the shock. He quickly learns that hitting the affixed lever will stop the discomfort. The researchers concluded that motivation and reward can have a powerful impact on learning ability even when those rewards vary from incentive or disincentive.[7]

What can we learn from the "hungry rat" experiment? Importantly, a variety of factors motivate behavior, and any assumption that a single factor can influence behavior is misplaced. Money alone is not universally motivating especially when substantial increases in effort only yield marginal reward. This may explain the disease of concomitant declines in productivity and modest wage increases experienced in the inflationary, post-COVID economy. In August 2022, the U.S. Department of Labor released worker productivity data as it has done since 1948. The department noted that nonfarm productivity, which measures hourly output per worker, fell at a 2.5% pace from the previous year. It also declined sharply in the second quarter at a 4.6% annualized rate, after having declined by an upwardly revised 7.4% in the first three months of 2022.[8] Similar trends were reported in most mature economies around the world. While wages have marginally increased along with inflation, net productivity increases have not.

If you've ever found yourself doing the bare minimum at work, you're not alone. It is a popular misconception that the lack of motivation experienced by today's workers, dubbed "quiet quitting," is a new phenomenon.

However, "quiet quitting" has been around for decades. The 1960s and 1970s saw a seismic shift in the workplace, with Baby Boomers leading an unprecedented wave of employee dissent as they sought to challenge traditional power structures and secure greater autonomy. This pushed some workers toward quiet disengagement from their jobs—helping drive meaningful change while enabling them to exercise personal agency within volatile social climates.

In the 1980s and 1990s, workers disengaged as economic globalization incentivized businesses to prioritize profitability over employee satisfaction. This was enabled largely by technological advancements that gave workers greater control of their own work schedules via remote productivity. Contract-based employment contributed to the shift as well with employees able to come and go during the workday without drawing attention.

In 2020, the pandemic disrupted boundary lines between personal and professional lives. Many employees worked unceasingly to preserve job security in uncertain times. This led to a surge of "quiet quitting" as burnout soared in the post-COVID era.

So-called "quiet quitting" occurs when an employee stays in their jobs long after they've lost motivation or interest. They may not overtly rebel or express dissatisfaction, but they disengage from their work, doing just enough to get by. This can have a major impact on productivity, as disengaged workers are less likely to go above and beyond or put in extra effort. So why is this happening and whatever is the conscientious executive to do? There are a few possible explanations. First, in October 2023, CNBC reported that job satisfaction has been declining in recent years, with many workers feeling undervalued and unfulfilled.[9] Second, the modern workplace can be stressful, leaving workers feeling overworked, burnt out, and unable to muster the energy to do their best. As a leader with a primarily remote team, even I get discouraged when my daily calendar is filled with meetings and no time to breathe. Ideally, only one-third to one-half of an employee's day should be filled with meetings. The rest of the day should be reserved for contributive rather than deliberative work. Finally, the gig economy has made it easier for workers to hold over between old jobs and new opportunities, leading many to simply wait until they land their next job before fully disengaging from their current one.

To combat the emergent social malaise around work, conscientious leaders should think holistically about motivation. In fact, the most motivated teams are composed of well-paid believers rather than mere hired guns. Studies show that employees who are motivated by factors other than financial rewards often outperform those who are motivated by money alone. In addition, employees who are motivated by nonmonetary factors such as control over their work schedule, freedom to choose their work location (such as remote work versus daily in-person work), autonomy in decision-making, power to direct financial matters (such as vendor selection and budget control), rewards for engaging in activities or achieving certain results, perks like working in an office where food is provided, proper administrative support, recognition for work successes beyond a "pizza party," authority to set office policy, and a sense of purpose, in addition to being paid well, are often more engaged and more likely to stay with an organization over the long term.

These strategies share a common thread. They are non-hedonic freedoms that convey a sense of ownership and control in the business to the employee. They devolve power and decision-making from traditional power centers at the top of organizational hierarchy to the team. They are more democratic and underscore trust placed in employees. As a result, businesses that fail to use all the tools to stimulate motivation may be missing out on the benefits.

Ironically, the traditional tendency of most executives during economically challenging times is to "streamline" and "optimize." We've all heard these words before. They are budget-focused words. They typically mean to "flatten" organizations (i.e., cut jobs), "centralize" (i.e., consolidate decision-making into a few people), and "transform" (i.e., reorganize with the goal of divesting assets and becoming smaller). All these approaches have merit in the right circumstances but none of them addresses the root cause of employee dissatisfaction and low productivity. In fact, they may compound them. Notably, every one of these strategies results in lessening employee ownership interest in business outcomes rather than expanding them! And it is axiomatic that employee dissatisfaction is directly linked to productivity and thus profitability.

Kou Murayama is an associate professor at the University of Reading, London, and studies the science of motivation. The literature on achieving goals is often split into two categories: "mastery" and "performance." The former refers to the desire for self-mastery, or becoming more knowledgeable about something; while the latter refers to the desire to surpass others' abilities in some way (e.g., winning contests). In one experiment, Murayama sought to understand whether self-mastery or performance have a qualitatively different impact on learning achievement over time.

Participants in the experiment were split into groups and asked to complete a memory test and a problem-solving task, but each group received a different goal. The participants who were told their goal was performance rather than mastery showed better immediate retention, but when the memory was assessed one week later, participants in the mastery group performed better. In other words, when asked to beat the other team, immediate short-term results were better, but when the objective was to become experts through learning, the long-term results were better.

Intrigued by this result, Murayama further sought to understand this phenomena's interaction with motivation and reward. While the Yale researchers demonstrated extrinsic motivators like rewards can influence learning in mice, Murayama believed that extrinsic rewards could also undermine motivation in some circumstances.

In a second experiment, Murayama separated participants randomly into a reward group or a control group. Both groups were tasked with playing a game while being scanned by an fMRI machine, which helps scientists monitor brain activity. Participants in the reward group were informed that they would be rewarded for their performance whereas everyone else played just for fun. In the reward group, participants demonstrated less voluntary engagement in the task than those in the "play for fun" group. Indeed, the fMRI brain scans showed decreased activation in the striatum, the part of the reward network in the brain, for participants in the reward group.

Murayama's work demonstrates rewards may not always benefit learning tasks, which begs the question: Would the rats in the Yale experiment have learned to trigger the lever if they weren't hungry or being electromagnetically shocked? Corporations can sometimes feel like a cage and workers like unsuspecting lab rats.

As leaders, one of the greatest things we can do for our teams and employees is help them find their passions and inspire them by connecting their work with the organization's bigger purpose. Doing this while providing innovative solutions and products to consumers is a win for everyone. Of course, monetary rewards are an important part of work because no one can be compelled to work for free. But few will be motivated to work in a hellhole for money alone. Some of our office environments are frankly terrible and leadership is directly responsible for that condition.

Humans are social creatures. We are connected to each other and the world in mysterious and profound ways. To be truly satisfying, our work must have a positive impact on something greater than ourselves that inspires us to get up early and carry on through difficult times. I learned this in practice by leading my team through the pandemic. Keeping the American economy moving and delivering over a billion vaccines made it mission critical that our planes operated all day, every day. Connecting everyone's work to this great mission was a badge of honor from the rank-and-file to senior executives. It was great to know a paycheck would be deposited every other Friday, but it was even greater knowing it was coming because we were saving lives.

In the old days, joblessness was universally derided, but employment was generally praised, even if an employee was underemployed and barely making ends meet. This was generally praised as industrious. Executives would usually meet employee complaints with the retort, "I pay you. What more do you want?" The callousness of the old meta overlooks the enormous personal sacrifice. We spend a considerable amount of time at work, often more than we spend at home. A work environment devoid of purpose makes the job a daunting task, and this is one of the reasons why some companies struggle to retain staff. Workers today desire a job that provides both monetary sustenance and fulfills their values, which fits in with the new meta game of life.

Unfortunately, this is not how tiger executives (as discussed in Chapter 2) think about inspiration. I will pick on lawyers because it's my profession. Lawyers, for instance, don't receive much leadership training or think about how to lead better; we usually just focus on how to win cases. Like corporate leaders, we tend to think about accomplishing tasks, gaining leverage, making a profit, and reducing costs but not about sharing a higher purpose, individual capacity building, and long-term employee satisfaction.

The importance of motivation became crystal clear at the height of COVID in 2020, when almost everyone worked remotely. In the transportation and logistics industry, knowing we delivered lifesaving vaccines added incentive to the work. But we also did more on Zoom than just meet—we had virtual get-togethers, celebrated milestones to stay connected, and gave out gift cards so employees could have a meal at home with their families.

As conscientious leaders, we operate in both a professional and personal capacity. Our employees are not just workers: they are humans with joys, heartaches, and unique stories. When one of my employees was going through a divorce, I did more than share platitudes. On invitation, I brought a beverage to their house to share, providing time and comfort in equal measure. When another one of my employees experienced the unimaginable loss of a parent and a brother in rapid succession, I put aside international business commitments and returned to Louisville. I planned for our condolences to be delivered to the family, shifted work schedules, attended the services, and was generally present. This may not have been corporate policy, but it was the only right choice—as our humanity demands that we be available for our team during difficult times. By embodying empathetic leadership in both words and deeds, we create an environment that fosters real commitment to the enterprise.

The new virtual-work terrain also created unexpected opportunities to improve. We realized that some of our reports, meetings, and other activities added little value, so we got rid of them. And we learned that without commuting, employees had more time with their families and a more flexible lifestyle, which made them happier and led to greater productivity and willingness to work late and early.

When vaccinations became available and we all went back to the office, the potential loss of those positive changes became real concerns. Some employees were afraid we would return to the inefficient, pre-pandemic normal compounded by potential health and safety risks. I promised my team that the benefits gained from remote work were too valuable to lose. Regardless of what other teams did, we would find ways to remain flexible. That reassurance was another motivator.

I also made sure we discussed how our work connected to the organization's post-COVID long-term objectives and our support for the local community in virtually every weekly staff meeting. Occasionally, we would even invite outside subject-matter experts to explain how our activities impacted theirs, and how our day-to-day tasks support the bigger picture.

Conscientious leaders create space for teams to connect and be vulnerable together because those high-octane moments are what inspire teams to collaborate and do their best work. In vulnerability is honesty, and in honesty, an actionable roadmap to improvement. This is what makes safety and authenticity among teams so valuable. Conscientious leaders realize that cultivating a culture of vulnerability within their team is the key to success. By setting an example for open communication, providing space for bonding and training opportunities, as well as celebrating vulnerability among members, trust between peers can be nurtured and emotional safety established. Strategic retreats or social events are great ways to build deeper connections while equipping teams with mindful tools that strengthens their ability in becoming vulnerable.

The Hierarchy of Inspirational Needs

Eric Garton and Michael Mankins are partners at Bain & Company and wrote an instructive article in the *Harvard Business Review* that uses an index to peg mathematically the baseline level of employee productivity and satisfaction. They make the point that if satisfied employees are productive at a baseline level of 100, then engaged employees are productive at a level of 144, and inspired employees are productive at an astonishing level of 225.[10] Inspiration is the level of productivity that we should strive for in our teams. It is clear that to reach peak productivity, our teams must strive to be inspired by the work.

Employee engagement can be divided into three components: satisfaction, engagement, and inspiration. Satisfaction is having the necessary tools to do the job. It manifests itself in employees showing up to work and using the tools as intended. It is like showing up to practice and on game day. Engagement is akin to thinking about winning the game and attempting to do so. It is about focusing on how to best use the tools provided to achieve better-than-expected results. It looks like a team that is hungry to win. Inspired teams become consumed with the task because they understand its importance. It looks like a team that is laser-focused on winning a championship. Inspiration takes the game to a new level, creating new strategies and finding out-of-the-box solutions with the tools available. Garton and Mankins surveyed over 300 senior executives worldwide who assessed productivity based on dissatisfaction, satisfaction, engagement, and inspiration and found that the truly noteworthy productivity scores of inspired employees were statistically significant.

Garton and Mankins concluded that building an organization that employees truly love requires a central focus on inspiration. Inspirational leadership can be assessed and developed through 360-degree feedback assessments, workshops, and individual training investments, all of which can help to increase employee motivation and lead to better workforce productivity results. Strategies like articulating the vision, purpose, and goals, building meaningful relationships between employees through off site engagement, and illustrating a message through story and example are core competencies for leaders who look to lead with inspiration.

Many people view inspiration as esoteric, as if it were an innate leadership style or personality trait, but Garton and Mankins point out that it can be taught and learned. Leaders can foster inspiration by satisfying a variety of employee requirements, which are like Abraham Maslow's hierarchy of needs and can be divided into the three tiers indicating employee level of engagement.

At the first tier, employees are satisfied when they have (1) safety, (2) tools, training, and resources, (3) efficiency over excess bureaucracy, and (4) are valued and rewarded fairly.

At the second tier, all of the first tier's needs are met. Additionally, employees are engaged when they (1) are part of an extraordinarily talented team, (2) have autonomy, (3) learn and grow every day, and (4) make a difference (i.e., have an impact on the organization and their community).

At the third tier, all of the needs of the first two tiers are met. Employees at the top tier are inspired when they (1) get meaning and inspiration from their company's mission and (2) are inspired by their leaders.

Other studies have also identified a strong correlation between inspiration and productivity. Addressing employee needs at each tier generates the kind of leadership mindset, and company culture, that produces amazing results.

Titans to Remember

In 1971, Herman Boone became the head football coach at a recently integrated high school in Alexandria, Virginia. The Alexandria City Public Schools (ACPS) determined that all high school students should go to one campus, which made T.C. Williams High School serve all local eleventh and twelfth graders. Before joining T.C. Williams, he was one of the best assistant coaches in the country when it came to program success, going 99–8 in a nine-year period, and was called the "Number One Football team in America" by *Scholastic Coach* magazine in 1966. Boone resigned from coaching at E.J. Hayes High School in Williamston, North Carolina, when he was told that the school board was "not ready for a black football (head) coach" despite his record of extreme success. Disheartened, but not defeated, Boone returned to coaching in 1969 at T.C. Williams as the assistant football coach and junior varsity wrestling coach. Few people knew of his pedigree, even when he was named head coach of the newly integrated high school. Years later, he said he originally thought it was a setup. All the other coaches in the system were White, and Bill Yoast, the White assistant football coach, had more seniority and would normally have been promoted to the position. Boone suspected that the school board hoped his team would be terrible and thus give them an excuse to fire him and end integration.

That made him even more determined to do the opposite.

Boone inspired his players to be a true team with one vision. One objective. One heartbeat. He presented the state football championship as the challenge to overcome. He encouraged them to celebrate their differences instead of fearing them, to respect instead of hate each other, and to show the state of Virginia and the world the power of diversity. Before the 1971 football season, he took the team on a field trip to Gettysburg, Pennsylvania, site of President Lincoln's famous address. The trip attracted such media coverage that President Richard Nixon sent one of his aides to take in the sight of an integrated football team getting along together. Boone's unwavering determination, values, and beliefs not only carried the T.C. Williams High School football team to their 1971 state championship, but the team also brought the community together—and inspired the blockbuster movie *Remember the Titans*. In December 1971, Nixon, an ardent football fan, was quoted as saying that Boone's Titans had "saved the city of Alexandria."

Coach Boone didn't set out to change the world when he got the head coaching job at T.C. Williams High School. All he did was identify a problem and was inspired to find a solution to it. He wasn't trying to be grandiose or flamboyant or draw attention to himself. Honestly, as a Black coach in America in 1971, if anything he would have been trying to deflect attention to focus on keeping his job. When you go 99–8 over a decade and you still get told that the town isn't ready for a Black head football coach, odds are that you keep your head down, work hard with the kids, and are grateful for every opportunity that comes your way.

Humility can be hard for leaders because most of us have that alpha personality that drives us to get to the top of our respective fields. That drive pushes us to show off our skills because we know that by asserting and proving ourselves, we can move up the ladder. But, when running a business unit or company, the most effective leader is often the one who leads quietly and lets the results speak for themselves.

Yet the highest tier of inspiration requires motivation by good leaders.[11] Let's look at an even older example. Newton Knight was a reluctant White Confederate inductee. It's unfortunate he isn't a better-known hero because his legacy is a testament to what we can do when we unashamedly live by our values. He wasn't rich and didn't own slaves. When he received a letter from his wife informing him that Confederate soldiers had harassed her while plundering their farm, he defected. He was captured—and purportedly tortured—but eventually escaped.

Rather than disappearing quietly, he created the Free State of Jones in Jones County, Mississippi, and led an integrated band of 125 Union guerrilla fighters deep in the South. Although constantly surrounded and outnumbered, the Knight Company, as it came to be called, evaded capture as its members raided Confederate supply caravans and distributed the goods to the people, like Southern Robin Hoods.

After the war, the government hired Knight to liberate Black children during Reconstruction from former enslavers who were refusing to emancipate them in Mississippi. He also led an army regiment to protect freedmen as they marched to the polls in 1875. He later had five children with a Black woman named Rachel, whom he loved but could not legally marry. Still, his children honored his last wish to be buried beside her, in direct opposition to the Jim Crow segregation laws at the time. (At that time, there was segregation even in cemeteries.)

Knight had a fighting spirit—he probably could have been a Confederate war hero. But he voted against seceding from the Union, like almost everyone else in Jones County, and actively fought against slavery, inequality, and corruption. By remaining committed to those values even in the face of personal hardship, he empowered all those around him to fight for justice.

When leaders take a stand and fight for values, it shows our employees and customers that we are rooted by principles and ethically strong. It also sets the tone for the kind of organization you want to be. In the end, you will be rewarded by customers and will be remembered, just like Coach Boone and Newton Knight.

7 | Value the Invisible

When the rail industry left Walterboro, capital investment left as well and the economy flatlined. The space left was occupied by a vexatious antagonist: poverty. Poverty is a unique adversary in that the longer it remains, the more entrenched it becomes. Like a bad habit, it's an episodic condition that becomes a feature if left unchecked.

The research is varied but generally suggests that poverty can have complex psychological consequences. Humans are wired to survive, and so, the experience of scarcity is bound to do strange things to us. Indeed, poverty is linked to several undesirable outcomes, including challenges of self-control,[1] short-term thinking,[2] stress, aggression, and feelings of helplessness,[3] risk-taking,[4] impact on cognitive functioning and neurological development.[5] Arguably foremost amongst those conditions is poverty's impact on the capacity to aspire. Aspiration is an inherently social practice, and as such, it is linked to social class.[6] I think it's striking how unanimous scholarship is on the point that poverty impacts, or at least has a relationship with, aspiration and by extension, motivation. The literature regarding why and how poverty impacts our motivation can be loosely organized into five schools of thought.

The first is the "diminished possibility" school of thought. It is championed by Professor Michele Lamont at Harvard. In it, the literature highlights that poverty constrains one's aspirations by curtailing the perceptual horizon of what is possible. In other words, people in poverty aspire to more modest goals because they would not aspire to something grander.

Dr. Lamont is famous for developing the idea of culture as a "tool kit" from which people draw different resources. The intersection of culture and poverty had something of a bad reputation for a good part of the twentieth century.

97

Dr. Lamont along with Mario Luis Small and David Harding contributed to the rehabilitation of the use of culture to understand poverty in part by suggesting that it constrains the "tool kit" of behaviors, values, and practices to which we have access (at least in relation to conventional values and goals). Using a largely interpretive research method, the trio suggest that underserved communities do not have deviant values, are not actively rejecting a society they see as stacked against them or are wracked with frustration from failed aspirations. Instead, what seems possible to them is limited or simply different by virtue of the scope of their experience.[7]

The second school of thought is the "resistance" school, and it is supported by the works of Rhodes Scholar Jay Macleod. In this school, those living in poverty do not aspire, but they are right not to aspire because in most cases they will largely remain poor regardless. Underserved communities lash out by rejecting the mainstream value of aspiration because they correctly recognize that the deck is stacked against them. Social structure is the problem. Macleod's book *Ain't No Makin' It*[8] is a sociological classic that started as an undergraduate thesis and is still widely cited and taught in the field. It uses ethnography, a powerful method of study that involves firsthand observation. I was first exposed to it in Professor Donna Minnich's sociology class at George Washington University, and even had my own experience using ethnography by living homeless in Washington DC during my undergraduate studies. I confess, I was probably within the "diminished possibility" school until I shared the experience of living homeless in Washington DC, sleeping under bridges and panhandling for food.

In his study Macleod found that one group (called the "Hallway Hangers") rejected aspiration, academic success, and conventional standards of social decorum. This group felt that the odds were stacked against them to such an extent that they did not feel it was worth trying to succeed in a system in which they were destined to fail. The ethnoracial makeup of that group was largely White. In contrast, the second group (called "The Brothers") continued to embrace conventional beliefs regarding social success, work ethic, etc. In this case, this ethnoracial group was largely Black. Both groups largely ended up in similar professional and life circumstances. Macleod concluded that while poverty might impact one's beliefs regarding aspiration and work ethic, a person is likely to remain in the same social class regardless of their social aspirations. And indeed, according to a September 2022 report by the Congressional Budget Office, the top 1% of Americans hold more than a third of America's wealth; and the top 10% control more than 70%.[9] Such gross inequality has predictably led to a precipitous decline in social mobility—empirically supporting Macleod's conclusions.

The third school of thought is the "culture of poverty" school. It is best articulated by the works of men like U.S. senators J. D. Vance[10] and Daniel Patrick Moynihan. In this school, academics theorize that the impoverished do not aspire because they embrace distorted values or dysfunctional goals. Culture is the problem, and it is durable, extending across generations. Obviously, this is a decidedly conservative school of thought. Moynihan was a U.S. senator (1977–2001) from New York, an academic, and an advisor to President Richard Nixon. He wrote a famous report[11] (or infamous depending on your perspective) arguing that the experience of poverty and racism (or the perceived experience of such) has led to cultural adaptations that persist independent of the reality of those conditions. Thus, cultural habits lead to outcomes such as lack of participation or trust in formal organizations, a lack of commitment to mainstream values, and deviant family systems. This decline in ambition and personal responsibility can lead to the perpetuation of social class positions.

The "fatalistic" school of thought is clarified by the work of Professor Laura Camfield at the University of East Anglia. In this school, people in poverty aspire, and they are aware that they aspire, but they willingly curtail their aspirations to a greater or lesser degree by virtue of their belief that they will not, realistically, or concretely, be able to achieve more. Camfield and her collaborators used qualitative and quantitative investigations of expressed attitudes in emerging economies to articulate this school of thought.

For example, the researchers suggest that the gap, between a new middle class in Thailand and those who are unable to achieve that lifestyle but have been exposed to it by virtue of Thailand's recent economic growth, measurably heightens frustration due to the inability to achieve those aspirations (lack of mobility).[12] This insight broadens the argument that we all have a psychological mechanism that activates when we are unable to achieve our goals (also known as "sour grapes"). This mechanism then leads us to aspire to less than we might otherwise. More directly, it expands the argument that a failure to aspire, is a result of poverty, though they don't get into the interpretive work of why or how.

Finally, the "working intervals" school of thought is crystallized by the work of Professor Natasha Warikoo at Tufts University.[13] In this school, people in poverty aspire, though they may appear not to aspire because they are balancing their aspiration with competing social goals. Alternatively, they may aspire but embrace "deviant" cultural values as a temporary response to structural barriers. Warikoo centers her work on race and education. She argues that underserved youth engage in what she calls "balancing acts": they aim to both succeed amongst their peers while still aspiring to achieve conventional success. In this regard, while they may appear deviant or as though they embrace anti-achievement attitudes, the reality is often more complex. Her arguments are direct challenges to those in the resistance school. And I somewhat agree because this generally describes my own life experience.

As a young man, I struggled with balancing the use of financial instruments with a lack of capital. It seemed I routinely siphoned away nickels and dimes to somebody else's piggy bank. When I took money out of an ATM, I was charged $3.50. That was a lot of money when I only had $50 in my checking account. I could never get ahead. I overdrafted on bank fees and made late payments in what would appear to be either a lack of concern for obligation or an inability to manage well.

Most people understand that banks have to make money. After all, somebody has to pay the salaries of the tellers, loan officers, and other employees who provide these services. And there are also the costs of maintaining the buildings, ATMs, and other infrastructure. But what many don't realize is that these costs are disproportionately borne by those who can least afford them. Consider, for example, the fees charged for using an out-of-network ATM. These can be as high as $5 per transaction, which may not sound like much to someone who is well-off. But for someone living paycheck to paycheck, that can be a significant amount of money. And it's not just one transaction—it's every time they need to access their money. Over the course of a year, those fees can add up to hundreds or even thousands of dollars. That's money that could be used to pay rent, buy groceries, or otherwise improve the quality of life for people who are struggling to make ends meet. It's yet another way in which our society stacks the deck against those who are trying to get ahead financially. I felt unseen, invisible to my bank.

Now that I have more in the bank, transfer fees, foreign ATM fees—all fees are waived even though I can afford to pay them. It feels like the standards are wrong and the rules are backward. Shouldn't present-day me, the person most able to afford fees, be the one paying those transaction costs instead of paying less? Maybe that question betrays my cultural bias. After all, Luke 1:48 is in the signature line of all my personal emails ("For unto whomsoever much is given, of him shall be much required"). Nevertheless, "traditional" banking is a system with blind spots.

That disregard of the working poor's needs has led to the rise of an increasingly serious disruptor to traditional banking—decentralized finance. "DeFi" projects are tossing out the old rule book, saying, "We can do better." DeFi essentially fixes banking's blind spots by democratizing financial operations. Of course, frictionless transactions have their own issues, such as cybersecurity. And DeFi will have to correct its own blind spots if it wants to be sustainable.

Still, correcting blind spots is a phenomenon that corporate leaders should take as seriously as addressing community poverty. The point is, no matter which theory of poverty you believe to be correct, the results are sociological conditions unsuitable for thriving business.

All too often we invest in well-resourced communities that already have existing infrastructure and human capital to address current concerns rather than imagining the possibilities of creating prosperity in places that need it desperately, like Walterboro. The battle for tax breaks for expanding development has become a paradoxical game which pits corporations against tax payers. Just as competition creates its negation, so too does capital investment in resource-rich areas entrench poverty in others. When we fail to consider the impact of our offerings (like banking services and fees) it foments resentment and causes communities to question the way the entire system works. Overlooking these concerns is short-sighted, unconscientious, and a threat to future business.

Corporate Parallax

Neil deGrasse Tyson discusses the parallax phenomenon in his book *Cosmic Queries*. If you hold your finger in front of you, close your left eye, and view your finger's position with just your right eye, you'll see where it is in relation to a wall (or whatever is in your background). If you switch eyes and now view your finger with only your left eye, you will see a shift in your finger to a different position. Only when you look with both eyes do you get the relative position of your finger. That's parallax. In basic terms, parallax is the apparent shift of an object against a background when viewed from different positions. This phenomenon occurs because our two eyes see objects from slightly different angles.

Organizations experience a similar phenomenon, which I call corporate parallax. It occurs when various stakeholders perceive corporate actions, policies, and strategies differently because of their relative positions to each other organizationally. Failing to understand these differing perceptions can have catastrophic results. To minimize the effects of parallax, leaders must obtain data from different perspectives to reach alignment. Just as our brain combines the two views from our eyes to create depth perception, so too does an organization to see a full picture. The brain performs this effortlessly, but it takes a little more work for groups of people to do so. Thoughtfully built systems for decision-making like use of an ombudsman and 360-degree evaluations can go a long way to seeing clearly and ensure we don't overlook a blind spot.

Functions within an organization can have drastically different views on a single issue. Take, for example, unionized labor matters. In labor relations, a different set of rules can often apply when it comes to addressing concerns for various classes of employees. Rather than relying on strictly enforced legal contracts, there is sometimes an informal understanding between union representatives and management that produces what are colloquially known as "paper napkin agreements." These agreements are usually enforceable, written without precision by non-lawyers, and based more on personality and relationships than strict legality. While this shift from conventional contract negotiation may worry HR and compliance stakeholders with stricter accountability standards, handshake deals have a track record of successfully building trust between corporate parties when formal channels fall short. These agreements also create friction between legal and labor teams that must be mediated. This is why an executive ombudsman can go a long way in drawing out the best approach for the company's many stakeholders.

Max Brooks's apocalyptic horror novel and subsequent movie *World War Z* highlights the concept of "the tenth man." In the movie, the world is ravaged by a plague that turns humans into zombies. And while the time from transmission to full infection is fast, the world's humanitarian and geopolitical calamity is a slow-moving disaster creeping in from the far corners of the earth. It's gloriously entertaining. And it teaches a serious lesson about the importance of listening to the whisper of the seemingly invisible contrarian. The theory goes: if nine people agree on a single perspective, the tenth person is obligated to disagree. She must assume the other nine's interpretations are flawed and propose a different view. That practice prevents tunnel vision.

At UPS Airlines, the ombudsman was almost always the region president, a business unit, apex executive. But, often, functional leaders had their own verticals and didn't always answer to the president. A designated ombudsman can often provide an impartial view that highlights concerns or issues that may be considered from a myopic, functional perspective. Consider a paper napkin labor agreement that broadens the definition of "time worked" in a small facility where clocking in or out is easy and relatively close to where an employee works. This informal agreement could create issues for accounting and HR teams in larger facilities where workstations are dispersed and where there is a greater distance between an employee's workstation and the time clock. A small facility may even set a legal precedent if it is in the same state as a large facility—or even a national precedent when local unions are part of a brotherhood. These broader issues may not be front and center for a local labor manager looking to resolve an immediate issue but could become major concerns for the organization at large. The tenth man, however, is obligated to address the larger issue. And in this way, she makes the organization more resilient.

In a paper titled "Resilience Attributes of Social-Ecological Systems" researchers David Kerner and Scott Thomas discuss key attributes of resilient organizations.[14] Resilience theory provides a comprehensive understanding of how individuals, organizations, and systems can effectively cope with adversity. Rather than being regarded as an inherent trait or characteristic, resilience is seen as a process that involves dynamic responses to environmental challenges. It can be an invaluable framework to understand how people, organizations, and societies cope with a variety of challenges. There are at least three attributes of resilient systems that are useful for the conscientious executive to help see issues clearly: stability, adaptive capacity, and readiness.

According to Kerner and Thomas, stability is the degree to which a system can continue to function if "inputs, controls, or conditions are disrupted." Adaptive capacity is the ability of a system to "reorganize and reconfigure as needed to copy with disturbances without losing functional capacity and system identity," and readiness is how quickly "a system can respond to changing conditions." Market volatility demands that each of these attributes evolve and improve as a mechanism of survival.

In Chapter 4, we discussed how organizations generally respond when economic headwinds rattle profitability. Their first reaction is to become more efficient and forgo substantial investments. Traditionalists believe that by prescribing goals and objectives that all employees must follow, they can bring a sense of order to their organization amid disorder. This idea is predicated on the belief that successfully achieving a discrete set of goals will bring in a steady yield that is intended to "stabilize" their business and generate predictable results. However, teams that are seen as "stabilizing" can often supplant individual thought and autonomy. Creativity is sacrificed at the altar of control. A top-down approach might work in a world where every variable can be accounted for and manipulated, but not in real life where we are often not in control of countless variables. Even the oft cited maxim "control what you can control" overlooks the fact that resilient systems, by their very nature, are based on a capacity-driven framework. In other words, they are designed to effectively respond to and adapt to uncontrollable events.

Kerner and Thomas conclude that integrating diverse sets of knowledge is one of the most important attributes to a resilient system because each stakeholder has their own observations, data, and experiences that leaders must understand to make good decisions. Leaders risk failure when organizational goals don't consider all points of view. Thus, conscientious leaders ask for input and direction from many stakeholders about the intended course, and then make decisions in view of the input. Debacles such as New Coke in 1985 and Blockbuster's refusal to buy Netflix in 2000 demonstrate how quickly billions of dollars can be lost due to ill-conceived endeavors that excite a small number of myopic tiger executives but ignores the point of view of a broader team. Clear vision means having both eyes open.

Think Long-Term

Imagine your team's point of view on a given issue as a circle. Each slice of the circle represents a constituency critical to the survival of the business and gives you information about its performance. Let's say, to completely fill the circle, your team needs feedback from seven stakeholder groups. Feedback, if received from only three of the seven stakeholder groups is insufficient and necessarily limited. To see clearly, an enterprise must have robust means for receiving and acting upon all feedback from each constituency. In this example, the vision pie chart (see Figure 7.1) includes stakeholders such as shareholders, employees, consumers, communities, governments, suppliers, and creditors. Let's go back to our labor example. If John, the labor manager at a

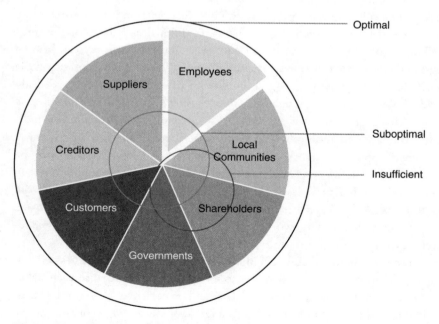

Figure 7.1   Stakeholder optimization.

small facility, wants to pay union employees from the time they enter the building, and he seeks only the input from town halls with union workers, then he may find out later that the local government relations team expressly lobbied for a uniform legislative approach, and that his actions undermine the organization's desire to gain common rules in all jurisdictions in which it operates. The same oversight could happen if John gets input from all the right stakeholders but only incomplete or partial input is actionable. Only by taking into consideration the complete and thoughtful feedback from all stakeholders can John make the right decisions.

Just as we expect our political leaders to enact legislation based on their whole constituency, not just well-financed interest groups, corporate leaders need to answer to all their stakeholders, including the often overlooked. Some stakeholders are well-understood like institutional investors, venture capitalists, funds, banks, and retail investors. Less considered stakeholders may be company retirees who earn pensions, local community members, and charities or foundations that depend on continued company giving. To ensure success, conscientious leaders consider the perspective of each of these routinely invisible stakeholders. The goal of the conscientious executive is achieving a prosperous outcome for all who rely on a business' success.

Leadership has always been about balancing priorities, but with today's dynamic pace, we need the speed of an Olympic hurdler and the emotional intelligence of a well-trained psychotherapist. Consider the pressure Amazon was under from politicians and worker advocacy groups to raise its wages in 2018. The Amazon team could have shrugged off concerns about its pay practices or tried to silence the criticism with hostility or ridicule, as many leaders do when facing criticism.

Instead, Amazon listened, raised all U.S. wages to $15 an hour, and openly supported the Raise the Wage Act that proposed a national $15-an-hour minimum wage by 2025. In 2021, Amazon announced an additional $0.50 to $3.00 an hour wage increase for 500,000 employees to help fill tens of thousands of new jobs, even though it would cost the corporation over $1 billion. Only five months later, Amazon dethroned Walmart as the world's largest retailer outside of China.

Amazon's actions did not eliminate all concerns about the wages of working people, but it deserves credit for establishing a positive precedent when new wage concerns arise. The reflexive reaction with a hyper-focus on economic bottom line rather than the long-term sustainability of the company, initially ignored the lesson of corporate parallax. The old meta overlooks the benefits of different perspectives, like the company's well-being and also its environmental impact. Amazon eventually got it right.

Deathly Myopic

Not all stories have a happy ending.[15] A lack of divergent thought is not just unsustainable—it often leads to malpractice as well. Flint, Michigan, had a $25 million deficit. So, in 2011, the governor appointed an emergency manager. To save $2 million in the budget, the manager ended the city's contract with the Detroit Water and Sewage Department (DWSD). Although the newly formed Karegnondi Water Authority (KWA) was supposed to be cheaper, its pipeline wasn't finished. As an interim solution, Flint spent $171,000 to upgrade its own water plant, which was not fully operational, to source water from the Flint River. Both DWSD and KWA sourced water from Lake Huron.

Many officials voiced concerns about using the Flint River for drinking water and using an inadequate facility to treat that water, but their voices were ignored because saving money was the solution for the deficit. However, even after the upgrades, the treatment plant could not properly monitor or treat the contaminated water from the river, which corroded the lead pipes it flowed through. Approximately 96,000 people, including thousands of children, were exposed to harmful bacteria, cancer-causing chemicals, and lead, which could affect them for the rest of their lives. They were invisible, until they were not. Subsequently, at least 12 people died of Legionnaires' disease. The emergency manager's myopic decision ended up costing the state more than $45 million to clean up.

Furthermore, the city lost faith in its leaders. Many officials have been criminally convicted, and many more lawsuits will be pending for years.

We cannot go back and change history, but this ongoing example of civic malpractice highlights why today's leaders must level up. No matter how "inconvenient" the voices of concern may be, they are essential. Had there been a tenth man in Flint, it could have prevented a horrific scenario and saved lives.

The bottom line can't be the end of the line for the conscientious executive. It simply no longer fits the narrative of how business functions in this country, or really any country. Cost cutting and efficiency are important, but they should be done from the top down, not by sacrificing the foundations of quality or safety.

The conscientious leader values the invisible and often overlooked. She sees a nearby distressed community as an opportunity for investment, mindful that there are many schools of thought on poverty and seeing clearly through those challenges to a path toward progress. She sees a vision of prosperity amid poverty to the mutual benefit of profit and the impoverished. She sees potential in forgotten places and people. She has clear vision because she appreciates that corporate parallax is all about point of view, and that her visual limits can only be fixed by including others.

8 | Attenborough's Lesson

My daughter. Claudia. loves animals, and this means we consume a great deal of animal shows like *Animal Planet* and the National Geographic channel. So, I have become an inadvertent student of Sir David Attenborough. One night, he was lecturing on adaptations. I reclined in my chair, propped a pillow under my feet, and prepared to take in my usual learning by dream osmosis. But I didn't fall asleep during this class.

Chameleons, octopuses, and even some flowers have a remarkable adaptive capacity to change in response to the environment. They do this by manipulating specialized cells called chromatophores. These cells contain pigments which reflect light differently to create colors and patterns. It's an ability managed through a complex mix of hormones, environmental stimuli, and neurological signals. Common examples of chromatophores include melanophores, which contain black or brown pigments; xanthophores, with yellow- and red-pigmented granules; iridophores for producing the appearance of iridescent colors; and leucophores reflecting light for a white hue. This ability is an invaluable adaptation among many species as it allows them to effectively camouflage in their environment, communicate intraspecifically and signal danger and other intentions toward predators or prey alike. Some species of chameleons are more capable of changing their color than others, and not all chameleons change their color for the same reasons. In fact, not all lizards can change color. Only the remarkable ones do.

As David Attenborough droned on in the background that evening, it occurred to me that adaptation is necessarily at the heart of nearly all

107

corporate strategy. In a dynamic business environment, new threats emerge every day. And so, it is essential for businesses to adapt to survive and thrive. In high-technology companies like Meta, Apple, and Google, the imperative is even more pronounced as innovation efforts may focus on one thing today, and then a breakthrough like Generative AI demands a pivot. My team sits at the fulcrum of these swings, managing patent strategy at Meta. Responding to dynamic shifts in the market is a difficult task, and like a chameleon responding to a predator, survival can often depend on how quickly we blend into the newly changed environment. It is a key leadership imperative, which like any other imperative, is easier said than accomplished. Maintaining adaptive capability requires effort and planning. Despite quarterly indications of success and progress, long-term plans are only as effective as the leadership team is prepared for change. It is important to remember that some chameleons are better at adapting than others (but only the remarkable ones change color).

I received some of the best lessons on adaptation in the oddest place, Sandhill Baptist Church, not far from where Wilhelmina's house once stood. There, Sunday after Sunday, and often throughout the week, I would be reminded of my smallness in the context of a greater plan. Scriptures like James 4:6, "God opposes the proud but shows favor to the humble," were written on my heart early and often. Perhaps the programming was too good. A friend once remarked, "I have some trauma from my youthful indoctrination as I find it hard to celebrate any of life's successes for fear of appearing too proud." Still, I draw great power from this singular truth, that adaptation is as much an exercise in humility as it is capability. At its core, adaptation demands that we recognize threats and our relative weakness in the face of them, conduct an honest assessment of current conditions, and make adjustments that account for factors outside of our control. Like Attenborough's most successful species of chameleons, the survivors are the most alert and quick to change. Similarly, an overconfident executive will be an unemployed executive and an overly proud business is a soon to be nonexistent one.

With lessons of humility firmly indoctrinated, at nine years old, I experienced the shock of culture clash when my family moved from America to Japan. Though I wasn't particularly tall by American standards, when I arrived in Okinawa, I felt like Michael Jordan. I was mobbed by strangers trying to touch my hair and skin and take my picture. It was the 1990s and Japan was again awakening to global interchange following nearly 40 years of isolation. I remember thinking it was somewhat odd. Why am I getting all this attention? It was uncomfortable for a child told to "walk humbly" before God and men. Humbly almost always meant unseen.

As I built relationships and learned about Japanese culture in the months and years that followed, I learned that, despite having an American military presence since the end of World War II, Japan remained, very stereotypically, an island nation. It was rapidly modernizing and opening up when I got there in the 1990s, but foreigners were still relatively new, particularly non-White foreigners. Many Japanese had never seen someone with such dark skin. Many wanted to take my picture, assuming I was a professional athlete or an *Oni* (a demon or troll). I like to think it was because I reminded them of admired players—after I was called Michael Jordan on more than a few occasions. Japanese culture places a high value on social hierarchy. So, I took the experience as a sign of goodwill and a desire to build a positive relationship.

If we are humble, we can learn a great deal from cultural exchange, especially from cultures that are older than our own. Growing up in Japan, a largely homogenous country with thousands of years of unbroken tradition, was an invaluable experience and a formative period in my life. To my adolescent mind, everything in Japan was different: we ate with chopsticks, slept on *goza* mats, watched TV from a low-seated position, and took off our shoes before we entered a house. I discovered the greatest honor I can do for someone is to mimic or exceed the level of respect they extend to me. And, because of this experience, seldom do I interact with someone even to this day and instantly assume negative intentions. Instead, I always try to see the positive and understand their underlying motives and feelings, as if painting on fresh canvas.

In Japan, I took the bus to school each day. A girl we kids named Aoi often rode our bus. The child of an American serviceman and a Japanese mother, her skin was as dark as mine. However, she had been born in Japan, spoke fluent Japanese, and was, for all intents and purposes, Japanese. I sometimes wondered how she managed to balance living in two different worlds with ever-competing norms and expectations.

One day, I got off the bus too early and couldn't find my way home. Standing at an intersection, all I could see were signs in katakana and hiragana calligraphy, the Japanese writing system. I didn't know what to do or where to go. I was lost.

While I was standing at the bustling intersection, my senses were awed by a symphony of sights, sounds, and smells. Aromas of sizzling yakitori and steaming ramen filled the air, along with the sweet scent of jasmine tea from street vendors. The streets were a vivid mosaic of colors with vibrant banners and intricate *kanji* lining the way. The buildings stood like stalwart sentinels, blending traditional Okinawan architecture with modern structures, celebrating the island's rich cultural heritage.

Pedestrians moved across the intersection in a choreography of traditional kimono and Western attire. Young men on mopeds zipped by in bold printed shirts and excited chatter filled the air. Women in elegant *yukatas* strolled along with delicate fans in hand, their faces adorned with vibrant makeup as they conversed. Vintage and modern cars rolled by in a chorus of engines, complemented by the syncopated rhythm of motorcycles and bicycle bells.

Music spilled from open windows, enlivening the soundscape. The energetic beats of traditional Okinawan *taiko* drums mingled with the melodies of J-pop and nostalgic *enka* ballads. The sensory symphony unfolded before me, celebrating the vibrant and dynamic essence of Okinawan culture.

In this melody, I was a blaring cacophony. I tried to ask for help, but no one spoke English. Then panic set in. All hope seemed lost, and then Aoi appeared as if summoned by my anxiety. She looked at me with a grin and without a word, grabbed my hand and guided me the few blocks home. To her, the street signs made perfect sense, and I am grateful that kindness is universally understood.

Aoi became a bridge between the foreign and the familiar. She was as adaptive as the most fit of Attenborough's chameleons in navigating different environments. She possessed the ability to reach others who would be lost in her community and, in so doing, taught me the ambassadorial role that we can play in bringing communities together.

Living in Japan was a fish-out-of-water experience. It reinforced the notion that humility and meekness aren't bad words. Blessed are the meek, for they will inherit the earth, right? A response is not always required, a concept that is often difficult for most Americans to comprehend. We tend to approach life and business as if we are always correct and our culture is implicitly right. Often this bravado by American executives betrays underlying fear. Fear of being wrong and confronting the humbling reality that a better way might be possible than they conceived.

In Japan, I became more resilient and adept in the face of challenges. Indeed, in our youth, we develop an unwavering trust in our own intuitions, confidently certain that our methods are superior. But with greater exposure we gain access to a wealth of alternative approaches and people from all backgrounds. Embracing the ideas of others and remaining receptive to novel approaches has made me a more effective problem-solver. Fostering diverse and inclusive environments does the same for companies.

Secrets from the Breakfast Club

The data are clear: travel and particularly studying abroad have enormous implications on performance and career success. In fact, in 2017 the Institute of

International Education (IIE) reported that study abroad impacts the development of modern skills and the ability to secure employment.[1] The researchers evaluated a broad sample of over 4,500 alumni of U.S. higher education institutions who participated in study abroad between the 1999–2000 and 2016–2017 academic years. They were trying to gain a more nuanced understanding of the links between study abroad and employability, with a particular focus on the aspects of study abroad programs that contribute to positive employment outcomes.

The researchers found that international exposure has a high impact on subsequent job offers and the development of most skills. Additionally, the skills gained through study abroad have a long-term impact on career progression and promotion. Intercultural skills, curiosity, flexibility and adaptability, confidence, self-awareness, interpersonal skills, communication, problem-solving, language, tolerance for ambiguity, and course- or major-related knowledge all improved dramatically. Teamwork, leadership, and work ethic were also reportedly developed or improved. In fact, of participants who studied abroad for one academic year, 68% reported international exposure contributed to a job offer at some point.

Let me tell you a little secret. Diverse experiences future-proofs organizations and generates similar benefits as cultural exchange. Despite this, it's a concept many profess to believe in but secretly fear. That "D" word is all the rage in elite social and corporate circles, but it's truly abhorred by old-school, rank-and-file corporate management. Corporate angst about diversity efforts among tiger executives has even given life to "anti-woke" political candidates for national office. In some instances, these same candidates are financed by donations from the very executives publicly claiming to support DEI (diversity, equity, and inclusion).

The truth is, we often talk about diversity wrong in corporate America. It is often leveraged to create unique distinctions between groups of people rather than, as Aoi demonstrated with her actions by grabbing me by the hand, to bridge cultural gaps and highlight shared humanity. As Robert Thurman points out in his book *Inner Revolution* diversity initiatives can sometimes cause us to

> . . . feel ourselves as individuals, irreducible someones, by identifying ourselves by race, sex, age, and religion; by ideology, nation, culture, profession, and health; by knowledge, skills, achievements, and experiences. These labels only ensure that we remain strangers to many aspects of our real selves and deeply alienated from one another. When we naively believe we are unique, independent, self-subsisting entities, essentially

apart from all other persons and things, all relationships becomes problematic. . . . This is what alienation means, that everything else seems "other," that each one sees a world in which he or she is the best, the only good one. Each self-identification as the best leads to a prejudice that all the others are worse.[2]

In March 2020, a Taft Communications and Rutgers-Eagleton Poll found that attitudes on diversity in American workplaces show significant divisions by race, gender, and political affiliation. When asked how important diversity is to an organization, three-quarters of Black respondents say it is "very important" (75%), compared to just under half (48%) of White respondents and a little over half (55%) of Hispanic respondents. Other notable viewpoint differences are accentuated by these drastically divergent attitudes on diversity. Where some groups see challenges necessitating progress, others see no problem at all. For example, the same poll found that 3 in 10 Black respondents (31%) say some employees are treated differently, compared to White (16%) and Hispanic (21%) respondents. And nearly 4 in 10 Black respondents (38%) contend some employees are treated differently, as compared to 16% of White respondents.[3]

This data certainly matches my own anecdotal experience. Early in my career, I realized there was a "breakfast club" at my company. The same group of about four or five men would go to breakfast every morning. They would arrive to work early and then proceed down to the cafeteria. They would always sit in the same place, "the football," we called it. It was an area within the cafeteria with large windows that permitted the morning sunrise to wash over the room and was shaped, as you might expect, in an ovular shape like a football. I began inviting myself to the morning breakfast clubs.

At first there was an understandably cold reception. Most of the men were middle-aged, White, and looking forward to an empty nest or retirement. I was, at the time, 28 years old, at the beginning of my career, and looking forward to filling a nest. But my mother always told me that those who desire friends must first show themselves to be friendly. Aoi confirmed that truth. And, so, I made a point to join this naturally uncomfortable troupe each morning until they would accept me as part of the club. I knew I had made it when I was sitting at my desk one day when a colleague, the marshal for that morning, stopped to pick me up as the breakfast club rallied by the stairs.

What I learned after several years of breakfast with these men is that they were not overtly antagonistic to diversity efforts, but that they saw no advantage in supporting them. By incorporating more groups into a community like UPS, which is often characterized by its male, heteronormative, Eurocentrism, the days of the breakfast club (in theory) would be limited because there are "only so many slots available." As one of my colleagues described it, "look out there, Andy," pointing in the general direction of the main highway, "not everyone turns into that garage. Many people drive on by. It's an exclusive thing to be a part of this club."

The point was not illogical but, perhaps, misguided. To me, organizations should be in a perpetual state of growth. Most executives learn the maxim "if you're not growing, you're dying," in business school. So, if we accept perpetual growth as the organizing principle of business, then there should be enough room for greater diversity at the breakfast table. But the concept of growing the proverbial pie is often missed by those who fear or misunderstand the point of diversity. With growth comes more pie. More pie means more opportunity to include those who are often underrepresented. And this, as I came to understand as a leader of a diverse team, is the goal of DEI initiatives.

Employees are generally uncomfortable talking about diversity. I know this because I acquired an asset long ago between the pews of a Black church and the hills and jagged cliffs of Okinawa: code-switching. This is the ability to adapt communication and deportment to different situations or environments. It enabled me as both a leader and as an employee to create meaningful conversations around difficult topics by learning about others in disarming ways. Not all lizards can change colors, remember?

In the classic, linguistic sense, code-switching means alternating between two or more languages in a conversation. In everyday life, it means customizing our style of speech, behavior, dress, and sometimes beliefs to match our audience or group. Think of mimicry as flattery as it would be in Japan. We work more effectively in groups when we naturally pick up some of their traits. (Note that this is the opposite of appropriation, which is when we adopt other people's traits without context, knowledge, or experience as our own.) Corporate code-switching is about finding common ground, minimizing cultural differences that may hinder understanding, and seeking to enhance shared tools like language that make us a community.

I have had to code-switch to a certain extent as a means of survival all my life—especially in corporate America, where the dominant community sets the culture. Though much of this book is about changing entrenched corporate behaviors, abrupt and radical change can alienate the very stakeholders who are needed to make progress. So, our leadership burden is relating to and communicating effectively within the dominant culture to be successful in both our personal career journey and advancing the shared goal of a more conscientious workplace.

Code-switching has opened doors to incredible opportunities for me and given me a seat at important tables that may have otherwise been inaccessible. For example, I recently found myself in Tel Aviv as a fellow of the Schusterman Family Foundation REALITY Tech experience. The charity supports long-term systemic change through investments in leaders, organizations, and U.S. public policy. Because of our common values and ability to articulate them, I took the 6,400-mile journey from my home in Atlanta to share in the foundation's commitment to the pursuit of justice (*tzedek*), repairing the world (*tikkun olam*), treating all people with civility and humanity (*derekh eretz*), and building inclusive communities. These shared values shape the beliefs that inform the foundation's work and my own.

But code-switching is not just for a minority group. Women have been doing it forever in spaces dominated by men. And, according to the Centers for Disease Control and Prevention, if you've ever been in a room with at least three other people, chances are, you've worked with a disabled person and didn't even know it.[4] Throughout the years, I have worked with numerous people who could be considered disabled in some way, though they did not always want others to be aware of their condition. However, their unique perspectives provided our team with valuable insight that made us stronger overall. The ability to connect with the neurodivergent or mobility impaired leverages their essential expertise for the benefit of the entire organization. In this way, reasonable accommodations become force multipliers rather than expense, and code-switching becomes a boon for the entire organization.

More expansively, we all have physical, psychological, emotional, cognitive, or other challenges. Yet, our challenges do not make us less able to function in the workplace. In this way, code-switching is essential to communicating in every environment. It helps us function better, and leverage differences for the shared benefit of the organization.

When we find ourselves in unfamiliar or diverse environments, seeking commonality is a way to anchor ourselves and feel connected. This is a natural human instinct, as it helps us to feel safe and secure in new or uncertain situations. Effective leadership comes down to creating a shared understanding of humanity among a diverse team. Whenever I start a new position, for instance, I give a presentation about my background, my upbringing, and my family, including pictures of my wife and daughter. I want others to see me as a human being before they see me as a peer, subordinate, or manager. I want them to connect with my humanity. This strategy of "humanizing" oneself is often obligatory for leaders who are not from a dominant cultural group. I came upon this practice after assuming responsibility for a large strategic communications team. This group of 30 or so professionals were part of a once-combined legal, public affairs, and strategic communications group at UPS Airlines. I was unknown to many in the group. To allay any unease, I suggested to my lieutenant that we have an "all hands" meeting and I would cover a slide deck with some of my initial thoughts as the organization changed hands. Instead of a business presentation, I merely provided slides of pictures with family and experiences that humanized me. As I spoke through the presentation, I could see mystery physically melting away from the faces of my new team.

Unease when facing the unknown is normal. The more we can reduce the unknown and find our shared humanness, the more our teams, colleagues, and everyone around us will be willing to communicate their feelings and work toward a common goal. This will make our organizations more generally able to respond to change when it inevitably comes. And the best way to prepare today for tomorrow's uncertainty is to hire conscientious executives who can demonstrably speak across cultural dimensions to fully engage a diverse group of talented people working toward common ends.

Benefits of Bidirectionality

Researchers published a study in *Scientific Reports* on open systems in living cellular organisms and their interactions with other organisms. Lead researchers Fumiko Ogushi at Kyoto University's Institute for Advanced Study and Takashi Shimada at the University of Tokyo's Graduate School of Engineering evaluated the impact of bidirectional influences on the robustness of open systems.[5] Bidirectional meaning influences from two directions. Robustness meaning resistance to collapse. They categorized the more resilient systems' key attributes, behaviors, and corresponding directional elements. For example, Ogushi's modeling found that systems with purely bidirectional interactions in ecological systems can grow twofold on average, in comparison with the purely unidirectional system.

A cooperative interaction between two organisms, for example, is bidirectional, characterized by positive feedback, mutualism, cooperation, and friendship. Conversely, a predatory interaction is unidirectional and characterized by negative feedback, predation, parasitic exploitation, and selfish actions. Using statistical and computational modeling, the researchers leveraged data, chemicals, genes, and animals of varying species.

Over time, the researchers discovered that organisms evolved differently depending on the type of interactions they experienced. The organisms in bidirectional interactions evolved faster since they had to adapt to a new environment or social situation. And because each organism assimilated to the other in some way, they were more resilient and stronger. The unidirectional parasites were less evolved and less robust.

The researchers concluded that, in the organic world, there is a clear correlation between a mutual exchange of interactions across environments and positive transformation and strength. In other words, where there are exchanges between two groups, the environment makes each group more robust and resistant to collapse. In keeping with our working thesis that any process, thought, experience, or emotion can manifest at an individual level, and therefore may manifest at an organizational level given the right conditions; we must accept, then, that organizations of people (groups of biological organisms) share instructive properties like their openness and responses to bidirectional interactions.

Anecdotally, Ogushi and Shimada's research makes sense. When my daughter stays home from day care, she is in a relatively closed system and has fewer illnesses in the short term. When she goes to day care, she's in a more open system where germs are freely shared with other toddlers, sometimes making her (and her parents) sick. But, in the long run, the exposure to other children strengthens her overall health and immune system (a willing sacrifice her parents make).

Interaction between organizations follow the same principle. It's no longer enough to merely be a unidirectional organization, absorbing the talents and resources of a community. That is a parasitic reaction, which is universally destabilizing over the long run. We must create open systems based on positive and collaborative interactions across environments. That's the new meta—and the essence of diversity.

The Benefits of Diversity

Many American companies were skeptical about doing business with China in the late twentieth century due to our major cultural, political, and language differences. But as soon as Wall Street saw the increased profits, they didn't look back. Even after trade wars, stolen technology secrets, and other political tensions that made doing business in China more complex in the early twenty-first century, few companies stopped. In fact, more and more started. And with good reason.

Corporations may be left behind if they don't tap into huge markets like China in some way. Companies that assimilate and combine the best minds from diverse perspectives thrive in new markets, where they naturally unlock more opportunities and more profit. For example, in 1999, Starbucks set its sights on establishing its presence in China, a time when Western-style coffee culture was barely existent in the country. To tackle this unique market, Starbucks built a diverse leadership team consisting of executives with both local and international knowledge, steeped in Chinese culture, language, and business practices, as well as leaders with experience in other Asian countries.

Belinda Wong, the Chinese American CEO of Starbucks China, was a key figure in the company's success. She demonstrated an in-depth understanding of Chinese consumer preferences, market dynamics, and cultural nuances, playing a vital role in steering strategic decisions. Wong's leadership ensured Starbucks tailored its offerings, aligned with Chinese tastes, and resonated with local customers.

Starbucks also established strong relationships in China by collaborating with local supply chains, engaging in joint ventures with Chinese companies, and actively seeking to employ local talent in their management positions. By including Chinese leaders in their top ranks, Starbucks not only showed commitment to respecting and understanding the culture but also fostered trust and acceptance among the Chinese people. Starbucks conducted extensive market research to understand the Chinese consumers' preferences, habits, and expectations and adapted their menu offerings, store designs, and customer experiences to align with Chinese cultural norms.

Through strategic efforts, Starbucks not only successfully penetrated the Chinese market but also experienced significant growth. By 2023, Starbucks was operating more than 6,500 stores in over 250 cities on the Chinese mainland, employing more than 60,000 partners. This success undeniably proves the importance of diverse leadership in understanding and effectively catering to the needs of complex and diverse markets.

Corporations frequently move upcoming leaders to different roles and locations to enhance their skills and provide a comprehensive view of the entire organization. This is done to ensure that future leaders have the skills and experience necessary to succeed in a variety of roles and to understand the company's overall goals and objectives. Leaders accustomed to working outside their comfort zones, who have a "breadth of perspective," are more effective in their roles and more valuable to the organization. International rotations, or at least roles with international scope, are increasingly necessary for success in the global marketplace.

One of the hardest things about doing business with China is navigating the regulatory differences. In the United States, we sometimes fight things all the way to the U.S. Supreme Court because adversarial interactions are typical in a democracy. It is expected and generally unprovocative to contest every-thing. In cultures where communalism and cooperation are the norm, however, corporations must align with the local community to resolve conflict. It is not uncommon to pay de minimis (minor) judicial fees to resolve issues in China and even apologize to authorities to remain in good standing. To succeed in certain jurisdictions, corporate strategy needs to be less adversarial and more culturally competent.

Taking risks to reach out and engage with new markets can be highly rewarding, but cultural competence comes first by having a little humility. It is easy to fall into the trap of believing that we are infallible in our actions and ideas; however, by humbly recognizing cultural diversity, we create a space for ourselves to learn from, rather than simply imposing our own values on others. Valuable opportunities come from engaging new markets for growth, as well as insight into dynamics that may have otherwise been hidden from us. In this way humility provides us with the tools to create open and trusting relationships with cultures around the world that will benefit us all in the long run, which is why conscientious leaders don't shy away from talking about diversity and inclusion.

Open Systems Are Better

Diversity is about recognizing the value each person brings to decision-making. It emphasizes that everyone's ideas, regardless of experience or seniority in an organization, should be considered and valued fairly. Equity demands we view people as more than just a dollar, a school attended, or a political connection leveraged. It also reminds us not to discount an individual due to their age, years of experience, or lack thereof, when appraising their merits and contributions, or considering their capacity for leadership. Inclusion demands that we look for, and ensure a meaningful voice is given to, underrepresented groups including women and minorities in all geographies and operations. However, it's impor-tant to note that DEI looks very different in Europe than in America. This reality reinforces the need for organizations to be open systems rather than regulated from the top down. Open systems account for geographic and cul-tural distinctions.

We've all seen a basic diagram for a cell in biology, the ultimate open sys-tem. It's often represented as a circle or sphere. Imagine an organization as a living cell, functioning as an open system with five elements: (1) core values, (2) feedback loops, (3) adopters and evaluators, (4) programmatic-consensus build-ing, and (5) assimilation (see Figure 8.1). These are the key structural elements

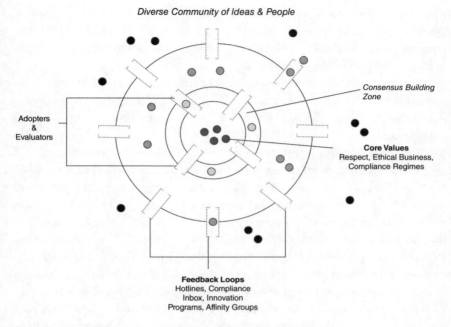

Figure 8.1 Ideation in a diverse open system.

for incorporating new ideas and roughly correspond to elements in a biological cell like the nucleus, cell walls, and nuclear pore complexes. Ideas, like little microbes moving around outside and inside the cell, interact with these constituent parts of the system.

Our core values guide how team members conduct themselves. They are the nucleus of the organization. The organization chiefs safeguard this essential core as a primary function.

Feedback loops are the processes and procedures that give stakeholders both within and outside the enterprise spaces to share ideas and collaborate without fear of retaliation. They resemble a cellular wall allowing things to pass between the interior and exterior of the system. The senior leadership team operates as gatekeepers to the organization's core decision-makers.

Adopters and evaluators are middle managers and team members from across the organization who evaluate and test new ideas. They are the nuclear pore complexes mediating and facilitating the transport of things inside and outside the system core.

Building consensus programmatically—the boundary around the nucleus—ensures that new perspectives are heard and considered, evaluated, and tried, and that a consensus is reached before adoption. They are often the nuclear envelope protecting the most sacred parts of the system. These are the truth-sayer functions like finance, compliance, and legal, that have professional obligations beyond profit.

Ideation and new implementation occur when there is organizational consensus for a solution. A diverse community of ideas and people can be leveraged only when a system makes a way for their incorporation with dispassionate consideration.

The conscientious leader understands that inclusion of diverse ideas and people within this type of system is not only a fortunate bonus, but essential. It is a feature of a well-run team. Without tapping into the vastness of perspectives that such a range of experiences bring to the table, any society or organization will remain limited in its achievements. It is only by cultivating inclusion that the full scope of a community's potential can be tapped into and leveraged. Rather than a pyramid, where information flows up to a select few at the top, conscientious leaders influence a more organic and circular flow of information within the organization's structure. Inclusive systems like this offer a place for each person to express themselves and use their unique contribution to support the collective good. Regardless of an individual's identity, inclusion should not just be preached but practiced for an organization to maximize innovation—and reap the rewards for doing so.

Grace to Be Uncomfortably Open

I remember making my way up to my new twelfth-floor office at my first legal job. Fresh out of law school, I was still bright-eyed and bushy tailed as I marveled over my beautiful wooden desk and view of Kansas City.

Soon, my new assistant entered with a worried look, closed the door, and sat down. We politely introduced ourselves, and then—I'll never forget this—she blurted out, "I want you to know I've never worked for a Black person before!" She laughed nervously. I thought for a second. Then I chuckled. Then laughed uncontrollably. "Well," I started, "I've never been a White person's boss. I guess we'll figure this out together. And I won't hold mistakes against you if you don't hold them against me." We shared a hearty laugh together.

She could have been quiet about her discomfort, afraid of what I would think or do. I could have reacted to her comment in a negative way. But there was something about her honesty and vulnerability that was both amusing and admirable to me. If feedback is a gift, then so too is safety in expressing feedback with sincerity.

Although most of us don't just come out and state our apprehensions, we've all been fearful, uncomfortable, or even narrow-minded when faced with new situations or people. I'm always aware that those around me may be uncomfortable—for whatever reasons—so I have to bridge those gaps. This was Aoi's gift to me.

Because my assistant and I were open with each other, we worked through the unknown and developed a strong and resilient relationship. In fact, we eventually became very close friends, but more importantly, we were able to produce meaningful work because of our mutual vulnerability. A system is not open if frank conversations are avoided. If management teams cannot share their discomfort with the ostensible homogeneity of a senior leadership team, or its lack of gender balance, then the organization will not adapt well to future market changes. Only when we face the realities of the areas where we fail to meet our aspirations today, and talk about those issues frankly with one another, can we construct more inclusive, open, and robust organizations that adapt to tomorrow's challenges like Attenborough's chameleons.

9 | Buckner's Law

A lifetime ago, in Mr. Buckner's middle school workshop class on Lady's Island, I sat with my fellow students learning about chemical reactions. We've all been there, half-engaged listening to a teacher discuss the transformation of reactants into products. This lesson, though, was on catalysts and fairly interesting as chemistry is concerned. Under lab conditions, Mr. Buckner filled a beaker with catalase and we watched the decomposition of hydrogen peroxide into water and oxygen gas speedily progress. This gentle conversion usually occurs over a long period of time, which is why hydrogen peroxide is shelf safe. "Catalytic reactions are not always this gentle," we were warned by Mr. Buckner. "This is why your knowledge of the materials and their reactions is important."

The boys in the class were often too busy to pick up subtle lessons when bubbling beakers were around, but for some reason, that lesson stuck with me. It was a life lesson, of course. A catalyst is really anything that can increase the rate of reaction between two things without undergoing any permanent change itself. Conscientious leaders exist for this same purpose. Often our task is to excite the reaction between work and worker such that the two increasingly react in an efficient way (and not losing ourselves in the process). While catalysts can affect the reaction rate and efficiency, they do not determine the fundamental properties of the reaction; in other words, whether it is a violent or gentle one. So, Mr. Buckner's point about the importance of knowing the materials undergoing said reaction, is a particularly relevant proverb. In teams, by understanding the personalities compositions, strengths, and triggers, a leader can either help to accelerate results with gentle or explosive outcomes. As the catalyst, we are the key.

122

The Real McCoy

My hero, Elijah McCoy, was born into a world of limitations. His parents, both former slaves, were unable to obtain a higher education. But, undaunted in their pursuit for a better future for their son, they made a difficult decision to give him up so he could pursue an education with abolitionists in Edinburgh, Scotland. A natural-born leader, Elijah's strong personality and determination ensured his acceptance in and graduation from a training program for mechanical engineers. Still, upon returning to the United States, his race made it impossible for him to secure employment in his field. But like his parents, Elijah was equally dauntless. He took a job as a locomotive fireman and oiler with the Michigan Central Railroad maintaining steam engines. It was menial labor, beneath an engineer of course, but it enabled him to earn a living.

As an oiler, Elijah's job was to lubricate all movable parts of the steam engine to ensure its high performance. At the time, the oiling and inspection was done manually. As you can imagine, this was time-consuming work. In fact, if Mike Rowe were alive during the time, there is no doubt he would produce an episode about it on his classic hit show *Dirty Jobs*.

One aspect of this job caused Elijah particular distress. He could only lubricate the engine when the train was stopped, which was incredibly inefficient. The design of early steam engines often required direct access to the bearings, pistons, valves, and other components for effective lubrication. Some parts were wholly inaccessible unless stopped. Additionally, oiling parts while the train was in motion was dangerous and could easily result in a one-way ticket to the hereafter.

We can all, perhaps, sympathize with Elijah. We have all been in a similar situation—working a job for which we are overqualified and suffering through a painstakingly inefficient process. But Elijah took matters into his own hands and became a catalyst for change not just for the Michigan Central Railroad, but the entire locomotive industry.

In 1872, Elijah invented an automatic lubricator cup that continuously supplied oil to the engine while the train was in motion, completely transforming locomotive travel in the nineteenth and twentieth centuries (see figure 9.1). The device, which consisted of a small piston-driven oil reservoir attached to an extensive network of pipes and valves, provided continuous and reliable lubrication to the engines' moving parts, resulting in longer journeys spanning greater distances at higher speeds than ever before. The new technology opened vast capabilities for industry and commerce; it enabled transportation on an unprecedented scale that transformed entire societies across Europe and America alike.

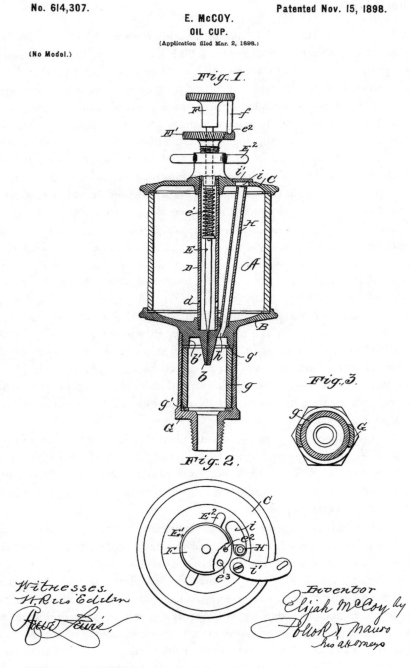

No. 614,307.   Patented Nov. 15, 1898.

E. McCOY.
OIL CUP.
(Application filed Mar. 2, 1898.)

(No Model.)

Fig. 1.

Fig. 3.

Fig. 2.

Witnesses.
H. Russ Edelen
Albert Lewis

Inventor
Elijah McCoy by
Pollok & Mauro
his attorneys

Figure 9.1   McCoy oil cup.

Railways began extending outwards from big cities like New York and Philadelphia and into the forgotten towns like East Palestine, Ohio, and Walterboro, South Carolina, bringing economic opportunity and development with them. In some ways, though I arrived 100 years after Elijah McCoy's invention, his legacy would even influence my life.

The railroad promoted McCoy to mechanical engineer instructor and sent him to Detroit, where he also consulted with various manufacturers. This was unheard of for Blacks of his time. Due to the elegance of his invention, many companies began producing similar oil-drip cups, though not always of the same quality. That prompted industry professionals to ask whether a given product was "the *real* McCoy" or just an imitation.

Elijah went on to invent over 50 other devices that further revolutionized nineteenth-century transportation and are still listed in the U.S. Patent Registry today. He continued patenting novel inventions into his seventies. Still, despite his many contributions to society, he often lacked money and was forced to sell his patents and licenses for a fraction of their worth. Many companies made millions off his inventions without giving him any credit.

After working hard to better understand patent laws and business, he opened the Elijah McCoy Manufacturing Company in 1920 so he could mass-produce his own products. Before he died in 1929, he had also invented a portable ironing board, rubber-soled shoes, and a circulating sprinkler. His environment could not thwart his ambition and determination. With each challenge that came his way, he rose to the occasion and demonstrated a strength of character that I could only hope to emulate. He was the difference-maker, a catalyst, in all his endeavors.

Conscientious leaders can take a few notable lessons from the life of Elijah McCoy. First, his age didn't constrain his productivity. Even in his seventies, Elijah was inventing and contributing his best. All too often we are ready to push out our more seasoned teammates to "make room" even when their contributions continue to be meaningful and relevant. Second, in his early career, McCoy's managers allowed his skill to determine his trajectory. They neither cared about his youth nor his race when they promoted him to mechanical engineer instructor early in his career.

Sometimes the young person on your team deserves to be the leader. In fact, the same Taft Communications and Rutgers-Eagleton poll discussed in Chapter 8 found that respondents under age 35 were more likely to say they felt passed over for a promotion due to their age (34%) than respondents aged 35 to 54 (25%) and respondents aged 55 and older (24%).[1] Tenure should never be a proxy for talent or a requisite for advancement. Talent should be the guide.

Promotions that follow tenure or a prestigious "name brand" school or firm perpetuates that same system of privilege that made it difficult for McCoy, and my grandparents, and their parents to succeed. We perpetuate systems that expose us to mediocre results by doing the same things repeatedly.

Third, conscientious leaders search uncommon places for talent. McCoy's story ran through Edinburgh, Scotland, an uncommon place to find an American engineer (not to mention a Black one) in the late 1800s. Sometimes, the talent isn't in New York City or Silicon Valley; sometimes the talent is in America's forgotten towns—like the one I grew up in.

From Pecans to Patents

Like Elijah McCoy's parents, mine were equally undaunted by their economic or academic challenges. Both sets of my grandparents achieved only a grade-school education from segregated schools. Their employment options were limited, but they were industrious enough to make ends meet, like collecting and selling aluminum for extra money. Or selling boiled peanuts and pecans on the side of the road. My grandfather Eddie became well-known in Walterboro as the "Pecan Man of I-95" and would go on to make friendships with travelers going up and down the eastern seaboard.

My mother, Beatrice, was among the first students to integrate the public schools in Colleton County. Two hundred miles south, my father, Andrew Sr., did the same in Ware County, Georgia. Beatrice graduated from high school and worked for many years as a bank teller. Andrew enlisted in the U.S. Marine Corps at the age of 17 with a waiver from his parents.

As each generation found ways to improve upon the last, a saying was passed down in the Cooper household: "Blossom wherever you're planted." This resilience mindset continues to enable me to tackle each of life's obstacles with an eagerness to progress. It is a characteristic often overlooked in establishments that focus more on archaic notions of "pedigree." From venturing through top technology centers like Silicon Valley to government hubs like Washington DC, I have accessed opportunities beyond my late grandparents' imagination using their gift of resilience. And, within those rooms, I've seen premiums placed on things like pedigree, family name, and school affiliation worth far less in value by comparison. I could not be more unimpressed by these résumé adornments; and when I lead a team, none of that matters.

By 2016, I was a patent lawyer, several years mature in practice, managing a company's global intellectual property portfolio. Julio Gil, then a prolific inventor at the company, was working on a drone delivery system. He'd figured out launching mechanisms but hadn't quite solved how to accurately land drones back onto UPS package cars, so I started brainstorming with him. I was determined to be the catalyst to a solution. Neither of us were aviators but rather natural tinkerers. It occurred to us that by incorporating some of the many implements within our warehouse operations, we could effectively guide unmanned systems onto package cars in several ways, including using a combination of sensors and railing. Eventually, our colleague Jeff Cooper joined us, and our ideas matured into United States Patent No. 10,586,201 (see Figures 9.2 and 9.3).

The distinctions between my experience and my hero, the real McCoy, made McCoy's experience all the more remarkable to me. Unlike him, I had the benefit of working within an open system to ideate with colleagues like Julio. "My lane" was not circumscribed to compliance or security or legal. My lane was doing whatever helped the company innovate, advance, and improve. The work became an opportunity to have an impact on the organization's future, and it gave me another edge as a high-performing leader. It was an opportunity to blossom where I was planted.

By contrast, McCoy experienced personal and professional loneliness from the time he left his parents' home and through most of his early career because of social views on race. He broke through that loneliness to produce amazing things. We both chose to be the catalyst to a solution. But so many within our organizations suffer in loneliness and lots of amazing ideas are lost because of it. For this reason, the conscientious executive makes it their mission to find these isolated team members, highlight their strengths, and encourage fellowship within the broader team to elevate performance.

In the late 1970s and early 1980s, Philip Uri Treisman, a renowned mathematician and distinguished professor of mathematics at Berkeley, noticed that his Black students were not performing as well as his Asian and White students on his examinations. Uri found this odd because Berkeley, as an institution, only admitted the very top students. Uri noted that, even among the Black students, "most were valedictorians and leaders of church youth groups, individuals who were the pride of their communities who had come to Berkeley highly motivated and under great pressure to succeed."[2]

Why, then, were their scores on his exams different from the Asian and White students? He began inquiring of other professors and colleagues, and shockingly, found that racist attitudes prevailed at this so-called liberal university. Clearly, racism is not circumscribed to a political affiliation.

The feedback Uri received blamed the high failure rates on the students' lack of motivation, lack of educational background, and lack of family emphasis

US010586201B2

(12) **United States Patent**　　　(10) **Patent No.: US 10,586,201 B2**
Gil et al.　　　　　　　　　　　　(45) **Date of Patent:　Mar. 10, 2020**

(54) **METHODS FOR LANDING AN UNMANNED AERIAL VEHICLE**

(71) Applicant: **United Parcel Service of America, Inc.**, Atlanta, GA (US)

(72) Inventors: **Julio Gil**, Veldhoven (NL); **Andrew Cooper**, Atlanta, GA (US); **Jeffrey Cooper**, Marietta, GA (US)

(73) Assignee: **UNITED PARCEL SERVICE OF AMERICA, INC.**, Atlanta, GA (US)

(*) Notice: Subject to any disclaimer, the term of this patent is extended or adjusted under 35 U.S.C. 154(b) by 155 days.

(21) Appl. No.: **15/582,187**

(22) Filed: **Apr. 28, 2017**

(65) **Prior Publication Data**

US 2017/0316701 A1　Nov. 2, 2017

Related U.S. Application Data

(60) Provisional application No. 62/329,491, filed on Apr. 29, 2016.

(51) **Int. Cl.**
G06Q 10/08 (2012.01)
B64F 1/02 (2006.01)
(Continued)

(52) **U.S. Cl.**
CPC *G06Q 10/0832* (2013.01); *B60P 3/11* (2013.01); *B64C 39/024* (2013.01); *B64D 1/22* (2013.01);
(Continued)

(58) **Field of Classification Search**
CPC ... B64D 1/22; B64D 1/00; B64D 9/00; B64D 45/04; H04W 4/70; H04L 67/26;
(Continued)

(56) **References Cited**

U.S. PATENT DOCUMENTS

3,053,480 A　9/1962　Vanderlip
3,526,127 A　9/1970　Sarkis
(Continued)

FOREIGN PATENT DOCUMENTS

CN　101124842 A　2/2008
CN　105438472 A　3/2016
(Continued)

OTHER PUBLICATIONS

ISA/206—Invitation to Pay Additional Fees dated Nov. 14, 2017 for WO Application No. PCT/US17/030157.
(Continued)

Primary Examiner — Jeffrey C Boomer
(74) *Attorney, Agent, or Firm* — Shook, Hardy & Bacon, L.L.P.

(57) **ABSTRACT**

Systems and methods include UAVs that serve to assist carrier personnel by reducing the physical demands of the transportation and delivery process. A UAV generally includes a UAV chassis including an upper portion, a plurality of propulsion members configured to provide lift to the UAV chassis, and a parcel carrier configured for being selectively coupled to and removed from the UAV chassis. UAV support mechanisms are utilized to load and unload parcel carriers to the UAV chassis, and the UAV lands on and takes off from the UAV support mechanism to deliver parcels to a serviceable point. The UAV includes computing entities that interface with different systems and computing entities to send and receive various types of information.

15 Claims, 67 Drawing Sheets

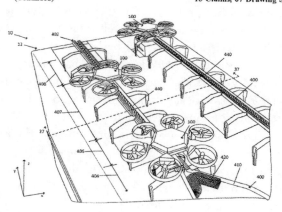

Figure 9.2　The 201 patent.

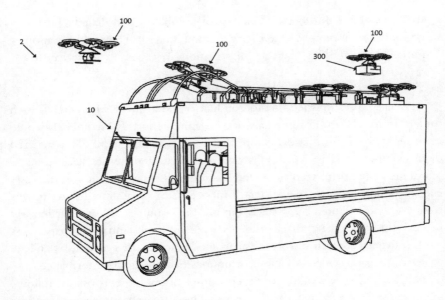

Figure 9.3   The landing rails.

on education. The arguments raised were reminiscent of Senator Moynihan's "culture of poverty" school of thought discussed in Chapter 7. But Uri wanted a more scientific exploration of the divergence and asked his Black students to allow him to observe their study habits over a period of time. He did the same with his Asian students. What he found was revealing. His Black students were often studying alone, in isolation, and had few linkages to study groups. Uri noted that he was "struck by the sharp separation that most Black students maintained—regardless of class or educational background—between their school lives and their social lives."

Uri saw something quite different among his Asian students. "Composed of students with a shared purpose, the informal study groups of Chinese freshmen enabled their members not only to share mathematical knowledge but also to check out their understanding of what was being required of them by their professors and, more generally, by the university," he observed. Further, Uri noted:

Chinese students in their study groups ask each other questions ranging from whether one was permitted to write in pencil on a test to how one might circumvent certain University financial aid regulations. More important was the fact that these students routinely critiqued each other's work, assisted each other with homework problems, and shared all manner of information related to their common interests. Their collaboration provided them with valuable information that guided their day-to-day study.

These observations led Uri to conduct an experiment. He required each student in his class to become part of a learning cohort. These cohorts would meet regularly to share information, check understanding, and cover material discussed in Uri's classes. The results were immediate and drastic. Black students' scores not only normalized across the classroom distribution but in some cases exceeded the performance of others. It turns out, the capabilities of his students were evenly distributed across races, but not the resources to learn, particularly in environments where Black students were in a substantial minority. Uri's work spurred adoption of the Treisman model across the academy as college professors began taking a hard look at notions of ability and performance.

Uri's experience should cause every conscientious leader to ask the following questions: How many ideas are we losing because team members are suffering in isolation? How much productivity is lost? When innovation and performance suffer because of isolation, a catalyst is needed—you and a community. This truism supports the notion among minority groups known as the "rule of three." Sometimes referred to as the "critical mass" doctrine, the rule of three states that any three minorities, when working within the same organization, will naturally form a support system to survive, thrive, and share information within a larger organization. I've led in organizations with lots of diversity and those with little. And I've personally thrived in the former rather than the latter.

Because of the Treisman model, and my own confirmatory personal experience, I now refuse to allow my team members to work alone. In 2020, my airline team was met with cost-saving measures when the "consultants" and "transformation" became the flavor of the day. Despite budget cuts that followed, productivity and innovation remained steady thanks to our ability to operate like a small firm. I rolled up my sleeves alongside others and ran an insourcing operation like a small firm ensuring that no one operated in isolation. That year we executed more contracts, addressed more administrative actions, and resolved litigation faster than any preceding year.

Teams that collaborate to reach common objectives are often capable of exceptional outcomes when good leaders are there to catalyze and engage. The key, though, is choosing the right leader. Not everyone in an organization is fit for leadership. In fact, leaders are often promoted based on personal relationships and occasionally on being outstanding individual contributors—neither of which is the best qualification for leading others. High-functioning teams operate best with trust, support, and camaraderie, which allows them the freedom to generate solutions beyond what any single individual could have done alone. When a leader lacks the ability to cultivate a high-functioning team, results and morale will reflect that dynamic.

Elijah McCoy shows us the tell-tale sign that an employee is prepared to lead. They solve, and excite others to solve, because they are intrinsically motivated to do so. Those who look for opportunities to augment their capabilities and acquire new skills are a step above those who remain complacent. They level up their hard and soft skills continuously, and ultimately their overall breadth of knowledge grows through demonstrated commitment to lifelong learning. In other words, they're willing to work outside their prescribed lane.

My baseline subject matter expertise as a lawyer doesn't mean that I can only contribute in a legal context. To stay intellectually fit, I read voraciously and share thoughts through writing, and encourage my teams to do the same. If we don't engage in thought leadership and share what we've learned, then we create unnecessary knowledge silos. There are thoughtful ways to encourage skill broadening. For example, UPS does a relatively good job broadening its executives through structured programs like its Executive Perspectives Program with Emory University and its Community Internship Program with Henry Street Settlement in New York. Both programs are designed to take executives with baseline expertise in a variety of areas and expand their business or operational acumen to become well-rounded. Most Silicon Valley companies do the same by liberally offering first-rate educational opportunities.

Conscientious executives are hyper-focused on cultivating everyone on their team and capitalizing on these learning opportunities. Cultivation is the process of developing or nurturing something, and it brings out the best in the team. It reinforces a "promote from within" culture and places the onus on leaders to inspire, rather than passing the responsibility for good leadership to HR. High-performing teams are cultivated by good leaders and set up for long-term growth and performance.

High-Performance Gardening

We cultivate high-performing teams in two ways.

First, we incorporate as many partners with divergent specialties in the decision-making process as possible without sacrificing efficiency, like when Julio sought help from Jeff and me as innovation partners. Remember, innovation suffers in isolation. Leadership is not just telling others what to do but is often diplomatically building consensus and leveraging viewpoints in ideation. The *esprit de corps* that comes from cross-functional teams and inclusion fosters creativity and inspiration. An engaged, high-performing team will become frustrated if left out of the decision-making process.

Second, teams require clear direction and ample communication. Being transparent and honest from the outset is a powerful way to establish authority through trust, as opposed to subordination through fear. It also creates an atmosphere of respect for team members, while listening and taking their advice to heart shows humility. Teams blossom under leaders who affirm and support them, even when mistakes happen, and who establish reasonable targets to achieve. When I reflect on the times when morale reached its nadir at any organization I have worked for, it was usually when leaders failed to communicate a clear and achievable objective, and then we failed to achieve that objective.

Recall, Mr. Buckner's law: "reactions are not always gentle." When communicating, it is acceptable for the conscientious executive to be firm in a way that still allows for honest conversation. For example, I often use the simple question "Can I be frank?" It seems to unburden others from the social constraints of formal conversation. When I express my views openly, it allows others to be authentic, question things, and air their concerns without fear.

It's human nature to seek signs of weakness, so if we're not confident in both our humility and firmness, our message, no matter how thoughtful, will be clouded by doubt. One of the most doubt-inducing questions I faced at the beginning of my career was, "Are you sure?" My boss would often ask his staff this question. It was always unnerving. This is because lawyers are never sure about anything. We live in a gray world with shifting landscapes. A sure footing is rare. The question would always make me second-guess myself. I soon realized I had to develop a way to be sure.

I set an attainable confidence threshold: 80%. When I hit that threshold, I can confidently say, "Yes. I'm sure." Even if I'm wrong—and 20% of the time I could be—it's probably due to variables out of my control or information that was unknowable at the time of the decision. Being 100% confident can lead to arrogance and blind spots. But, by satisfying a high confidence threshold each time, it can raise self-assurance and decision-making.

The Leadership Power Curve

In 2021, I completed a management program sponsored by McKinsey & Company (hereafter "McKinsey" or "the Consultants"). The course was designed to help high-performing executives gain skills in preparation for senior leadership. McKinsey, for better or worse, has a well-deserved consulting reputation for high-flying theoretical approaches and use of analytics. In the course, the instructors explained McKinsey's concept of the "economic power curve." The curve is one of those high-flying theoretical approaches to understanding business strategy. It is, nevertheless, useful as a tool for our purposes.

The curve, according to the Consultants, helps us understand the role of making strategic decisions and its link to profitability. The framework notes that businesses that make strategic moves year over year generally reap greater economic rewards than less strategic competitors who are in a constant battle to recoup capital costs. Among other things, companies with a strong presence in the market can benefit from strong capital expenditures, productivity, and efficient resource allocation in ways that help them gain even greater advantage against competition. This is all represented when plotted on a graph with three distinct zones.

Roughly 60% of companies fall within the three middle quintiles where the curve is relatively flat. This middle zone indicates that economic profit does not vary wildly for the cohort. Generally, these companies work hard to recoup their capital costs. Whereas in the top end of the curve, the top 20% of companies capture drastically more profit per year. These companies consistently make strategic moves that help them move into, and stay, at the top of the economic power curve.

At the bottom end of the curve, an inverse reflection appears. Companies in the bottom quintile (the bottom 20%), have drastic economic losses. These bottom quintile organizations have made inadequate decisions or have made no strategic moves at all.

The power curve can be represented graphically in a two-dimensional space where the relationship between a company's relative economic profit is plotted along the x-axis and average profitability for all companies is plotted along the y-axis. The curve has a sideways S-shape, with the most profitable companies to the right of the curve, and the least profitable companies to the left. The most profitable companies are exponentially more so than others on the curve. Figure 9.4 is my own version of McKinsey's Power Curve of Economic Profit with only the key elements. For our purposes, the shape of the curve and its theoretical framework is all that's relevant.

Generally, McKinsey supposes there are definitive steps that can be taken to move a company from the quagmire of the middle quintiles where economic profit is flat, to the top quintile where economic profit is exponentially higher.

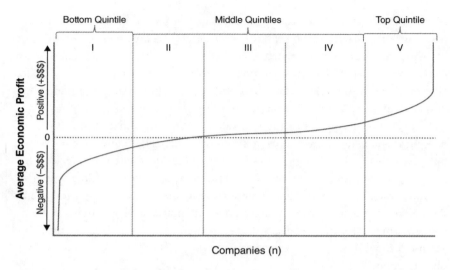

Figure 9.4   McKinsey's theoretical power curve.

That key difference between the top quintile and the other quintiles of the model are primarily leadership and structure driven. This model resonates with me because it aligns with a reasonable notion that companies are also the sum of all the individuals in the enterprise. That's why good companies make it a point to hire exceptional people and help them grow. The baseline of a team with exceptional people will be naturally higher than competitors with less talented teams. I see this firsthand daily at Meta Platforms where every employee I encounter is a veritable genius. And the exceptional human capital at top quintile companies make the organization as a unit more efficient in capturing economic value, reducing waste, and making bold decisions.

Notably, companies in the bottom quintile are just as broken as companies in the top quintile are exceptional. It's almost as if they're professionals at being bad. They have poor leadership, poor procurement processes, poor auditing procedures, and so on. Because it is almost statistically impossible to be wrong by chance alone, it means they're systemically wrong—like an amateur athlete whose shots are usually far away from their intended targets.

In the top quintile, the opposite is true. They are almost always right—from the people they hire to the processes and protocols they use. Like top-quintile athletes Tom Brady and Rory McIlroy, they make most of their shots and are close even when they miss. They know how to move themselves and their teams up the power curve.

McKinsey concludes its model by suggesting there are at least five moves that are essential to propel an organization up the power curve.[3] These moves are:

1. Programmatic mergers and acquisitions: investing in deals frequently and allocating a significant portion of capital to them.
2. Dynamic reallocation of resources: shifting nearly half of all capital expenditures among business units.
3. Engaging in strong capital expenditure to invest in industry-leading innovations.
4. Strengthening company productivity to the point where it is industry leading.
5. Implementing innovation that enables competitive advantages.

However, while the model applies to organizational moves that can improve economic profit, the truth is that the moves are only as effective as the executives who oversee them.

And this brings us right back to our thesis. Any process, thought, experience, or emotion that can manifest at an individual level may manifest at an organizational level given the right conditions. The McKinsey model is missing something. It doesn't capture the myriad of ways an organization's people need to level up to make strategic moves. Is it possible that organizations can manifest better economic profit if we improve the same way individuals within the organization lead, think, and create experiences?

Unquestionably—yes! Organizational culture largely impacts individual executive behavior. Some cultures are stifling and others less restrictive resulting manifestly different approaches from running meetings to interpersonal communication. And, as a result, corporate economic results will differ too. If your boss is yelling at you, then it says as much about acceptable behavior within the organization culturally, as it does the individual manager's ethics.

But my experiences are largely limited to Fortune 500 companies like UPS and Meta, and a large international law firm. For example, I would never imagine rank-and-file employees at UPS penning the types of posts on the company's internal communications page as employees do at Facebook. The cultures of communication are vastly different between the two companies. So, I embarked on a quest to informally survey colleagues at other publicly traded companies, large private companies, and entrepreneurs with small operations of less than 100 people. In nearly every case, the story was the same. Company culture has a profound impact on the deportment of individual contributors.

It is important to note that McKinsey's power curve is a theoretical frame-work for strategic decision-making. It has been criticized by some, but it is fundamentally about how leaders choose to allocate resources. The essence of strategy is when, where, and how to invest resources. The same framework can be useful in thinking about developing leadership competency. That is my leadership power curve. The following concrete steps are loosely analogous to their McKinsey counterparts, but instead they focus on the moves that matter to improve individual performance as conscientious leaders. The steps are:

1. Dynamic Omnidirectional Relationship Investment (DORI): achieving alignment among key relationships.
2. Human capital investment: investing value in human resources.
3. Strength and balance training: efficiently distilling various operating environments.
4. The maximization default: understanding the connection between effort and outcome.
5. Growing a trustworthy brand: tying productivity to a reputation and behaviors.

These moves that matter are particularly important today as we navigate cultural firestorms that rage across our society from the local community school board meetings (think book banning) to corporate boardrooms (think ESG: environmental, social, and governance investing).

Implementing these steps creates a virtuous cycle of professional growth. Now that we have discussed the qualities needed to address tomorrow's challenge, in the next several chapters we will unpack how the leadership power curve can help elevate your individual leadership away from the bottom quintile, where negative value is placed on your contributions as a leader, and away from the large middle quintiles, where most executives are stuck in neutral and not advancing relative to their peers. The goal is to move toward the top quintile of leaders who perform better than the rest in virtually every way and can lead corporate America, and America's free enterprise system, into a better tomorrow.

III

Level Up the Leadership Power Curve

"Sometimes our strengths lie beneath the surface. Far beneath, in some cases."

— Claudia's favorite movie, *Moana*

10 | Move 1: Dynamic Omnidirectional Relationship Investment

In 1985, America Online (AOL) forged a path for the future of online communication by introducing subscription-based services like dial-up internet access, email, and instant messaging. Under the leadership of Steve Case, AOL became an early leader in digital transformation. By 2000, it had grown into one of the world's largest providers with 23 million subscribers worldwide. At that point, faced with increased competition from high-speed broadband companies like Google, AOL merged with Time Warner, a merger that ultimately faltered due to disagreements between the two companies.

In the last decade, I've managed billions of dollars in mergers and acquisitions (M&A). They can be powerful instruments for companies to gain strength in the market, with mergers allowing two firms to create a greater asset than either could have individually. Acquisitions, generally, involve one larger firm taking control of a smaller one or their assets. They may remain separate from the acquiring company or join under one enterprise. So, by their nature, acquisitions tend to focus on cash flow opportunities. Mergers, on the other hand, tend to combine organizations with the goal of gaining more share in target markets. Both strategies are often referred to as "inorganic" growth because they allow companies to access new markets more quickly than if they had only used organic methods of development like expansion of existing resources.

As the AOL–Time Warner merger was under discussion, their corporate cultures clashed. The young energy of a tech-driven start-up met an old-meta media industry culture head on. Opposing strategies caused heated disagreements over how to manage their newly shared enterprise. AOL leaders wanted to focus on growth in its internet venture and Time Warner preferred to nurture its existing traditional holdings. Conflict was inevitable when the merger was complete in 2001, resulting in the two companies struggling to reconcile their diverging corporate cultures and priorities. The contrasting corporate cultures caused deep divisions in management decisions, which significantly hindered growth potential of both businesses. The result? An unprecedented $100 billion loss by 2002, prompting several key executives to leave—including the CEO from AOL—and ultimately leading to the company's divorce seven years later.

Over a decade after the separation, Steve Case was asked to reflect on the failed merger. He noted, candidly, that AOL and Time Warner "failed to capitalize" on the extraordinary moment of linking emerging internet technologies and traditional media assets. He further pointed to issues with "culture" and too much "short-term orientation" as challenges, suggesting that there were people in the combined company who were not as enthusiastic about its digital path. In sum, Case concluded, "[Time Warner] tended to play defense, trying to protect what already existed as opposed to playing offense and try[ing] to create what the future would be."[1] The tension between old meta and new could not have resulted in a more spectacular, public meltdown.

Let's return to the 1980s. In 1986, a year after AOL was founded, a small animation studio was opened in Richmond, California, by Edwin Catmull and Alvy Ray Smith. Catmull was a computer science nerd from West Virginia who would later get a PhD from the University of Utah. To make ends meet, Catmull moved to New York and worked at various institutes where he researched computer animation. Smith was an electrical engineer who had worked at Xerox for years before joining Lucasfilm in California. He would later get a PhD in computer science from Stanford. Together they founded the iconic Pixar Animation Studio.

It wasn't long before the continued success of Pixar caught the attention of another giant, Disney, and in 2006 there was a seismic shift within the entertainment industry. The two merged. This collaboration resulted in an unprecedented integration where both companies' talents meshed seamlessly, leading to rejuvenation of Disney's animation division that can still be seen today.

In 2021, three years after Steve Case's CNBC interview detailing the failure of AOL–Time Warner, Disney CEO Bob Iger was similarly asked about the Pixar deal. Iger could barely contain his enthusiasm as he described the merger as his "proudest decision." He would go on to highlight the co-creative work and integration of the two companies as critical to the deal's success.

Two mergers, two different outcomes. What made the AOL deal fail and the Pixar deal succeed?

In a word: relationships. Integrating relationships into a shared, forward-looking strategy can make or break inorganic growth plans. The relationships between executives and their influence on corporate direction can be decisive in business. Put plainly, Pixar and Disney had compatible visions of the future, and AOL and Time Warner did not.

The same is true for our professional growth. Integrating relationships can make or break one's leadership journey.

McKinsey suggests that the first way an enterprise moves up the economic power curve is by undertaking a healthy inorganic growth strategy. The recommendation is to look for a steady stream of deals every year with each amounting to no more than 30% of market cap, with the goal of the deals adding at least 30% of a company's market cap over 10 years.[2] That's pretty big. Inorganic growth, then, is where we will start our movement up the leadership power curve too. But how does a conscientious leader grow inorganically?

In contrast to organic growth, which is reflective and internal, inorganic growth occurs through methods other than self-discovery. Methods of inorganic growth include mentoring, networking, collaboration, and 360-degree feedback. Just as it is beneficial for an organization to expand inorganically by acquiring assets through mergers and acquisitions, it is equally important for conscientious leaders to grow in this way. And the risks are the same. Engage in improvident or ill-advised mergers, and the result will be no better than AOL–Time Warner. Alternatively, engaging in synergistic transactions can result in a professional windfall, like Disney Pixar.

A simple strategy to grow inorganically is to engage in what I call DORI: Dynamic Omnidirectional Relationship Investment. I coined the term while journaling about the innumerable investments made by my own mentors while Claudia watched Pixar's *Finding Nemo* in the background. In the Pixar classic, two fish, Marlin and Dory, set out on an adventure across the ocean to find Marlin's son, Nemo. Along the way, the duo receive help in big ways and small from all sorts of sea creatures. Marlin's stake in his relationship with Dory pays huge dividends and they eventually find Nemo. Dory's character is symbolic of the incalculable value of relationships. Likewise, here, DORI means investing professional currency to acquire and maintain key relationships that are professionally additive. Here are three steps to do this:

1. Identify relationships that will add skills, knowledge, training, or insights that you cannot develop alone as a leader.
2. Choose the type of investment you can make into said relationship.
3. Ensure that at least 30% of your effort is invested to build trust in these relationships.

DORI is an ongoing effort with the goal of fostering trust, respect, and mutual benefit across professional channels. This holistic approach emphasizes flexibility, responsiveness, and proactivity as essential for building lasting connections that are not limited by hierarchy or directionality. In other words, it's about understanding that inorganic growth can come from any connection within the corporate environment, including in the places that you least expect them. Conscientious executives who embrace DORI are more likely to listen to employees and consider different perspectives because they are wired to grow no matter the source of the growth. In this way, the boundary between a coachable future leader and their discernment is illuminated.

I was exposed to DORI in practice in the late 2000s, long before I could give it a name. The Great Recession (2008–2009) was a terrible time to be looking for work. Many industries were cutting internship classes and clawing back employment offers. Overeager to impress and with practically no experience, I sent out a four-page résumé applying for jobs I wasn't qualified for.

Somehow (I would later learn how), I was granted an interview with the Coca-Cola Company. So I conducted my due diligence on the position and showed up prepared. Thankfully, my hard work paid off, as I had few other options!

Dinisa, my mentor in the program, took me out to lunch one day and told me that when she saw my lengthy résumé, she had thrown it straight in the trash. However, Coca-Cola, or at least that particular interview panel, had a unique selection process. Each member could pull one résumé from the circular filing bin and give it a lifeline. Her colleague, Jennifer Manning (Coke's future corporate secretary), thought my résumé was interesting—partly because her son's name is Andrew.

Looking back, I'm embarrassed at how my résumé had almost cost me such an enormous opportunity that changed my life. I had been so focused on getting all my experience and skills on paper that I hadn't stopped to think about how it would actually look to a potential employer. My résumé was so long that it made me look like I was trying to overcompensate for something. That was my first hard lesson in corporate America. It is important to be strategic and concise in communication or an essential message (like "hire me") could get lost in the noise. To my credit, I realized that I needed to learn this new terrain to be successful, and Dinisa could not have been a better teacher. She was exactly the person I needed to learn from. I needed her as a coach and began investing all the time that I could spare to support her practice and learn along the way.

In exchange, I acquired her trust and the relationship synergy helped me grow. Dinisa would go on to provide a small window into how she managed key relationships in her career and helped me to understand the unspoken rules of corporate life. She showed me how to present myself in a way that would stand out from the competition. Without her guidance I wouldn't be where I am today. Dinisa was my first and my dearest coach for the next decade, until her untimely passing in 2020. She never stopped giving advice and encouragement from helping me pass the bar, navigating big law, and ultimately thriving as a corporate lawyer. Her pushing never stopped. In her own career, she would rise to become a leader at Nike and Hershey. Anyone who knew Dinisa will attest that, despite her many accomplishments, she always made time to help others in their career journeys. It was her hallmark; a gift from her to me, and now it is my gift to my own mentees.

For many years, I wondered what I did to deserve such an awesome advisor and advocate. Perhaps it was luck. Perhaps it was my own willingness to be taught and to take steps to incorporate Dinisa's advice. Whatever the case, Dinisa's example rang loud and clear: growth from the experience of others (inorganic growth) pays unmatched dividends. The magnum opus that Dinisa composed in her life centered on building meaningful relationships in all directions.

Traditionally, career relationships can be broken into three categories: mentors, sponsors, and boards of directors. In this old meta, mentors coach us in our day-to-day careers and help us overcome challenges. They transfer their time, energy, and personal stories from one generation to the next. And like all great corporate (and mentoring) deals, each party benefits. She went above and beyond expectations for traditional mentors. Dinisa invested time and effort because growth could be tangibly observed, and her own legacy enriched simultaneously.

It is not always easy to attract a good mentor. One must first demonstrate coachability. We must devote our full care and attention to acquiring the lessons and put our entire efforts into living the advice practically. Mentors do not invest their time, trust, and values in someone who stubbornly resists their advice or ends up publicly humiliating them because of a job done badly. That is the path to a quick divestiture.

An observable willingness to be mentored begins the mentor-mentee relationship. When I moved to Louisville, Kentucky, one of the first people I met was Larry McDonald. Larry was a long-time director at Humana and the former president of the Lincoln Foundation, a charitable organization offering outside-of-school academic enrichment and college readiness programs for underresourced youth throughout the Louisville metropolitan area. After a few meetings, Larry looked me in the eye and said, "Keep your nose clean. We like you very much and will follow your development with great interest." It was quite an intimidating but also flattering statement. I had no idea who the "we" included. In his trademark deadpan manner of speaking, it was his way of telling me, "I've heard good things about you, but before I decide for myself, I'm going to see what you do with my time and knowledge." I must have passed the test because Larry would later invite me to join a well-regarded social community of state politicians, judges, businessmen and women, and Kentucky Colonels (after a period of keeping a sufficiently clean nose).

Larry and Dinisa were not conventional mentors. Conventional wisdom advocates for prearranged, position-based mentorships, but those can feel forced, lack depth, or generate unease and mistrust. Mentors and mentees should have a natural inclination toward each other and a mutual spirit of cooperation; mentors should see a part of themselves in their mentees. Businesses structure episodic mentoring events but they are often sterile and nowhere near the 30% of time needed to be effective. Given the level of investment needed, it is hard to have more than one or two mentees.

Traditionalists promote sponsors as another career essential. Sponsors are higher-level decision-makers who don't have much daily contact with us but nevertheless advocate on our behalf to give us opportunities. They also say you should have a personal board. Personal board members are people with whom we may have very little contact, but we can rely on them when faced with major career decisions, challenges, or questions. Whether they are at the pinnacle of their careers or retired, they are often in our industry but not our organization, which adds a breadth of perspective (and avoids conflicts of interest). They don't have the time to be sponsors or mentors, but in more limited ways they enjoy helping others flourish. A personal board may take years to cultivate but can make all the difference to a young professional trying to level up.

But there are three nontraditional archetypes of professional relationships that are essential to career growth for the conscientious leader and are not routinely discussed. Dinisa shared these with me, and I now share them with you. These archetypes are distinct from the mentor, sponsor, and personal board; they transcend hierarchy and represent the kinds of relationships that sustain the conscientious executive through the most difficult challenges. These archetypes are the Shifter, the Connector, and the Benevolent Antagonist.

Nontraditional Archetypes

Cars were once built with large, joystick-like controls in the center console known as a gear lever. We called them "sticks" or "shifters." I first learned to drive using my dad's manual, pearl white Ford F-150, which had a big shifter right in the middle. The shifter had a few purposes. Lower gears provided more torque for climbing steep inclines, while higher gears offered better fuel efficiency and higher top speeds. We shifted to lower gears for slower speeds and greater power like when starting from a standstill or driving uphill. In other words, manual shifting allowed for more precise, context-specific choices for moving forward. In many ways the Shifter archetype mimics the utility of having manual control over a car. In this case, the car is your career.

In the professional context, the Shifter archetype can impact our careers by reminding us of the importance of adaptability navigating uncertain and dynamic situations. Our professional journeys often require us to adjust our strategies, perspectives, and even our life plans to meet new challenges. The ability to embrace change, think creatively, and adapt to different circumstances can be invaluable in career advancement and personal growth.

The Shifter reminds us to be discerning and question appearances or surface-level impressions. In our careers, we encounter people and situations that may not be what they initially seem. By adopting a Shifter's ethos, we can develop a keen sense of observation, the ability to read between the lines, and the discernment to navigate complex professional relationships and environments. For me, Dr. James Stephenson continues to play this role in my career. Dinisa, according to her nature, often doubled in this role as well. James is a former NASA fellow and currently a researcher for the U.S. Army. For nearly 20 years, I've invested in a strong relationship with James, which developed from our shared love of PC strategy games. We once worked in the same organization as peers and now we routinely connect over career development. As one of the "big brains" for NASA and the Army, James is comfortable questioning the way things are done: in fact, it's his job. Like most science guys, he gets paid to prove the world exists by questioning what we think exists. He then proceeds to test assumptions for proof. He does the same for me. Whenever I think

I have it all figured out, James challenges me to think differently or provides another way to think about a problem. He helped me work through the loss of a job in the Great Recession as an opportunity to grow in a different direction. And that has made all the difference.

Conscientious leaders need a James, a Shifter within their organizations. This person can be organically cultivated or inorganically assigned as a career ombudsman. This archetype is a reminder that our career journeys may involve encountering individuals or circumstances that defy easy categorization or traditional definitions of good or bad. They encourage us to embrace the uncertainties, adapt to changes in the road ahead, and approach our careers with curiosity, flexibility, and a willingness to explore different perspectives.

The second archetype is the Connector. This archetype functions as a liaison or facilitator, akin to a social butterfly. They possess a vast array of contacts and actively foster the extension of your professional affiliations. They introduce you to noteworthy people, endorse your endeavors, and generate opportunities for linkage and cooperation. They exhibit an aptitude for cultivating meaningful connections and forming a supportive network. To provide a concrete illustration, envision a business development specialist who excels in cultivating rapport and frequently brings together coworkers, consumers, and industry leaders for mutual gain.

This second archetype is like Mycroft Holmes, Sherlock's brother. A Connector is a trusted intermediary whose judgment can be trusted implicitly. They are steadfastly loyal and dependable. Accordingly, they are often in possession of good information. Unlike the Shifter, the Connector is nearly omnipresent. Instead of forcing reconsideration, they are willing to triage and resolve matters with you. Their ability to fit into different social circles allows them to establish connections with individuals from diverse backgrounds. Whether mingling with professionals or interacting with individuals from different social classes, their social adaptability forges relationships and gathers valuable information we occasionally miss. This archetype is a naturally diplomatic and affable person who helps to navigate complex interpersonal webs and maintain a positive rapport with various individuals. They are tactful and disarming, which allows them to extract information.

For me, Leonard Searcy continues to play this role in my career. I, by nature, am happy to play the role for others as well. My dear friend Leonard speaks so many languages that I have lost count. He is a renaissance man who plays multiple instruments and has such a good taste for wine that he once held an importer license. We met 10 years ago while working for the same organization. We bonded over our shared home state of Georgia and ethnic roots in the

Lowcountry of South Carolina. There is rarely a week that goes by that he doesn't point me in the direction of someone I should meet. We are both motivated by the belief that blessings return to those who sow blessings into the lives of others. This "good works" karmic approach to relationship building is often a depthless wellspring.

The conscientious executive needs many Connectors because building bridges to the communities is part of our work. Connectors are the key to constructing those bridges personally and professionally. Today's challenges often combust and spread quickly, sometimes requiring innovative solutions that can only be achieved through cross-sector partnerships. This archetype forges long-lasting relationships that can bring valuable resources to the table that will prove useful far into the unforeseeable future. Connectors are often organically found rather than inorganically assigned. But organizations can ensure that its leaders are likely to develop these relationships by getting employees in rooms where Connectors are found, namely charity boards, good-will galas, and other community giving organizations.

Finally, Dinisa always cultivated a relationship with the third archetype, a Benevolent Antagonist. Even when one didn't exist naturally, she created an atmosphere of light-hearted competition that would invariably draw out this essential archetype in someone. Traditionally, an antagonist is viewed as oppositional to a main character. They are often a peer who creates conflict and obstacles to overcome, which drives the narrative forward. But antagonists need not always be "bad" characters. In fact, in many cases, they are not malicious at all. They may simply have different goals or motivations. For example, in *Les Misérables*, Detective Javert is pursuing convict Jean Valjean. Javert sees the world in black and white and believes in strict adherence to the law. While Javert is technically an antagonist, his pursuit of Valjean inadvertently leads to Valjean's redemption. In many ways, Javert's commitment to justice forces Valjean to confront his own past and ultimately transform his life for the better.

Similarly, in *Harry Potter*, Professor Snape is initially portrayed as a menacing and antagonistic figure, particularly toward Harry. But we later discover that Snape's actions were really driven by love for Harry's mother, Lily. Snape's behavior is ultimately part of a carefully constructed plan to protect Harry from the dark forces aligned against him. In fact, Snape's actions, though often misunderstood, contribute to the ultimate defeat of Voldemort. This archetype of Benevolent Antagonist has the same effect as a straight edge on a whetstone.

For years, my colleague Nate Smith played the role of Benevolent Antagonist. Nate, now the CEO of the billion-dollar Sydney-based company Tellus Holdings, first came to my office upon his arrival at UPS in the mid-2010s and offered to take me out to lunch. It was a scouting mission to check out the competition in the department. Unbeknownst to me, Nate had spent a few weeks inquiring around the department who the high-potential team members were. After my name came up a few times, he reached out. I was at first hesitant to become friends with the proverbial class "gunner." But we ended up in the gym with each other every day after lunch. Then we began working out together with a personal trainer. Then we began spending more time together outside of the office. I learned Nate was naturally competitive and that he needed that competition to push himself. We developed an entente and would go on to complete several incredible transactions for the company. To this day, I can call up my friend the CEO for advice when I need a devil's advocate, or generally a kick in the rear end to pick up the pace on accomplishing goals. And, yes, we still compete with one another.

The conscientious executive needs at least one Benevolent Antagonist. This archetype unlocks so many essential benefits for personal and professional growth. They can promote innovation and creativity by pushing you to explore new ideas and approaches. They can enhance your decision-making by helping you uncover potential blind spots and consider a broader range of perspectives. They can foster your personal and professional growth by encouraging self-reflection and self-improvement. They can build your resilience and adaptability by teaching you to handle criticism, setbacks, and opposition. They can facilitate your learning from failure by providing candid feedback and alternative perspectives. And they can support your decision-making by questioning your decisions and ensuring ethical considerations are considered.

We often hear about mentors, sponsors, and personal boards who support your growth. But the most conscientious executives seek more than these traditional relationships. They look to be challenged for growth, tasked with seeing things differently, and connected along their career journey to those who can help make real impact. The Shifter, the Connector, and the Benevolent Antagonist, are not adversaries but are trusted allies who play a crucial role in your growth and success. They genuinely care about your well-being and the success of your endeavors while offering constructive challenges and alternative viewpoints. Cultivating such relationships can help you become a more effective and conscientious executive, capable of leading with resilience, innovation, and ethical decision-making. When combined, the mentor, sponsor, personal board, Shifter, Connector, and Benevolent Antagonist create a structure of social support for the conscientious leader that leads to personal growth and a sense of purpose. Organizations built on leaders who have this entourage of support, in the aggregate, make better decisions than those with isolated, socially awkward honors students from name-brand schools.

Social support is key. In a 2022 study of over 2,000 students in China from seven universities, researchers found that social support, personal growth initiative, and academic self-efficacy were all significantly associated with a sense of purpose.[3] Researchers Jingxue Cai and Rong Lian defined social support as "material or psychological resources from individuals' social networks that help them cope with challenges." Social support mainly includes support received from family, teachers, colleagues, and peers. They then undertook to measure responses for various categories like social support, personal growth initiative, and academic self-efficacy. For the social support element, the results were generated from student use of the Multidimensional Scale of Perceived Social Support, a tool where individuals responded on a 5-point Likert scale, ranging from 1 (strongly disagree) to 5 (strongly agree); the higher the score, the stronger the sense of social support.

The researchers found that "[a]s with most psychological constructs, purpose does not develop in a vacuum; purposes are discovered, fostered, pursued, and realized with the support and guidance of friends, parents, and teachers and a variety of activities." The findings were largely consistent with the results of American researchers Heather Manlin (Stanford) and Sara Weston (University of Oregon). Namely, a sense of purpose was found to be significantly related to the influence of important others. This is a powerful indication that conscientious leaders should aim to build a community around themselves to reinforce their effectiveness and sense of purpose.

Developing relationships requires strategy and can be charted like any other framework.

Imagine we are standing at the center point of a planar diagram with an x- and y-axis (see Figure 10.1). The vertical (y) axis represents our relative position to others in the organization; the higher up the axis, the more senior on the corporate pyramid. The horizontal (x) axis indicates the relative effort it takes to nurture a relationship. Connectors and Benevolent Antagonists are relationships nurtured out of the leader-follower dynamic because of information asymmetry. Generally, the Connector and Benevolent Antagonist know something that you don't and integrating their knowledge into action demands moderate-to-high investment in the relationship. Peers and Shifters are relationships formed out of the peer-subordinate relationship. Generally, information is available to peers and subordinates in equal measure, but there's value in different perspectives on and interpretation of that information. In all cases, acquiring the information or perspective held by these groups are an asset to the conscientious leader but do not come without consideration.

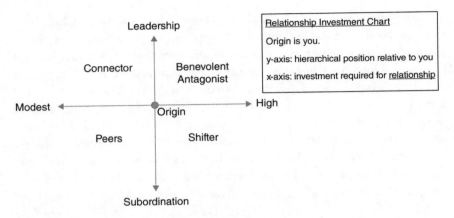

Figure 10.1 Plotting relationships.

Dinisa would similarly map out relationships and discuss with me how to nurture them strategically and consistently on several levels, both within and outside of my organization, to gain knowledge, tap into others' expertise when needed, and build consensus among various stakeholders. As those connections moved in different directions, these relationships proved essential to my future as an organizational leader.

It is impossible to predict how interactions with others, from the building security guards we pass every morning to the cafeteria workers who prepare our lunch every day, might impact their lives or our own. A small relational investment, or act of kindness or generosity, can have a profound effect on someone, and it is important to remember that we never know who we might be helping or who might be helping us. This lesson has been beneficial to me as I often gain valuable insight from those who are often overlooked within an organization.

In accordance with the McKinsey's recommendations for business acquisitions, we should invest approximately 30% of our social currency each year in DORI. For me, this includes relationships such as those with superiors and subordinates, connectors and shifters, mentors and sponsors, and the personal relationships that naturally develop from teamwork (see Figure 10.2).

The people who work for you and with you are exceptional, no matter their level of commitment to the organization. All are motivated by something that, once understood, can unlock a deeper sense of ownership in the business. They deserve more than a silent nod in the hallway as you sip your coffee to avoid having to make actual conversation. They deserve your engagement, your exuberance, and your grace every day. They are willing to come to work as part

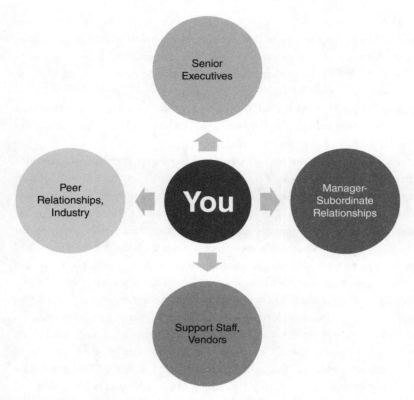

Figure 10.2   360 relationship investment.

of your company or your team and willing to turn their skills into your successes. Celebrate them. Appreciate them. Pick their brains about problems that you are having a hard time unlocking in your own mind. Ask them their opinions on current events, both in your industry and in your community, and engage with them about their answers. Be the approachable leader, the person they can ask a favor, shoot the breeze, celebrate the big sports victory, or laugh at a viral video with. The leader might look bigger than the rest of the people when viewed from the outside in, but you never want that to be true in your own mind, lest you become far less human and out of touch. These are the social mergers that must succeed.

The need for solid relationships cannot be addressed in a vacuum. It is a manifestation of a much bigger and connected problem. The social strain has led to a sense of disconnection among people. In a February 2023 interview with CNN, Starbucks' CEO Howard Schultz noted that much of the angst around labor and workers in enterprise in America are "in many ways a manifestation of a much bigger problem." He continued, "I've talked to thousands of our Starbucks partners in these co-creation sessions. And I was shocked, stunned to hear the loneliness, the anxiety, the fracturing of trust in government, the fracturing of trust in companies, fracturing of trust in family, the lack of hope in terms of opportunity."[4] Schultz's remarks are a poignant reminder of our need to invest in personal relationships as well. Investing in relationships through deep conversations and meaningful interactions may not solve the larger problem immediately, but it is a start.

How much time do you spend during the week proactively engaging with team members whose roles aren't to engage with you? How much time are you in the break room, walking the floor, visiting the warehouse, or taking a few different coworkers out for lunch, drinks, or both? If you can't remember the last time you took time for a genuine conversation that wasn't 100% focused on something going on in your workflow process, then it's been way too long, and chances are you're tone deaf to the present pulse of your organization. It also means your organization needs to dedicate more resources to that purpose. Giving someone our attention is a powerful way to gain their trust and respect. You can't lose sight of the most important resource of your company and your community: people. Corporations can work without technology, they can work without an office, heck, they can even work without certain finances after a fashion if they are clever and frugal. But no company can succeed without people. So, remember to value yours and stay humble about who you are among them.

Strategic Currency

Time is just one of the currencies you can use to build trust. Because our time is limited, and "time is money," as they say, we may be tempted to spend less of our time currency on relationships. But giving someone our attention is a powerful way to gain their trust and respect.

Trust is an asset that can be purchased with five currencies: (1) time, (2) political capital, (3) financial capital, (4) emotional energy, and (5) talent. Each has a different and unique impact on the recipients.

When you pay attention to someone, you're investing time in them, and as most therapists will attest, when a professional gives their full attention to a client, actively listening to their concerns and showing empathy, it can create a strong sense of trust and respect between the two. In fact, research has shown that a therapist exhibiting these qualities encourages clients to disclose more personal information, allows them to feel understood, and helps them view the therapist as credible and trustworthy. In turn, this can lead to more effective therapy outcomes, as clients are more willing to engage in the therapeutic process and work collaboratively with the therapist.

Political capital, another form of social currency, manifests when leadership publicly supports or recommends a person professionally, which is what sponsors do. Good leaders spend their political capital whenever people deserve it—unlike those who speak well of others when things are going well but are the first to pass blame when things go wrong. Something will always go wrong, and relationships that can weather those storms become even stronger and more valuable in the future.

The pandemic highlighted the impact of emotional energy as currency—building relationships can be draining when personalities (or technology) don't align. And while we may be tempted to abandon professional relationships where there are low returns on invested political capital, the resulting trust deficit between leader and employee can create more problems down the road. While it may seem self-evident that one should nurture relationships and avoid burning bridges, it is surprisingly easy to forget to do so when one is preoccupied, or emotions are high in a moment.

Financial capital means leveraging money to ensure a team has the right tools and people to accelerate success. When leveraged right, this currency often complements collaboration because well-funded efforts are often easier to get off the ground and sustain.

We use our talent as currency when we share our knowledge, decision-making processes, and years of experience with others. Some may feel the need to closely guard their expertise like a precious secret, but that fuels distrust because others may feel that they are no longer a team player. When we spend our talent currency on others, it helps them level up for the greater good.

Over time, making the effort to invest in these five currencies develops trust with our mentees and other subordinates. They not only get to know us on a deeper level, but they also see that we genuinely care about their success. As we see them succeed and invest their currencies in others, we, in turn, develop trust in them.

Use of Currency, an Example

In 1996, Linda Duffy watched as a small crowd of figures wearing ski masks burst into her forest ranger station in Ashland, Oregon. Her staff was terrified, and so was she. But unlike most other Forest Service employees, Linda had studied human behavior in college, not forestry or biology. She got the masked group's attention, brought them outside, and asked what they wanted.

Then she asked for their help.

Like so many rural towns across the United States, Ashland had been deeply divided for years between the logging industry and environmentalists, a rift so deep that it's often called the "Timber Wars." By that time, environmentalists had successfully backed many laws against logging. Yet the Forest Service used logging companies to make fire breaks and access roads for fire-safety personnel. The Forest Service then paid the logging companies with the revenue from selling the timber. While it seemed like a win–win situation, environmentalists were convinced it was just a way to override legal hurdles and make extra cash while destroying precious forest.

Linda genuinely wanted to know why the environmental protestors who stormed her office were upset, and what she could learn from them. After that first meeting, she called a local conservation group leader and skilled negotiator for help and began holding meetings with the activists. Some protestors refused to believe the Forest Service would listen and wouldn't attend, but many others showed up.

Eventually, Linda and her staff led walks through the forest so the activists could see for themselves what the Forest Service was doing and why. A young National Park Service employee happened to attend one and explained the then-experimental concept of controlled burns to prevent wildfires. He also pointed out that a lot of the big trees the service had marked for removal weren't really a threat. Large trees have higher branches and thick, fire-resistant bark, making them the most likely to survive a wildfire and the least likely to help it spread. Linda agreed that thousands of the marked trees should remain standing.

That pleased some of the activists, but many were still unconvinced, and it didn't please her staff. Those large trees were the ones the logging companies wanted—the ones that would fund the operation. In addition, the city of Ashland, which relied on the forest's watershed for its drinking water, also wanted to be involved—as did the local American Indian tribes, who agreed with the "new" and "experimental" idea of controlled burns that left larger trees standing. Their ancestors had done the same for millennia.

Linda listened and negotiated with the different stakeholders for four long, painstaking years. Finally, she decided to stop the Forest Service's logging operation altogether and let the community take charge of protecting the forest.

Linda's boss was not happy. He felt she was trying to gain impossible consensus instead of listening to the Forest Service's experts and, in the process, had wasted valuable time, money, and resources. The forest needed its fire breaks before disaster struck.

So, he reassigned her.

But the environmentalists and community groups had built relationships with her and knew she was listening to their needs, which no one had done before. They called everyone they could think of, and as a result, the Forest Service received letters from both of Oregon's U.S. senators opposing her dismissal.

A few days later, Linda got a call from her boss's boss. She was back on the job.

One year later, the new Ashland Watershed Protection Project was up and running. That didn't mean the meetings were over and everyone was on board—in fact, the project extended an open invitation to residents and business owners with concerns. If anyone objected to the removal of any one tree, they could visit that tree with project members and discuss other options. The city organized dozens of tours, which further extended knowledge and consensus around the project as more people understood what was planned and why.

Eventually, Ashland residents saw trucks and even helicopters removing trees, and few complained. The Timber Wars were over.

Now the work of removing brush and managing controlled burns is funded by grants and nonprofits, and the Ashland Forest Resiliency Stewardship Project has become a model for healthy forests and community action around the country.

Linda invested significant time currency to build meaningful relationships with key stakeholders of her enterprise. It is not always easy, but it should never be underestimated no matter how long it takes.

The term "majority rules" might win you an election, but it's not going to build the best sort of community when you are at the top of an organization that touches an enormous number of lives. Everyone's opinion matters and investing in the relationships with external groups raised the white flag on the Timber Wars.

If a sparrow sings in the factory and nobody hears it, is its song still beautiful? The voice of truth, no matter how small, deserves attention in any issue that affects your company and community. Often, simply explaining the situation to someone who does not understand or feels wronged is all that is needed to help them see things from your perspective. This simple act of kindness can win you the trust and respect of a community member, which is priceless. When the stakes are higher and more people are involved, it is important to remain the voice of reason and have patience with everyone involved. Ensure that everyone has a fair say, feels heard and respected, and comes away understanding the outcome, even if it is not what they wanted. This is a fine line to walk, but it can position your organization as a trusted and valued member of the community.

Essential and Personal

Building dynamic omnidirectional business relationships is critical, but don't forget that you are not defined exclusively by your job—and neither should your relationships. In *Finding Nemo*, Dory was a cute, blue tang fish with an innocent charm I couldn't help but love. Despite her short-term memory loss that always put her orange-and-white clownfish friend Marlin on edge, she was integral in finding his son, Nemo. Dory's saving grace was to sing the one phrase she never forgot: "Just keep swimming!"

Business relationships, like personal relationships, require that we engage with challenging personalities, but they are nonetheless important and necessary. When confronted with difficult personalities, I hear that refrain in the back of my head: just keep swimming. The relationship that is difficult to build may be the one that impacts your life the most.

Sitting with my grandparents at Sandhill Baptist Church decades ago, we would sing an old song, "This May Be the Last Time, I Don't Know." It's a melancholy tune but the lyrics underscore that we don't know what tomorrow will bring, and this may be our last time together, so let's make the most of it. I certainly didn't know that Dinisa Folmar's life would be so short, and I'm glad I'm one of those fortunate enough to have known her well. Had she not been intentional with investing in me, even when it was difficult, my story would be drastically different.

And I certainly would never have enjoyed enormous career growth if not for my wife, Amy. One of the most consequential mergers you will ever make in life is the person you choose as your life partner. Our personal relationships also have a strong impact on our careers and the kind of leaders we are and should reflect our values just as our professional ones should.

Amy and I met at Emory Law School, where I sought her assistance with family law, and she sought mine with business law. We studied together in the library, a purely platonic relationship, until one day she asked if I was dating anyone. I would later learn that she did not need my help at all—in fact, she graduated a few seats ahead of me. It was all part of a calculated plan to see if I was husband material. Amy is by far the smartest lawyer I know. I trust her judgment implicitly, a function of the time we've spent together, and seek her opinion and approval on everything. She has sacrificed a lot for our family as I have moved from job to job; she is the partner every man wishes he could have. Asking her to be my wife was the defining relationship decision of my life.

To be a more conscientious leader, at least 30% of your investments should be in DORI. These relationships should be professional and personal, internal and external, and require the use of all of the currencies available to you. In a year's time, these relationships compound and should fill at least a journal page of reflections on impact. When conscientious leaders within organizations are invested and engaged in the daily work of developing dynamic omnidirectional relationships, the results show dramatically in every metric, from retention to profit. Just keep swimming.

11

Move 2: Human Capital Investment

Amy was pregnant. We were cautiously optimistic, this time, because the pregnancy progressed further than any other. My daughter Claudia would later arrive after a difficult and prolonged labor, ultimately delivered by cesarean. It was December 2018, a few days before Christmas, and although late, Claudia arrived a healthy baby. I couldn't have asked for a better Christmas gift.

Nothing about the experience of having my first child was as I expected. We hadn't expected she would be emergently delivered by a doctor, in a manner we hadn't expected, and at a time we hadn't expected. Several months earlier, we moved to a town that we didn't know, purchased a house we didn't love, and I started a new job that wasn't fully known to me. We were so new to the community that we hadn't even met our neighbors, and to make things more interesting, both sets of grandparents lived nine hours away.

Like most executives at Ford, Humana, and UPS, we found ourselves buying a house in a suburb of Louisville—a small town called Prospect. With a population of 5,000, Prospect is situated on the banks of the Ohio River about 20 miles northeast of Louisville and about 60 miles north of Knob Creek, where Abraham Lincoln was born. The town sits beside U.S. Highway 42 on one side, and by Harrods Creek, a tributary of the Ohio River on its southern end.

Much like my hometown, Prospect grew thanks to the railroad, part of a network of rail lines that never quite reached completion. We ended up settling alongside a historical and an invisible railroad, too. Kentucky became the last stop for enslaved people escaping on the Underground Railroad's northern route to freedom. And this part of Kentucky and Indiana, including the town of Prospect and the nearby town of Goshen, became important stops along the way.

If life is a tapestry, then there are times when the hand of destiny weaves circumstances that defy rational explanation. These seemingly random events often point to an underlying truth such that coincidences guide us toward discovery. This small town in which I found myself for the next few years, with its good-natured people often forgotten by coastal elites, would underscore the importance of its existence and contributions to a broader national story. When the pandemic raged, Louisville's Muhammed Ali Airport became America's staging ground for airlifting vaccines.

Like most executives, I was fully enmeshed at the time. I fully aligned with the company narrative requiring sacrifice by its senior leaders, and so it was a no-brainer when I sold my Atlanta home and moved my pregnant wife to Kentucky's Sand Hill.

The next spring we were veteran newborn parents. Instead of expecting Amy to cook every day, I dutifully assumed that responsibility by ordering take-out. One day I ordered from Uber Eats and noticed the driver arrived in a relatively nice car and business attire. Let's call him Don.

I asked Don what he did for a living.

"Oh, I'm a systems engineer at a major hospital," Don replied.

"Why do you drive for Uber?!" I asked.

"It's my way to save for my daughter's college," Don responded.

"Is it really that lucrative?" I pressed.

"No, not really. Well, it's okay. I just need a way to make a little more than I can get from my job." Don concluded.

How strange. I imagined someone with Don's credentials would be compensated enough to save for his child's education without needing a side job. I wondered how working two jobs must have limited his family time. Before Claudia, I would have never thought about Don's predicament. It's funny how growing a family changes you. It has a profound impact on your life and influences your leadership style as well. As a parent, you learn to be patient and improvisational, skills that are also fundamental to being a successful leader in any industry. Late nights with newborns certainly make you more self-aware— particularly regarding energy limits. You become a more balanced and thoughtful decision-maker as you juggle the daily demands of teaching and correcting while also striving to meet the expectations of your team at work. Although it may seem unexpected, parenthood can propel you forward in your leadership journey, helping you to become a more effective and compassionate leader.

The gig economy is full of Dons who have regular jobs but also freelance, either because their salary is not enough to cover basic living expenses or to save for the future. Indeed, talking to Don validated a concern I had for months after Claudia's birth. How was I going to make everything work financially? No one really tells you how expenses balloon after having a child, but your pay does not. And the social support for working families in America is virtually nonexistent. Few things enrage younger workers more than out of touch, empty nester executives who are tone deaf to this reality. This fact blew up in Dave Ramsey's face, a self-styled financial guru, who guffawed at a caller on his platform *The Ramsey Show* for spending $25,000 per kid on day care. The problem is, I and every parent of young children I know spends that much or more today because of inflation. It's standard for working families. For weeks Dave was roundly lambasted by the internet from podcasts to social media influencers, pointing out what appeared to be a disconnect from reality.

I contemplated a gig even as a company vice president.

Understand the State of Play

One of the first things covered in new management orientation at UPS is the benefits package. All eligible employees were enrolled in an exciting "portable" retirement account that operates differently from the old pensions of "legacy" employees. The new plans were called "defined contribution" plans and were billed as superior to the old-school "defined benefit" plans our dad's generation were given. This type of benefit is broadly used in corporations across the United States. In actuality, the old "legacy" employees with pensions had more certainty in retirement and generally more loyalty to the company over a longer term. This delta in loyalty partially created by defined contribution plans make gig work increasingly a normal occurrence for employees at companies today. Combined with lower wage growth, this also makes child rearing difficult for younger employees, which followed a well-established trend by 2020 of critically low birth rates in the United States.

Caroline Hartnett at University of South Carolina and Alison Gemmill of Johns Hopkins write extensively on population trends, and in 2020 published a study published in *Demography* that found that the delay in having children, sometimes referred to as "tempo distortion," is often linked to the sociological challenges of achieving milestones necessary to maintain a reasonable standard of living with children.[1] Thus, it's not an outright rejection of children but rather a sober realization of the world today. Amy and I were, after all, not spring chickens when Claudia arrived. We were caught in the same vortex that today's employees struggle to escape.

Rising childcare costs, stagnant wages, and increasing cost of living have made it hard for many families to afford children. Financial uncertainty stemming from economic recessions and rising student debt levels is delaying childbearing. These stressors weigh heavily on those considering their options for building a family, ultimately presenting significant psychological and emotional challenges. As leaders, it is important that we recognize and address these concerns, and work toward creating more stable and secure economic conditions for families. Stable families create committed teams, tenured employees, lowers churn, and helps stabilize wage costs.

The economic terrain of the American workforce has undergone tremendous transformations in the last 50 years. The trend of declining purchasing power for the average worker remains a constant point of concern. Real wages flatline, while the cost of living skyrockets. This worrisome trend casts a pall over the ability of many individuals to innovate while struggling to make ends meet, which leaves them grappling with financial insecurity and anxiety.

The soaring cost of housing is a key factor in the erosion of purchasing power. This is particularly true in urban areas where there is a high demand for housing. Many workers find themselves unable to purchase a home due to the exorbitant prices of real estate that keep climbing with no sign of slowing down.

Renting, which has become the only viable option for many workers, has also become more expensive. Rental costs have outpaced wage growth in many areas, making it challenging for workers to afford decent housing without sacrificing other essential expenses. For example, one of my mentees is a young lawyer in Atlanta making an extraordinary salary at a respectable law firm. She struggled with housing insecurity as landlords escalate rents into the high five figures for apartments the size of closets. On my recommendation, she began looking for a townhome outside of Atlanta in one of the smaller surrounding towns. While this is a better option for her financially, even a modest loan on a townhome at current interest rates yields a higher monthly payment than I make on a much larger, single-family home purchased only a few years earlier.

But that is not all.

The burden of health care expenses has also grown significantly over the past five decades. Health care costs have consistently outpaced wage growth and inflation, leading to higher premiums, deductibles, copays, and out-of-pocket expenses for medical care and medication. The Peterson Center on Healthcare, a New York–based nonprofit focused on health care policy found, on a per capita basis, health spending has increased in the last five decades from $353 per person in 1970 to $12,914 in 2021. Researchers found, "[i]n constant 2021 dollars, the increase was from $1,951 in 1970 to $12,914 in 2021."[2] These rising costs not only limit access to quality care, but also put pressure on workers' finances by limiting their ability to meet other essential needs. In fact, in 2022, I suffered from severe abdominal pains for which I went to see a doctor. Even though I have medical insurance, it cost me nearly $2,000 to conduct diagnostic tests, including a colonoscopy. I was aghast.

But that is not all.

The same story plays out in education. The cost of higher education has increased much faster than wages. This makes it challenging for anyone seeking a college education or trying to finance that education for their children. Many workers find themselves saddled with student loans that can take years or even decades to pay off. This situation has significant implications for the future. As a young man, for example, I had to rob my 401(k) retirement account as a means to fund a down payment on my first home; otherwise, I couldn't secure the loan, even with my wife's income, because we both carried substantial student loan balances. These are the unfortunate choices that America's young workers have to make.

But that is not all.

While productivity has increased consistently year over year, wages have little parity with these gains. Many workers are earning the same or even less than what their counterparts were earning decades ago, in real terms adjusted for inflation. This has left workers with limited or no real wage growth. Years ago, one of my hourly employees received a 2% merit increase in an environment where inflation was escalatory. This was the amount authorized by HR. I can't remember the exact amount, but he countered his merit increase with a request for a modest hourly adjustment around 20 cents per hour. I encouraged him to formally request the increase, and I was supportive of his salary expectations as his direct manager. However, the request was inexplicably denied by my senior manager. This decision would go on to greatly impact the employee's commitment to the organization. Years later, after I moved on to a new role, he sent me the following message on LinkedIn:

> Andy, I honestly regret staying here longer. Our last conversation before you left is always in my head. I was comfortable with what I was doing. You were right. It does not make sense to be loyal in the absence of loyalty in return. I want to see what is out there.

Because HR wouldn't budge over a 20-cent increase, a tenured employee who was comfortable performing at a high level lost all desire to continue producing for the organization.

The shift toward gig jobs, part-time work, and contract work has taken a toll on the value of full-time work. However, the gig trend has also resulted in increased job insecurity, reduced access to employee benefits, and decreased financial stability. Gig workers are faced with lower wages, irregular hours, and limited job security, all of which increases the variability of their wage by subjecting it to wild swings in consumer demand and few safety nets. Many gig workers struggle to make ends meet, facing financial stress and insecurity. This can have detrimental effects on their physical and mental health.

In August 2022, Jeanna Smialek and Ben Casselman published an article in *The New York Times* detailing how the working poor face inflationary pressure with substantially fewer tools.[3] They reveal that a big chunk of a worker's budget is devoted to food and housing, and lower-income families have less room to cut back before they have to stop buying necessities. To cope, many workers are going into credit card debt, putting off replacing cars, and even buying fewer groceries. In practice, all these options are terrible for social stability. The options boil down to defaulting on unsecured debt, which is terrible for lenders and the banking system; reducing consumption, which slows economic growth in a market built on consumer spending; relying on old cars, which is bad for public safety, the environment, and the auto industry; and, finally, malnutrition.

Why should corporations care? These precarious conditions have implications for corporate productivity. In Don's case, the hospital and Uber were competing for his loyalty and best efforts. When workers need a second job to make ends meet, or to save for a child's college education, or to achieve the middle-class life they deserve, it divides their time, energy, and creativity between endeavors. The ability to focus on their highest and best work is diminished. Conscientious leaders consider the challenges of the average worker and find ways to help their teams give their full effort to one job. This often means investing heavily in our human assets to mitigate the market's worst pressures. It also means that we must know about the financial health and well-being of our workforce. As Henry Ford once noted, the rule for the industrialist is not just making quality goods at a low cost, but also "paying the highest wage possible." That last part conveniently gets lost when deciding whether to grant a nominal pay increase to a tenured employee.

Instability Costs

People are the most important resource of any enterprise. Trying to run a company without investing in people is like rushing into battle without an army or building a house without tools. It's impossible. For over a decade I led service-oriented teams. UPS, at its core, provides a delivery service. You simply cannot provide service without teams of people working together. Similarly, my old law firm provides a service requiring both trust and effective advocacy. Neither service is possible without talented and hardworking providers.

In the service profession there is an old saying attributed to Harry Gordon Selfridge: "the customer is always right." It's a powerful adage that has endured for over a hundred years. But Gordon Bethune, former CEO of Continental Airlines, noted that Selfridge's saying had to be tempered with a singular admonition. "You can't treat your employees like serfs. You have to value them. If they think that you won't support them when a customer is out of line, even the smallest problem can cause resentment."[4]

Customers aren't just the people paying for a transaction but includes all people touched by a service, such as internal customers like employees. They have the potential to be both payer and producer over the years. So, they are arguably a customer of the most important sort. When we invest in our internal customers, we don't just fortify our businesses, we help to stabilize our communities in the process.

Take, for example, the town of Greenville, South Carolina. Like Walterboro before the demise of the Walterboro railroad, or Prospect before the collapse of the Westport Railway, the sleepy town of Greenville had similar beginnings, but the outcomes diverged substantially.

Greenville underwent a significant renewal during the 1970s and 1980s when the local textile industry faced a decline. Attracting investments from renowned global manufacturers like BMW and Michelin, the city transformed into a flourishing economic hub with a varied industrial backdrop. This not only created ample work opportunities for the locals but also helped in boosting the overall economic growth of the region.

BMW built one of its largest manufacturing facilities in the world near the community of Greer. It produces a range of BMW models there, including the X3, X4, X5, X6, and X7. The company has made substantial investments in expanding the plant and increasing its production capacity over the years. Consequently, the Greer community has grown from a population around the size of Walterboro in 1980 to nearly 40,000 today. The median income there today is over $54,000, well above the federal poverty line. Michelin, too, has a significant presence in Greenville. The company operates multiple facilities in the area, including a manufacturing plant and the Michelin North America headquarters. The Greenville plant produces passenger and light truck tires and has undergone expansions and investments to support increased production.

Greenville is a prime example of how proactive efforts toward economic development can turn a city's fate around and the economic prospects of employee families as well. As *New York Times* reporter Justin Baer noted in 2021, places like Greenville, Des Moines, and Provo benefited dramatically from the pandemic as the precursor plans for growth and investment made them attractive to industry and workers alike. This planning windfall inured those communities from major economic disruption.[5] Walterboro, on the other hand, failed in planning and attracting the same investment from corporate interests, and suffered accordingly.

Forgotten towns inhabit underserved areas in every state and generally exemplify food and job deserts, lack public services, have greater social inequality, and put a strain on the surrounding economy. Companies operating in such destabilized environments face lower net profits, higher infrastructure and security costs, and increased crime and property loss, not to mention less reliable employees due to their increased divided loyalties. A degenerative spiral begins until either business or community are nonexistent.

But they are also ripe for economic opportunity. The U.S. Department of Agriculture's 2021 report on rural America reveals that nearly 50 million potential customers live in America's rural areas. They have a higher propensity toward subscription services for things like broadband, and there are many able-bodied potential workers looking for stable, good-paying jobs.[6] This is why McKinsey and Company analysts Mike Kerlin, Neil O'Farrell, Rachel Riley, and Rachel Schaff, noted that "rural is rising" in a report detailing economic development strategies for America's heartland.[7] Future infrastructure development in these areas will make them prime opportunities for business and underscores the importance of Senator Tim Scott's 2017 Opportunity Zones[8] initiative setting aside nearly $30 billion for economic development, and President Joseph Biden's Infrastructure Investment and Jobs Act in 2021 setting aside another $40 billion for rural internet infrastructure.[9]

Among McKinsey's recommendations to move up the economic power curve is the pursuit of a "big push." By funneling a significant amount of investment into areas of need to create "a sustainable, long-term, virtuous cycle of economic growth." This can take many forms but is most frequently associated with the attraction of a major employer or the construction of large-scale infrastructure. This was the same strategy used by BMW and Michelin in the Greenville region. While the McKinsey analysts suggest that the size of a big push investment would normally require the involvement of a government body such as a federal or state government, that is not a foregone conclusion.

Conscientious executives, with a big picture in mind acting singularly or in collaboration with like-minded corporate leaders in other organizations, can accomplish this feat without the government. For example, in 2017, Nate Smith and I worked tirelessly on a big push to make investments in a joint venture with China's delivery behemoth SF Express. As reported by Reuters, the joint venture between UPS and SF "combine(d) SF's 13,000 service points in 331 cities in China with UPS' global network spanning 220 countries."[10] This deal was really important to me because it created the infrastructure necessary for entrepreneurs in small towns and rural areas to sell goods into the Chinese market, thereby opening greater Asia to the Prospects, Walterboros, and Greenvilles of the world.

This is just one example of a private sector "big push": two companies working together to invest in the infrastructure needed to specifically benefit rural economies and small business. Alternatively, there have been big-push investments in electric vehicles in places like Tennessee. The state has offered Ford Motors and its partner, South Korea–based SK Innovation, hundreds of millions of dollars in incentives to develop BlueOval City, a site to produce electric pickup trucks and advanced batteries. Leaders expect the project to create nearly 6,000 jobs in Stanton, Tennessee, a town within distressed Americana Haywood County, an area experiencing uneven economic progress.

Destabilization makes it harder to tap into the potential economic reward of a place and to share in prosperity together. Physical safety concerns and poor infrastructure can make doing business an expensive undertaking. Shifting social dynamics like tensions with local law enforcement can also make it difficult to establish and maintain relationships with customers and suppliers.

One effect of this destabilization is higher theft. Walmart CEO Doug McMillon often cites shoplifting and theft at Walmart Stores as a cost driver noting in a CNBC interview in December 2022 that "[Walmart] stores across the U.S. are grappling with an uptick in shoplifting that could lead to higher prices and closed stores if the problem persists."[11] McMillion's claims were corroborated by Target's CFO Michael Fiddelke, who reported that shoplifting at the Target stores had jumped 50% year over year and could amount to nearly half a billion dollars in losses in the fiscal year.

A few months later in April 2023, Walmart announced that it was closing four of its stores in Chicago. When asked about the reason for the decision, a spokesman for Walmart demurred, "There was no single cause for the increase in losses and that theft wasn't a driving factor." But the *Wall Street Journal* would go on to correctly note Walmart's own public statements reveal, "[Walmart's] Chicago stores have not been profitable since [they] opened . . . and [t]hese stores lose tens of millions of dollars a year, and their annual losses nearly doubled in just the last five years."[12] When an operating environment becomes cost prohibitive, the resulting closure of businesses is bad for everyone, especially the folks left behind in an increasingly expansive food and job desert.

Conscientious executives see the possibility in places that are written off and treat the instability costs of any investment as a variable, not a constant.

To be successful in an unstable environment requires leaders to seek to understand why destabilization exists and develop an investment plan to help mitigate the root cause. Yes, your sales solutioning teams need to become socially curious and aware of how they can positively influence local dynamics. Gone are the days of the easy sell. Prime markets are saturated. The endeavor requires key entrepreneurial traits such as adaptability and creative risk-taking that demonstrates a laser focus on the good will and profit that can be achieved in equal measure by working to stabilize the operating environment.

So, what kinds of instability can corporations help resolve?

A common and obvious source of community destabilization is a lack of good jobs. A "good job" for our purposes is one that pays a wage that places the worker above the federal poverty line and includes benefits like health care and retirement plans. A conscientious leader works to ensure every job in the organization is a "good job" and that those jobs are located where you want to sell. Some issues faced by Wilhelmina Nesbitt, who died in her home in a Walterboro house fire, were due to a lack of access to health services and transportation, and food insecurity, but corporate leaders can influence each of these issues. Still, the most immediate impact on social destabilization can be made by merely offering good jobs and benefits in underserved areas. These areas tend to be in poor neighborhoods like Walterboro (roughly 54% White) or Chicago's South Side (approximately 74% Black). They are America's railroad towns and inner-city wards. They cut across racial and ethnic lines. They are hard to reach places or hard to secure places, but they are, nevertheless, important places that influence the overall stability of the national community.

If too many forgotten places falter, then America's free enterprise system may share the same fate of 100 Ann Court—a collapse. And the fall is often heaviest on historically disadvantaged groups. Notably, in October 2021, the U.S. Census Bureau released a bombshell report on wealth inequality in the United States finding non-Hispanic White householders had a median household wealth of $187,300, compared with $14,100 for Black householders and $31,700 for Hispanic householders.[13] The implication of this historical trend provides a guidepost for organizations looking to be a stabilizing platform for local communities. Clearly, the target environment is rich and full of opportunity.

So, what can you do as an individual leader in a large, matrixed organization? Here's what I did.

Operationally, my personal goal is to make sure everyone in my department is compensated well. Even though Human Resources makes salary recommendations based on its own metrics, hiring managers often retain some flexibility. I used that flexibility. Whenever possible, I also seek out local talent and qualified candidates from underrepresented groups in my organization, which varies by location. And I make it a point to offer them the best salary possible for the job classification.

The same is true for the contractors, vendors, and all outside workers I hire. For instance, one of the most powerful decisions I can make within a corporate legal function is who I choose as outside counsel, because millions of dollars flow from our in-house legal department to external law firms. Paying and treating workers well creates stability through turbulent times.

For years I served on the Chief Legal Officers committee for the aviation industry group, Airlines for America. The committee was composed of general counsels from major airlines like JetBlue, United, American, Delta, FedEx, and UPS. Patricia Vercelli, a colleague and friend, would lead the meetings. She and I would often talk about the impact we could make to increase participation of women within the aviation industry, which lags behind virtually every industry in gender balance.

During one committee meeting, Patricia was facilitating a legal discussion, and we were debating proposals for assigning counsel to a matter, which typically results in millions of dollars of legal spend. Our work narrowed the field down to two proposals, one of which seemed like the winner. As we were getting ready to vote, I asked the team, "So, what does their diversity picture look like?" Bob Rivkin, then general counsel of United, flashed a trademark boyish smirk. Priya Aiyar, general counsel of American Airlines, adjusted in her seat and noted that it was a good question. Brandon Nelson, then general counsel of JetBlue, nodded his head in agreement to hear more on the topic.

No one had asked that question before. When we asked the preferred finalist this question, they responded by presenting a team that was both qualified, and more inclusive than its competition, and included geographic diversity from America's heartland. We went with that firm over the name-brand, east coast elite law firm. And just like that, we gave average Joe from middle America, a seat at the table and a nice paycheck to boot.

If I hadn't spoken up at that moment, we probably would have gone with either firm; their teams would have done good work, and it would have been business as usual. But because I asked the question, a diverse team of women got an opportunity to receive the investment of experience and resources that can often be elusive. Their children got to benefit from the boon and more importantly, we invested in a place that needed and deserved the work.

Sometimes all it takes to get an organization to move in a different direction—a better direction—is one person asking the right question.

That's the kind of impact needed across industries. The conscientious executive has a keen understanding of the bigger picture, which includes the market stabilizing needs that are an important predicate for business to thrive. Imagine the good that would come from supply chain operations in Greenfield, Ohio (population 4,300), auto manufacturing in Strasburg, Pennsylvania (population 3,100), and solar panel manufacturing in Lewisburg, West Virginia (population 4,000). Leaders must be willing to level up by making a big push so that our investments will impact broader society and stabilize the free marketplace today.

Total Value

Harvard Business Review routinely conducts surveys of leadership teams to assess how they spend most of their time. Since 2017, the results have generally followed a trend. In a typical survey of roughly 1,000 CEOs across six countries, CEOs spend over 56% of their time in preplanned meetings with other leaders. The topics vary but usually focus on future strategic plans and production. In other words, CEOs spend the bulk of their time evaluating the "big picture" with a focus on the future.

Future investments, future growth opportunities, future marketing product plans, board meetings, and potential legal issues consume the days of the most senior executives. A central question that runs parallel to all these issues about the future is simply how the enormous platform that comes with capital should be deployed. For the conscientious executive, the question is the same, but with the added concern of how the enormous capital platform should be deployed in ways that develop society for good *and* profit. In other words, how do tomorrow's decisions leverage the enterprise as a platform for positive change? A slight calibration in the question can raise major differences in investments and strategy. Decades ago, when the executives of the Coca-Cola Company considered how to leverage their capital platform in ways that could develop society for good and profit, they made the conscientious decision to invest heavily in research and development to develop the world's first recyclable plastic bottle made with up to 30% plant-based material.

Coke's 2009 innovation was aimed to directly address the concerns of the company's youngest consumers who were increasingly conscious of the pollutive byproducts of their purchasing decisions. At the same time, the company set upon an ambitious plan to become water neutral; focusing on how the company could capture and replace water used in its production processes.

By 2021, Coke unveiled its first-ever beverage bottle made from 100% plant-based plastic and was returning the same amount of water to the environment and communities as the amount of water used in all beverages and production around the world. But 2021 is just one stop along a continuum. Coca-Cola's executives were thinking about 2031 before arriving at the 2021 milestone. The drive to invest well doesn't stop at one victory. Dr. Paul Bowen, Coke's director of sustainability, notes, "We have to really think and make conscious decisions to do things like reuse water, capture water, and make sure that it doesn't go down the drain."[14]

Social good and profit need not be in constant tension, though it can often feel that way with at least one corporate stakeholder—the investor class. The typical investor targets a predictable financial return over a predictable time horizon. They often avoid investments that seek to address ancillary social concerns in favor of those that are directly related to the enterprise's bottom line. I call this form of investment "entrepreneurial myopia," and it is arguably the root cause of much of the environmental and social decay making business increasingly risky in the long run. A hyper-focus on discrete economic decisions and the resulting profit is an economic fallacy of reasoning that results in palliative rather than innovative risk-taking.

A hyper-focus on profit and without regard to source, caused investors to overinvest in "bundled" financial instruments in the early 2000s. A lack of concern for the impact that variable interest rates could have on mortgage notes within these instruments directly led to the mortgage-backed securities catastrophe of 2008. It's the same force that led investors to create SLABS, student loan asset-backed securities, causing a real impediment to addressing college financing and debt relief policy. The same diagnosis of entrepreneurial myopia can be seen in the failures of enterprises like Silicon Valley Bank, the sixteenth largest bank in the United States at the time, which was shut down by federal regulators on March 10, 2023. There are strong indications that it may be the cause of the post-COVID inflationary economy referred to derogatorily by some commentators as "greedflation."

Greedflation is when inflation occurs because people in the market act greedily, ignoring fundamentals by artificially boosting demand for goods or assets. Market distortions created by greed and speculation, could trigger a vicious cycle in which inflation feeds greed and vice versa. Theoretically, this market condition can lead to an economic bubble and a period of economic and social instability if left unchecked. If all investors want to hear on an earnings call is "we've had another quarter of record profit growth," then pricing and other variables that factor into profit become as unmoored from performance reality as Steven Temares' salary at defunct Bed, Bath, & Beyond.

Albert Edwards, a global strategist at Societe Generale, also known as SocGen, notes that pursuit of corporate profits has become so extreme that it could even trigger the "end of capitalism." His words, not mine. SocGen is one of Europe's leading financial services groups and a major player in the economy for over 150 years. It's one of the few banks in the world to be considered as "systemically important" by the Financial Stability Board, the G20's international body dedicated to safeguarding the global financial system. Using data from the U.S. Federal Reserve, Bureau of Economic Analysis, SocGen, and his own personal insights over 40 years in finance, Edwards makes a compelling case in *Fortune* magazine that "he's never seen anything like the 'unprecedented' and 'astonishing' levels of corporate Greedflation in this economic cycle."[15]

Edward's notes that the Federal Reserve Bank of Kansas City found, "that markup growth—the increase in the ratio between the price a firm charges and its cost of production—was a far more important factor driving inflation in 2021 than it has been throughout economic history." Similarly, the Bureau of Economic Analysis data showed profit margins for corporations remained near record highs relative to costs in the 2022 fourth quarter data. Most economists would have expected a sharp decline at the end of 2022 given the economy slowed, but instead, corporate profits soared, which defies traditional economic logic—but not the logic of greedflation.

The drive to maximize profits is strong, even paramount for unenlightened capitalists. But this approach is frankly unsustainable. The lack of conscientious capitalists could cause a systemic failure resulting in all companies becoming victims to a rapidly destabilizing social environment that is hostile toward free enterprise.

People-focused leaders with a big-picture view can overcome entrepreneurial myopia. Our job is to think about opportunities for forgotten towns, forgotten people, and the forgotten art of social care. Tactically, this means understanding what benefits your employees desperately want—like the chance to convert part of their paycheck into a college savings fund. It's not enough to drive your company to record levels of profit if the result is a wasted society. The market is shifting its focus from flashy profit headlines to the broader impacts of financial success on employees and community welfare. This shift is driven by a generation of consumers who seek to avoid the harmful consequences of unchecked corporate power. While record profits may grab attention, companies must consider how their financial achievements translate into meaningful benefits for those beyond their boardrooms.

Leveraging vast corporate resources to make employee lives better is the single biggest move that matters to establishing a happy, passionate team. When you do this, you're sending them a direct message that employees are worth even more than what their paychecks read, and that you are aware of that fact. The same is true of the communities in which you do business.

20% Tithe

McKinsey consultants traditionally suggest that companies engage in strong capital expenditure to move up the power curve of economic profit. For our leadership curve, this 20% annual tithe is invested in human capital. Capital allocations to labor vary depending on organization but most estimates put the average cost of labor between 20–35% of gross sales. Similarly, you meet the bar on this step if you are among the top 20% in your industry in your ratio of human capital spending to sales. So, that typically means spending 1.7 times the industry median. Like a tithe, you should see this contribution is not a maximum requirement, but rather a minimum annual investment in your workforce.

Uche Enemchukwu is a lawyer turned CEO who now owns Nelu Diversified Consulting Solutions, a benefits consulting firm focused on developing strategies that account for the diversity of a workforce. It's not unheard of for lawyers to turn entrepreneurs, but it certainly is a less traveled path. I was excited to reconnect with Uche, who I'd met working at a competing law firm in Kansas City and learn about her journey.

When I asked about her motivations for creating Nelu, Uche said that a one-size-fits-all benefits structure cannot satisfy every employee's needs. As a lawyer she consistently managed benefits and compensation matters that rarely addressed the fundamental challenges of the wage worker. "Millennials like us," Uche explained, "often experienced economic hardship at critical points in our lives and face a dramatic wealth disparity compared to other generations." This is certainly true: we took on higher student loan debt, entered the workforce during a near-depression (the Great Recession), and were hit by a dramatic rise in housing prices right when many of us were getting ready to buy our first home.

If a company gives two executives from different generations $100,000 each in stock, the older executive can let that stock grow over time and make money on it, but the younger executive is likely to cash it in within just a year to cover present life expenses—which means paying regular income taxes on the sale of that stock and no longer having that investment to grow. In other words, although the dollar amount of that stock is technically the same for both, it has vastly different value for people at different life stages.

To remedy this, Uche explained, the company could allow the worker to instead elect paying $100,000 directly toward their employees' high-interest student loans. If more businesses did that, more employees could pay off their student loans in a few years, instead of 25 or 30 years. That would decrease the loan's accrued interest, which in turn, would allow the employee to start building wealth instead of fighting debt interest. This would also help to mitigate the risk of default in the event of job loss and provide powerful, long-term support for consumer spending. Further, if the government incentivizes companies to adopt this benefit plan through favorable tax treatment, it could alleviate the need to forgive those loans through certain income-based repayment plans, which results in a net loss for taxpayers.

Thinking differently about employee retention, including benefits structure, is how we construct a win-win proposition for business and workers alike today. Uche is an example of subject matter expertise that leaders should look to for ideation in the new, post-COVID economy. To gain commitment from the workforce today, a benefits plan needs to look more like a student loan repayment plan rather than a tired buy-and-hold stock plan.

Most of us have taken employee satisfaction surveys that ask us to rate our responses on a five-point scale, where five means extremely satisfied and one means extremely dissatisfied. Gallup uses 12 specific questions, called Q12, that are based on more than 30 years of accumulated quantitative and qualitative research, to understand employee satisfaction. The Q12 includes statements like, "I have the materials and equipment I need to do my work right." "There is someone at work who encourages my development," "I have had opportunities at work to learn and grow," and so on. Generally, Gallup's business surveys focus on employee development and support. The results are then used to help organizations solve problems and excel in their industry.

Over the years Gallup found a trend. Organizations that had more employees with "extremely satisfied" responses showed overall higher performance indicators and less employee turnover, mishaps, and other negative indicators. In 2020, Dr. James Harter and a team of researchers set out to validate the correlation by conducting an in-depth analysis of 456 Gallup studies covering over 2 million employees from 276 organizations and 54 industries across 96 countries.[16] In their analysis published in 2022, Harter's team not only confirmed the correlation was correct, they also learned that the quality of an organization's human resources is perhaps the leading indicator of its growth and sustainability, noting that "optimal decision-making happens when information regarding decisions is collected at a local level, close to the everyday action." In other words, how organizations manage human relationships is as important to growth as, for example, innovation.

When leaders decide to act conscientiously the result resonates deeply throughout an organization. Harter's meta-analysis got me thinking about how to best achieve these resonant and impactful human connections. Coincidentally, Samantha Gesel, a professor at University of North Carolina has been thinking about a similar question, particularly for primary and secondary school educators.

In most organizations, receiving feedback on a regular cadence is doctrinal. Spend a day in any American company and it will not be long before you hear odd phrases like "feedback is a gift." The present cultural fad demands the suppression of personal sensibilities, notions of pride in authorship, and the acceptance of criticism, no matter how brutal, in the hopes of uncovering errors, omissions, and alternative solutions. I've witnessed managers use this cultural norm to unburden themselves from social expectations of decency, eloquence, and sometimes respect in addressing issues. But more concerning is that today's "feedback culture" without appropriate moderation can demotivate, lessen creativity, and even lead to groupthink if only applied in a one-way direction.

Professor Gesel and other researchers challenge the notion that merely conducting assessments and telling teachers how to improve generates significant results. An in-depth analysis of studies spanning 40 years revealed an irrefutable connection between the amount of professional development teachers received and their students' positive achievement.[17]

The same is true for us in the corporate environment. Just telling our employees what to do is not enough. We must continually train, support, and engage them so they can provide the company and its customers their best work.

Tracy Roberts was the VP of human resources during my tenure as UPS Airlines's chief lawyer. Our central mission as a duo was to resolve employee concerns. We often promoted training to managers and frontline workers as a key deterrent in addressing employee concerns before they were even conceived. Conscientious leaders incorporate "training culture," which is a form of people investment, into every layer of their organization. After countless employee versus management resolutions, I instituted a new policy in my group. When a new employee was hired, I would meet with their manager first and explain my expectations for professional development, and warn them that no negative feedback about a new employee could be submitted either in writing or orally unless the employee was first trained on the matter of the complaint.

While I'd love to take credit as a pioneer in training culture there are rarely new ideas under the sun. Training culture is an honored tradition at many companies. Schneider Electric, for example, has not one but two "universities" available to its employees: Schneider Electric University, which teaches customer education, energy solutions, executive development, functional skills, leadership, and sales excellence, and Energy University, which provides more than 200 free online courses and resources on energy efficiency and data-center topics. Schneider understands that professionally developed employees are more committed to the organization, better able to work multiple positions in multiple locations, and better future leaders.

When Amazon announced it would upskill a third of its workforce (about 100,000 people) over six years at a cost of about $700 million, it included virtual training for remote employees as well as a month-long training and leadership program. The company also offered to prepay 95% of employees' tuition for English-as-a-second language classes, high school completion programs, and associate degrees in certain fields.

When Amazon later expanded the program to include more than 750,000 U.S. employees, it also included 100% of tuition and books for bachelor's degrees to attract more hourly workers. Amazon leadership recognized that many working adults don't have the financial means to go to college, which further hinders their ability to progress in their careers or change to one they find more rewarding. Although this initiative had a price tag of $1.2 billion, the company knows this investment will generate even bigger profit in the long term.

Amazon believes "good jobs" have three basic elements: (1) a good wage, (2) robust benefits from day one, and (3) the opportunity to create a career—which requires upskilling to keep pace with rapid technological advances. Microsoft, Apple, and Meta, with market capitalizations of $3 trillion, $2 trillion, and $1 trillion, respectively, as of the date of this book, ensure their packages are such "good jobs" that talent is essentially assured.

As more companies realize the old-meta benefits are no longer alluring, they are offering better benefits in addition to higher wages. Start-up Dockwa, a marina-reservation app, changed its workweek to give employees Mondays off permanently, without changing other time-off benefits or pay. The result a year later was nearly 100% revenue growth and increased productivity. Employees said the shorter workweek helped them focus, work more efficiently, and made them happier. Indeed, countries like Belgium and Denmark have instituted four-day work weeks because of its many benefits.

The old meta had people investing in the company. Today, the company must also invest in its people.

Compassion

The final but critical investment in human capital is compassion. Compassion is a deep understanding of others' suffering and a desire to help. It's expressed through acts of generosity, empathy, and support. And it is rooted in our shared humanity. It can help build stronger relationships and a more compassionate society. Unfortunately, compassion is not an emotion that corporate executives are known for, and when leaders lack it, there is high turnover and low morale.

My teammate Bob suffered two great personal tragedies at once. I knew his extraordinary hardship required an extraordinary response. I told him to take off as much time as he needed. This was not policy, and I was unsure whether he would return. But it was the right thing to do. Doing this meant personally taking over a lot of his responsibilities for an indefinite period. Our actions communicate more to our teams, and those around us, than our words. Great leadership means putting ourselves in others' shoes and being flexible enough when necessary. I would go on to lead other teams and Bob subsequently retired. Still, I made it a point to travel back to Louisville at my own expense to see Bob into retirement. Small gestures matter especially when budgets are tight.

Too many leaders today lack compassion and shouldn't be in leadership roles. Lacking compassion should be disqualifying. In the vast desert of indifference, compassion is an oasis of care, providing relief and restoring hope. It is a bridge that spans differences, connecting individuals with shared humanity and fostering unity amidst diversity. It is an anchor that grounds us in our shared humanity, reminding us of our capacity for love, understanding, and healing. It is a powerful force that can heal wounds, mend broken spirits, and create a more compassionate and caring world.

Compassion is not a weakness. Showing compassion means you can recognize that your employees, your customers, and your community are first and foremost people, flesh and blood, with feelings, doubts, worries, and emotions that complicate their days but make them imminently more interesting, passionate, and capable of great things. Nobody wants an army of robots working for them; well, at least most companies don't. Sure, they'd have round-the-clock efficiency and never need a lunch break or a holiday, but they'd also never go past exactly the tasks they were intended for.

Humans are built differently and are better than that. They surprise you when you least expect it with innovations and remarkable flexibility when they are in tune with a job, a company, and a leader. They can use their original drive to create, while at the same time mentally multitasking about ways to make it all even better. One of the biggest keys to unlocking all that remarkable potential is consistently reminding teammates that you know they deserve more than simply financial compensation for what they are giving to you. Show that you celebrate who they are, learn their passions and pastimes, learn about their families, their cultural practices and their favorite places and things to go, see, and do. Motivate them individually as much as you motivate them in group settings. Find out the ways that they best enjoy being communicated through and engage them there with frequency. Make sure they feel valued and trusted and integral to your organization on a consistent basis.

Consider this: if you opened your company directory and picked out an employee at random, could you name three things about them that have nothing to do with work? No? How about one thing? Could you even pick them out of a lineup? The personal touch is what transforms you from a leader of employees to a leader of people. Knowing not only what people can bring to the table in the work venue, but who they are and what makes them tick is a huge bonus for any leader to possess. Take the time to know your people, so you can celebrate and care for them as they deserve. This is the essence of human capital investment and a distinguishing feature between top quintile organizations on the leadership power curve.

12 | Move 3: Habitat Discordance

As I stood chest deep in the cold water, the vastness of the ocean before me was breathtaking. Dressed in an all-white robe, a staid atmosphere cloaked the entire experience as I contemplated the enormity of the place and the smallness of my existence. Words of scripture were read from nearby Okuma beach in Japan, but they served as background to the moment. Had I been in my grandfather's church, the baptismal would've taken place in a pool beneath the pulpit. But I was more than 7,000 miles from Walterboro and the Pacific Ocean was the nearest and most magnificent analogue.

This was a moment of spiritual significance. I knew that I was about to be fully immersed, a symbolic cleansing and rebirth, but my mind drifted, as it often does, to the seraphic. Then I was brought back to reality in a sudden and unexpected jolt. Paster Webster had concluded performing the rite, ending in something along the lines of "father, son, and holy ghost," and I was administered the ceremonial dunking. My momentary lapse of concentration left me completely unaware of how quickly the sequence of events would occur. And, with one hand firmly clasped on my nose, and the other behind my neck, I was submerged, freezing water rushed all around me, in what was an unceremoniously jarring experience. As I surfaced and fought for breath between streams of water running down my face, the salty sea water rushed into my eye causing momentary blindness and burning.

In that moment, as I struggled for breath to the rhythm of handclaps and song, I felt a sharp, electric prick that shot through my body. It started as a slight irritation, but quickly escalated to a burning pain that spread like wildfire. It felt as though my skin was radiating, with needles piercing every inch of the flesh on my forearm. "Perhaps this is what it feels like for the holy spirit to enter my body," I thought as I let out a whimper. But, of course, I was forsaken. I looked down to see a jellyfish tentacle unfurl and then fall off my wrist.

I resisted shouting for that might start an interlude of uncontrolled dance and song that would only prolong the service.

At a mere 10 years old, baptism was the beginning of my realization that things are rarely what they seem under the surface.

After wading back to shore, I hugged my mother and explained what happened. Confused, she protested that jellyfish do not venture so close to shore, and that it must have been something else. That was the narrative. But it couldn't be true. I saw the tentacle with my own eyes and felt the fiery sting. Indeed, we would later find a nearby sign in Japanese that read "Warning Jellyfish." Apparently, by the 1990s, warmer water temperatures and changing tides were already pushing jellyfish closer toward beaches.

Magellan's choice to name that great ocean "Mar Pacifico" is ironic. The name Pacific Ocean, meaning "peaceful sea," has endured in the lexicon of both explorers and cartographers alike for centuries. But it is far from peaceful. To the contrary, it is often characterized by powerful storms and turbulent seas that have challenged seafarers throughout history. And below the surface, as I know well, things lurk that surprise and defy explanation.

My not-so-pacific baptism in the so-called peaceful sea revealed how language can become rooted in our collective consciousness despite how well or poorly it reflects reality. The frequent dichotomy between words and reality is evident in our personal lives and organizations. What I learned that day in the Pacific is that we must often look deeper, below the surface, to gain a clear picture of an operating environment. This means shedding over reliance on precedents and stories that may color our perception, and instead, seeking out the underlying facts, which invariably reveal a more authentic picture.

The connection between the power of language and effective leadership is significant. Conscientious leaders understand words can shape how people view the world and so use them carefully and parse them intently. According to the *Harvard Business Review*, many CEOs spend a lot of their time in meetings with other leaders just to ensure that they can distinguish fact from fiction.[1] In other words, they are unsure of how true the stories are when presented. This recognition of the power of language is crucial for conscientious leaders who strive to bridge the gap between constructed narratives and real-world data. Let's call the delta between narrative and reality "habitat discordance."

This term gives us the language to address the next move that matters to move up the leadership power curve.

In the context of moving up the power curve of economic profit, McKinsey believes that dynamically reallocating resources is key. This process involves moving at least 50% of capital expenditures among different business units over a period of 10 years, with the aim of targeting each part of the business for optimal performance at different times. This approach helps identify problems being obscured by large budgets, avoids creating unrealistic expectations of future support, and allows starvation cycles to produce efficiencies naturally. By constantly rotating resources to new areas, business leaders can ensure that no single part of the business falls significantly behind. The same strategy is reflected in the leadership power curve.

Dynamically allocating resources also helps groups to benefit from the investments of time, political capital, money, and emotional energy. The conscientious leader is mindful that, all too often a select few "high potential" employees receive an outsized amount of attention, resources, and opportunities. This over investment can lead to an overvaluation of an individual's value to the organization. Worse still, employees who are not identified as high potential can become neglected and underdeveloped.

Dynamic reallocation of resources helps to deconstruct false narratives by stress testing an organization and specific teams. Stress tests uncover true weaknesses and provide opportunities for improvement. Notably, our organizational struggles to overcome weaknesses are deeply rooted in individual social development.

Researchers at the University of Pune in India noted a remarkable trend among parents of young school age children, namely, that negative beliefs about media and how it may create a gap between the real self of the adolescent mind and the created "imaginary self" are deeply rooted such that even educational applications encounter adoption skepticism. Discordance is top of mind for these parents. The researchers collected qualitative data through in-person and online interviews with parents from urban communities to derive a questionnaire. The instrument covered datapoints such as communication channels, influences of sociotechnical factors on technology adoption, the attributes of innovations, the characteristics of adopters, and the social support system of the subjects. They also noted the parents' educational background, as well as their comfort and attitudes toward technologies. Finally, they collected data from 400 pairs of respondents—800 parents. Importantly, parents professed interest in access to the technology but inherent concerns about adolescents being influenced made adoption difficult even when supported by advertisements featuring celebrities.[2]

This analysis supports the hypothesis that concerns about habitat discordance occurs at the individual level and social unit level, often as young as adolescence. Essentially, we are influenced by both the environments and the narratives constructed by the people in them. We carry this discordant behavior into our adulthood and often manifest them in our organizations. This aligns with my own experience. Like most Millennials, I grew up alongside disruptive technologies like broadband internet, the personal computer, and social media, and I became a prime target for the often-distorting impact of habitat discordance. What I knew to be true and what others claimed to be true were often in tension as technology amplified the distance between the two. For example, I didn't think I was as smart as the other kids in school because social media said so. The constant messaging from society that I was not smart enough weighed heavily on my young mind. However, I was fortunate enough to have a strong management team: two great parents who instilled in me the value of never hiding weakness. With their unwavering support, I worked tirelessly to get into the International Baccalaureate (IB) diploma program in high school.

Math, particularly, was my Achilles' heel. I spent a lot of time in remedial math trying to catch up during my freshman and sophomore years because I knew I had to take advanced math my junior and senior years. In that first advanced math class, I felt so outmatched and out of place; I honestly didn't think I would pass.

After years of internalized doubts, it took an iconic moment at graduation to awaken me to the realization that I belonged among my high-achieving peers. I received the coveted IB diploma unlike some who tried. This moment served as a catalyst for me to parse discordant behavior to grow. Committed thereafter, I set out on a journey of personal growth by actively seeking out areas for improvement to challenge myself instead of just accepting any narrative about my own abilities.

I would go on to graduate from college with a degree in economics—a far cry from what was possible had I listened to the wrong voices.

Recognizing and resolving pain points is what differentiates extremely successful people and enterprises from average ones. But the key to breaking through habitat discordance lies in taking an honest accounting of weaknesses and applying laser focus to fix them. No matter how tranquil (dare I say, pacific) an organization may appear, what often lurks beneath the surface is what may cause real pain if ignored.

We often hide weakness, in the hopes of minimizing the damage that may be caused by it. This reflexive behavior may be hardwired from adolescence. And we've all developed work-arounds to avoid a weakness at some point in life.

But conscientious leaders recognize that strengthening a weak process, team-mate, or product is a better remedy than protection.

Armor has a psychological effect on both the wearer and the adversary. Research suggests those who use protective gear may feel more confident and emboldened. But the insidious downside is that the flaws and weaknesses still exist. The vulnerability remains subject to exploitation. Conscientious leaders look to eliminate vulnerability by supporting those who are struggling. The solution as you may have guessed is dynamically reallocating resources among teams and projects to encourage growth. This allows everyone to be empowered to achieve.

To be an effective leader in this way requires both intelligence and emotional maturity—the ability to assess a situation and respond appropriately, rather than simply punishing mistakes. Often, individuals struggling with weaknesses may attempt to mask them through secrecy or aggression. In such cases, a good leader reads through the discordant narrative and provides transformational support that will help the individual grow and succeed.

The medical start-up Theranos claimed it had the technology to run hundreds of tests on a single drop of blood. Its founder and CEO Elizabeth Holmes raised over $700 million from venture capitalists and private investors. Eventually, the company reached a valuation of $10 billion. Ten years after its launch, Theranos leaders claimed they finally had the technology right and started using it on patients—except it didn't work at all. When a *Wall Street Journal* exposé resulted in federal investigations and several lawsuits from both patients and investors, the Securities and Exchange Commission charged the company, Holmes, and the company's former president, Ramesh Balwani, with fraud.

It wasn't just Theranos that took the fall, however. The Safeway grocery store chain invested about $350 million in changing clinics at 800 of its national locations for in-store blood tests. Red flags were raised when deadlines for the Theranos products kept being missed. The company put on a trial clinic with its technology at Safeway corporate headquarters that left a lot to be desired, and the grocery giant eventually pulled out of the deal altogether. A similar thing happened with Walgreens, which went from agreement to confusion to disallowance to a lawsuit in the span of just four years.

Holmes was independently wealthy thanks to a trust fund set up by her parents, which allowed her to drop out of school at Stanford and devote money to her idea of the wearable patch that would help deliver drug dosages and test blood. But Stanford isn't exactly the sort of place that tends to get snowballed by dropouts claiming big ideas, and in February of 2015, Professor John Ioannidis wrote in the *Journal of the American Medicine Association* that Theranos and

Holmes had zero published research in medical literature,[3] basically the most standard form of practice for getting new technology recognized and accepted in the medical field.

Holmes went on the defensive, inviting sitting Vice President Joe Biden to take a tour of the facility to help prove its legitimacy. Biden praised what he saw, but in one of the more remarkably unbelievable scams you'll hear about, it was later revealed that the lab Biden visited was fake, constructed and staffed solely for his visit.

So, what happened here? Habitat discordance was unchecked at Theranos HQ. Former employees testified that the company's culture was based on secrecy, paranoia, and retaliation against anyone who spoke up. Even the company's advisors didn't parse fact from fiction. Facing failure in front of so many investors would have been difficult, but these leaders could have avoided much worse scandal if they had just addressed their shortcomings, switched to an open culture from one of secrecy, and focused on finding better technology. Instead, they chose to continue hiding behind their self-generated smoke-screens and expensive armor in the form of respected political figures on their board of directors, hoping no one would notice. But underlying weakness persisted.

When you make bold claims and refuse to back down from them, that sort of unchecked bravado is short-lived. The Department of Justice got involved after Theranos kept failing to get FDA approval, and soon the states of Arizona and California, where Theranos had laboratories, were on the hunt as well. Refusing to back down, Theranos was finally the subject of a criminal investigation by federal prosecutors, the SEC, and the U.S. House of Representatives Committee on Energy and Commerce. After employing 800 people at its peak, the company was down to fewer than 25 by April 2018. Holmes's personal wealth, at one time thought to approach $4.5 billion, fell to virtually nothing by 2022 when she was found guilty on four counts of defrauding investors.

A similar tale played out in New York at WeWork. It was a brilliant idea on paper. Start-ups and SMBs could rent eco-friendly coworking spaces in the Big Apple, paying pennies on the dollar to rent what would be difficult pieces of real estate to buy. Locations were originally all over the five boroughs and gave companies the opportunity to see beautiful, inspirational views while creating and crafting the next best thing. WeWork quickly expanded nationwide. I, myself, occupied a WeWork office for some time in Atlanta. By 2013, there were 350 start-ups listed as customers of WeWork and in 2014, its investors include the likes of Goldman Sachs, JP Morgan, T. Rowe Price, and the Harvard Corporation. Every year, WeWorks seemed to earn a new honor, a new place on a "top new" or "fastest growing" list, and more clients. The company got the former CFO of Time Warner Cable, Artie Munso, to come on board as COO and president in 2015, and in 2016 raised a staggering $430 million in financing, a valuation of $16 billion.

But within just a few months, the wheels fell completely off the wagon. First came layoffs of 7%—an early warning. Then an employee was fired and then sued for leaking information to the press that not only was WeWork going to miss its financial goals that year but miss them badly. Still, the company continued to raise money in the billions and invested heavily in its presence in New York City and beyond with a luxury health club near Wall Street, partnerships in India, China, Singapore, Germany, and Canada, a location at the University of Maryland, and more. People wondered how WeWork could afford it all, and the truth was that it couldn't. WeWork lost more than $2 billion in 2018.

Astoundingly, the investments kept coming in, and WeWork founder Adam Neumann kept buying more and more assets with the funds until it was announced in April 2019 that the company would go public with its initial offering. Over the next few months, Neumann liquidated a stunning $700 million of his private stock. The reason why became painfully apparent in August 2019, when the company revealed huge financial losses and obligations. Moreover, Neumann was hit with multiple sexual harassment complaints brought against him, which revealed a sordid corporate culture that permitted employees, among other things, to have unlimited access to beer during the workday. Neumann was ultimately asked by investors to keep his family members off the company's board of directors and to step down as CEO.

In its first nine years, the company had reached a $47 billion valuation—despite the fact the company had lost more money than it made and unrealistically claimed that its potential customer base was every American with a desk job. The habitat discordance was unmistakable.

What still amazes me about both Theranos and WeWork is that they were publicly backed and financed by some of the biggest names in business. Where were those investors' values? Why didn't they notice that Theranos had only a few medical experts and no peer-reviewed studies of its product? Why wasn't WeWork stopped when people reported Neumann was running it "like a frat house"? Why didn't anyone look below the surface? Because the truth would have been inconvenient. It was easier to not look and to hope no one got stung. It was easier to focus on strengths instead of weaknesses. In the case of WeWork and Theranos, it was because they chose to back the "next big thing" rather than take the long, hard road to success.

Money is blinding. In the same vein, leaders can be blinded by their own ambition in the pursuit of money. And when a leader decides that the ends justify the means, there's no stopping them until someone takes a stand. These people aren't leaders; they're narcissists who believe the only way forward is through their own zeal, and they seek validation by changing the world no matter the cost. Both Holmes and Neumann had great ideas, ideas that quite literally could have changed the world had they been managed correctly.

The problem was that both individuals, and the blind followers who wanted their own share of the pie, could only see the beginning and the end. They did not see all the work in the middle that must be achieved for greatness to happen and everyone to benefit from a visionary idea. But at some point, a point that only Holmes and Neumann knew about, things started going in the wrong direction. But they didn't want to admit that they were wrong. They couldn't be wrong, and they couldn't admit weakness, so they just kept spinning the lies larger and larger until they got so far out of control that they destroyed their companies and the lives of the people who had worked for them.

Play the Long Game

Like investing, building and leading strong and profitable organizations is a long-term endeavor. It requires careful planning, execution, and patience. I've often heard amateur investors say, "Man, I wish I had bought Apple or Google or Amazon stock when they were worth nothing." But when those stocks were worth nothing, no one knew if they would last.

Blue chips may hold the highest value in poker, but "blue chip" stocks are not necessarily the highest priced in the world of finance—they're the most durable. They're big companies that have operated for decades and have manageable or no debt, large market capitalizations, stable debt-to-equity ratios, and high returns on equity and assets.

Even better than "blue chip" stocks are "dividend aristocrats," companies that, in addition to all the attributes mentioned earlier, have increased their stock dividend for 25 years or more.

Then there are the "dividend kings"—companies that have increased their dividend payouts for 50 years or more. The top five most consistent are Lowe's Companies, Lancaster Colony, Parker-Hannifin, Hormel, and 3M. Some of these may not be household names like Apple and Google are, but they are respected because of their reliability and their utility as a barometer in the market to parse facts from fictions. Unlike start-ups such as WeWork that claim everyone will want or need their new product or service, these stable companies first considered the needs and concerns of their industry and then devised products and services that addressed those needs. They understood their purpose was to solve problems, not just hype investors to get rich.

These companies endure because they constantly shift large portions of capital to improve where they are weak. And, from decade to decade, their business models go from strength to strength.

The final move that matters to level up the leadership power curve is shifting resources to resolve weakness. Conscientious leaders devote at least 50% of their resources to training, supporting, and improving areas of weakness in themselves and among their teams. Organizationally, this means utilizing at least half of the training budget in areas that are identified as weaknesses on measurable instruments like corporate surveys.

Feedback Loops

Overcoming weaknesses requires feedback loops, which should be an integral part of every team's process and procedure. These feedback loops should be safe and supportive environments where employees feel comfortable sharing their thoughts, experiences, and ideas without fear of retaliation. This can be achieved by providing employees with the opportunity to provide feedback anonymously.

In 2020, there was a lot of bad market news. Concerns about the pandemic impact on our business performance were at their peak. As I looked for ways to convey bad news to an already uneasy team, it became important to me to convey the idea that challenging environments are also opportunities to improve. I encouraged my team to embrace looking beyond the surface and strengthen our weaknesses. I penned an article in our company newsletter describing the five critical steps for delivering bad news and avoiding pitfalls during the environmental pivot. The five steps are:

1. **Acknowledge bad news as a failure.** Just apologizing or saying, "Unfortunate things happen," is not as helpful as "This isn't right—we have a problem." While denying or minimizing our customers' or employees' pain may ease our own discomfort, it only further misaligns our organization from the very people who support our business.

2. **Be honest about the cause of bad news and its impact on real people.** This involves sharing two truths: what senior management knows about the problem and what employees and customers experience. Failed organizations share a misalignment caused by the lack of

honest, productive, organization-wide conversations—in other words, an absence of feedback loops.

3. **Apologize for failure.** Half-hearted apologies often come across as damage-control attempts that allow leaders to move on without fixing anything. A real heartfelt, empathetic apology is not only extremely refreshing; it also helps mend broken trust with stakeholders.

4. **Commit to fixing the problem.** Although this may seem obvious, it's all too common to avoid that commitment because it means admitting error or weakness and possibly even overhauling internal procedures—no small task. Yet aggressively and transparently responding to a problem's root cause makes the organization more resilient, boosts productivity, improves employee morale, and restores trust with stakeholders.

5. **Detail a plan to avoid future failure—and invite employees to refine it.** When we share weaknesses or failures collectively and give serious consideration to others' criticism and proposed solutions, we not only learn from our failures; we change problems into inspiring challenges we can solve together as a team as well.

As individuals, we should incorporate constructive feedback as part of our annual performance reviews. Too often we share only the positive because it makes the conversation easier and, on paper, reflects better on us as leaders. But no one is perfect, so we must strive for candid conversations that identify weak areas, develop a plan to overcome them, and pledge continued support.

The Peter Principle claims employees are always promoted to their highest level of incompetence, but in today's world, that's no longer true. If we're good at covering up our incompetence, we can go even higher until our fall from grace becomes completely humiliating and damaging, like Theranos. Accepting honest input from others requires an insatiable desire to learn and improve, and a bit of tough skin. It is also the best way for leaders to avoid plateauing and a public downfall.

An old proverb says, "There is safety in a multitude of counselors." And, even when their advice was sometimes hard to hear, it helped me avoid a lot of pain and heartache. When we become adept at providing effective feedback, overcoming our weaknesses, and accepting input from all our stakeholders instead of just a select few, the potential for growth is limitless.

13 | Move 4: The Maximization Default

Donnie Yen plays a martial arts master named IP Man (pronounced "eep man") in the big screen anthology by the same name. He has a great line in the inaugural film that aptly describes what makes conscientious leaders so different. In the first movie, Donnie's character confronts a duelist named Jin, who is attempting to make a name for himself and his northern style of fighting. Jin sets out to elevate himself by humiliating the local martial arts schools in the city of Foshan by defeating their leaders. When Jin meets Master IP, he is handily defeated. Jin later concedes that Master IP's southern fighting style, called Wing Chun, is superior to Jin's own, to which IP Man replies, "It's not about style; it's about you."

Wing Chun has a rich history and a reputation for being a practical and efficient fighting technique. What sets Wing Chun apart is its emphasis on economy of movement and minimal use of brute force simultaneously minimizing effort and maximizing impact by default. In this context, the statement "it's not about style; it's about you" highlights an important philosophical point of the martial arts school, namely, when we expend maximum effort to achieve nominal results, we must ask a deeper question about the person rather than their methods. There is only one way to fight and that is efficiently.

188

A gem is hidden in this principle for the conscientious executive. Finding the best ways to conserve effort while achieving maximum results *as a matter of course* is what I call the maximization default. It's seeking out and occasionally innovating the newest meta available to ensure the greatest conservation of resources. Finding the most efficient means to achieve results today saves precious time and energy in the future, and as Donnie Yen notes, it defines a leader.

Martial arts films always resonated with me as a child. Bruce Lee inspired a generation, not only making martial arts a worldwide phenomenon but also spurring greater appreciation for Eastern philosophical wisdom on how we can develop our potential.

In 1971, Bruce appeared on the Pierre Burton show in Hong Kong, fresh from the success of *The Big Boss* and the anticipated releases of *Fists of Fury* and *Way of the Dragon*. When asked to discuss his philosophy on martial arts, Bruce replied:

> Empty your mind. Be formless. Shapeless. Like water. If you put water into a cup, it becomes the cup. If you put water into a bottle, it becomes the bottle. You put it into a teapot, it becomes the teapot. Now water can flow—or it can crash. Be water, my friend.

Bruce was ahead of his time. When he made this comment about the strength of water, it was generally understood that water could cut through hard materials, but large-scale commercial use of water cutting implements were not conceived of for another decade. It turns out that this soft and formless thing, when pressurized to over 100 gigapascals, and forced through a .05-millimeter nozzle, transforms into the world's sharpest and most efficient blade.

Growing as a leader means being flexible enough to mold ourselves to whatever situation is at hand while focusing our efforts to have a sharp and incisive impact.

Business consultants like McKinsey would say that one of the moves that matters most to ascending the economic power curve is improving differentiation. Corporate leaders should leverage a company's business model innovation and pricing advantages to accelerate gross margins into the top 30% in your industry. What they won't tell you is that such an achievement is impossible without dynamic, agile leaders. You see, it's not about style, it's about you.

Most video games today offer an immersive experience that lets players make a limited set of choices in the game. Players can choose different characters that have their own strengths and weaknesses, weapons that fit their play style, and pathways that can convey an edge in battles. Each choice has its own set of pros and cons, and players must weigh the options carefully when leveling up. It's not possible to choose every skill. Instead, players need to choose what skills are most appropriate for the situation they find themselves in. It's these trade-offs that teach players valuable decision-making skills and make the gaming experience more engaging and replayable.

The real world is similarly made up of finite resources, limited time, choices, and trade-offs. None of us can do everything well, so we must make informed decisions about where to focus. The most self-aware among us recognize our natural strengths and where we need help. For example, when looking for a new job, I always seek the assistance of a professional résumé writer to help. Leveraging external expertise saves time while also developing a strong résumé. My former Facebook colleague Paul Grewal is a LinkedIn influencer and general counsel of Coinbase. He often leans into his self-awareness by asking the brightest minds to help him through public invitation. Here's just a taste of Paul's self-awareness. In a June post, Paul noted his often-hectic schedule and lamented the inability to read all the latest patent cases. You may have guessed that Paul is a big brain. He then invited his over 20,000 followers to share cases they've read that resolved favorably for industry. What makes Paul's posts so refreshing is his sincerity and public embrace of his own limitations.

Like Paul, I've embraced my own limitations over the years. Society often puts immense pressure on individuals to perform exceptionally in all areas of life, but the reality is that we all have unique capabilities. And while strengthening weaknesses is a virtue, it's also important for conscientious leaders to know when to get help. Teams overcome challenges by bringing a set of capabilities that can be adapted to the circumstances—like water. Instead of a single individual trying to excel in everything, a mix of capabilities makes the team malleable. Because the C-Suite requires a varied set of leaders with different capabilities, a strong cohesion is built when each member embraces the capabilities of others; short of this, feelings of inadequacy can set in, feeding a condition called altitude sickness.

"Altitude sickness" occurs when higher levels of leadership lead to equally high levels of interpersonal conflict. It's what happens when we ascend to organizational leadership much like the altitude sickness someone might experience at a higher elevation. Many leaders become disoriented as they struggle to adapt to the new high-level demands of their role. The higher you go in leadership, the greater the expectations upon you; and the more your relationships may change with others, especially if you are raised up from within an organization.

Leaders at the highest level of their organization may experience tremendous pressure and stress, which can manifest in detrimental ways that adversely affect those under their guidance. Just as new runners to Denver are counseled to regulate their exercise pace when beginning in the new environment, similarly leaders transitioning into higher positions or roles must carefully adjust habits and behaviors. They can't operate in the same way at a higher elevation as they did at a lower level—otherwise there's a risk of quickly becoming overwhelmed.

Altitude sickness was the cause of my first missteps as an executive. When I first joined the airline leadership team, I tried to operate as if I was still a portfolio lawyer, demanding control and visibility over all aspects of ongoing legal work by all departments. This approach led to swift conflict with the labor team, who were accustomed to dispatching outside counsel at their leisure, and often without oversight from the airline legal team. Seeing this work as core to my department, I quickly sent an email to the head of labor explaining that, from then on, his team would route legal requests through my office. This, of course, unsettled a long established precedent. And, of course, there were deep relationships involved that would be disrupted by my decision. For example, an old labor lawyer named Tony didn't take kindly to this new approach. My desire to move quickly and exert control, rather than evolve long-standing behavior over time, was misguided.

Basically, I made a rookie mistake that could've been avoided merely by slowing down. I realized quickly that I needed an experienced deputy. But I should have known. On my first day at the company, I met Richard "Rick" Rufolo, a high-level executive in the legal organization. Instantly, I knew who he was because, in preparing for my interviews, I read a story about Rick and his friend Steve Ensor, an outside lawyer (like Tony) at the Alston & Bird law firm. The article in *Corporate Counsel* magazine titled "Blood Brothers"[1] detailed how Steve underwent major surgery for kidney cancer, and when Steve survived, his first thought was to pick up his BlackBerry and check emails. Steve then learned of an impressive victory his team secured on behalf of the company and, while convalescing in the operating room recovery unit, made his first phone call to Rick. Not to his wife. Not to his priest. To Rick Rufolo. The level of dedication the article promotes, while an interesting relic in time, was culturally emblematic of the value of relationships back then. It was this environment I entered. The clear implication is that this is an environment where almost nothing would stand between the long-standing relationship forged over the years. Of course, it was a relationship supported by millions of dollars and the expertise of some of the best lawyers in America.

While it is important for leaders to have a broad understanding of all areas of running a business, it is not necessary to be an expert in every area. In fact, trying to be an expert in everything can be counterproductive, as it can lead to spreading oneself too thin and not being able to focus on the most important tasks. It is more important to focus on developing expertise in a few key areas and outsourcing or delegating the rest.

Assembling great teams not only helps ensure success but will also lighten the overall load. Knowing when and how to combine forces enables those involved with maximum faith in each other's competency while strengthening relationships. Perhaps not as closely as "blood brothers" forsaking family first in lieu of work, but close enough to have a reasonable degree of trust. You can't sit at a massive control panel and run every single phase of your company; even the Wizard of Oz couldn't handle that pressure after Toto pulled back the curtain. What you can do is delegate, trust, build relationships with, and rely on the leaders of your individual units and teams to deliver what you are all building together. It's not about style, it's about you.

I was once a favorite student of Wallace P. Mullin, an associate professor of Economics at the George Washington University. Professor Mullin joined the GW faculty in 2002 after receiving his PhD from MIT. He will be pleased that I retained some understanding of fundamental economic theory, which applies so readily to the present concept. The trade-offs that a conscientious leader makes to focus on impact, while relying on capable deputies, is empirically supported. Because our lives are constrained by things like time and available resources, the best way to achieve an advantage is by exchanging effort with others.

The concept of comparative advantage is both simple and powerful. It explains the gains from trade and why countries specialize in producing certain goods and services. Developed by economist David Ricardo in the early nineteenth century, the idea is based on opportunity cost. If a country can produce a particular good or service at a lower cost than another country, it has a comparative advantage. Countries should specialize in producing goods in which they have a comparative advantage and trade with other countries for goods that are less efficiently produced at home. This results in more efficient production and greater overall welfare. By understanding and harnessing the power of comparative advantage, countries can benefit from global trade and promote economic growth.

The same dynamics are understood by the conscientious leader who, like water, is willing to recede from the spotlight with grace at the right time, rely on a team when appropriate, and then return with a crash in moments when decisive leadership is necessary. They exchange efforts with equally capable peers and focus on their comparative advantage. There are many examples of this type of leader.

A Lesson from Johns

Although not as famous as other civil rights leaders, without Vernon Johns, there would have been no Dr. Martin Luther King Jr. as we know him. One of the fathers of the Civil Rights Movement, Vernon was the pastor at Dexter Avenue Baptist Church in Montgomery, Alabama, a few years before Dr. King took over. His activism and fiery sermons against inequality paved the way for Dr. King's leadership, and Vernon continued to galvanize the Civil Rights Movement up until he died in 1965.

Born in 1892, Vernon loved theology and recognized his passion was his strength, even in his youth. Although his goal was to attend college and become a pastor, his father passed away when he was 15, forcing him to leave school and tend the family farm.

Still, he continued reading and learning on his own even as he farmed. He earned his Bachelor of Arts from the Virginia Theological Seminary and College in 1915 and Bachelor of Divinity from Oberlin College in 1918. He pastored several churches, was a professor at and then president of Virginia Theological Seminary and College, and even plotted small farms to see the produce and to earn extra income for himself and his congregations. With his photographic memory, he often recited lengthy biblical and literary passages—including Shakespeare—and was fluent in Greek, Latin, Hebrew, and German.

Of course, Vernon also had his weaknesses. His sometimes-unrelatable intelligence, unfiltered honesty, and quick temper often alienated those he worked with, causing problems throughout his career. Perhaps he could have accomplished even more had he recognized and overcome those faults and learned to foster better relationships. But because he focused on his natural strengths—theology interpretation, persuasive public speaking, instruction, and a flair for farming—he excelled despite his flaws.

Just like Vernon Johns, fine-tuning our strengths makes us ever more productive and valuable to our organizations while enriching ourselves and others. But we must also know when to pivot like the changing flow of water. At the right time, we gain from interchange with others as Johns did with King. Johns stepped back and allowed MLK to lead Dexter, while supporting in the background. This became a pivotal decision that changed the course of American history. As a senior leader, he knew when to step aside and let someone younger and more capable lead. Martin also brought with him a comparative advantage in building interpersonal relationships that Johns acknowledged and respected.

We have to strategically decide what's most important for our growth because we cannot go to every conference, mentor every subordinate, or have every sponsor. Or, in my case, control every legal decision. Instead, we must ask: Am I going to the *right* conferences? Am I mentoring the *right* people? Do I have the *right* sponsors? Am I moving my leadership in the *right* direction? Is it time for me to step aside?

Those questions demand that we declutter to focus.

Decluttering

Let's return to Costco as a corporate case study. Todd Miner, a butcher who ran the best Costco meat shop on the East Coast, worked six days a week performing every task in the shop. That's why he was surprised when Costco founder Jim Sinegal visited his shop and told him, "Stop working so much."

Jim knew the biggest mistake any leader can make is to not delegate, or in other words, to use comparative advantage in the workplace. He spent about 200 days each year visiting his warehouses around the country, but he knew for everything to be done right, he also had to hire, train, and support the right leaders, who would do the same for their people down, and for themselves. That meant knowing when to take tasks off their plate and rely on others.

While Jim could have probably stocked the shelves and rung the registers himself, he kept his professional life decluttered so he could focus on what made him, and Costco, so good.

I do this, in part, by actively finding ways to filter out disruptions. For instance, I leave myself an hour of reading time on my professional calendar every afternoon. During that time, I purposely don't answer phone calls or emails so I can sit and digest important information. Also, I rarely give people my personal phone number, and I put my phone away when at dinner with my family.

I strategically identify which relationships are important to maintain and which I can allow to naturally progress to their end. And sometimes I spend less time at work so I can be with family and friends—and I make sure my employees are allowed to do the same. All that protects those sacrosanct moments and declutters my professional life, which helps advance personal and professional goals alike.

In fact, we all start out with a healthier, less cluttered view of life. As I watch my now-five-year-old daughter grow up, I notice how she sees the world and how everything to her is so simple.

And as I would listen to my nearly 90-year-old grandfather's basic explanations and descriptions of all that he's seen and gone through in his life, I noticed that as we get older, things appear simple again. Wisdom akin to the saying, "try a little bit and then see where you're at," reminds me to not bite off more than I can chew. Occasionally an incremental approach is best.

Leadership can be a weighty, complex topic that is often hard to convert into conversations or training. But when we focus on our strengths and declutter our lives, we realize we need to do only a few things well to reach our goals.

The smallest things turn out to be the best quite often in our lives. Reading a good book. Watching a sunset on the beach. Quiet conversations with your favorite people. As leaders, you must respect your distinct, intrinsic need for downtime where you can detach your fearsome, always on-the-go attitude for the conquest of the next stage of business and allow yourself the time and space to reflect on what it's all for. It's not easy, trust me, I know! But the simple things that we enjoy are the perfect counterbalance to all we achieve during the workday. When we are always putting our best selves forward for the purpose of achieving and offering more for our employees, our customers, and our communities, there comes a time when we must rest and recharge. This is why companies like Meta allow for its teams to take a sabbatical every five years. This month-long retreat is essentially for recharging dedicated employees. This is the time when it's okay to be selfish. To be greedy about how we spend our time and who we give our attention to. Without the small, personal moments, you won't have the motivation over the long term for the big, noisy ones.

A Lesson from U.S. Grant

After reading *Personal Memoirs of Ulysses S. Grant*, I was impressed by how several of Grant's attributes as a military commander during the U.S. Civil War emphasized being malleable to changing circumstances. His success, willingness to engage, and perseverance all reflect a leader willing to be fluid and shapeable by circumstances and intensely focused when necessary.

When Grant was promoted to head of Union forces, he enacted a new strategy—and lost 17,000 soldiers in the first battle, several thousand more than General Robert E. Lee. Neither side gained any ground after two days of fighting. Lee probably expected Grant to retreat, as most other Union generals had done after suffering heavy losses.

But leaning on his previous wartime experience and success, Grant saw the bigger picture. He knew the Union had more troops and supplies in reserve than the Confederacy; if the North could persevere, it would win the war by attrition, not by one major battle. Instead of retreating, Grant quickly out-flanked Lee and continued pushing south. His soldiers were overjoyed that they finally had a leader willing to engage.

Lee's forces attacked Grant's a day later, leading to one of the bloodiest battles of the entire Civil War: The Battle of Spotsylvania Court House. Again, both sides suffered dramatic losses, and again, the battle was inconclusive. But Grant continued.

After four more extremely costly battles, Grant wasn't sure how much more his army could suffer. He paused to consider his options, but he knew Lee's army had suffered horribly as well, which was the ultimate objective. So, he kept leading his troops south and eventually laid siege to Petersburg, Virginia, cutting off supplies to the Confederate capital of Richmond.

That campaign officially changed the course of the war in the Union's favor.

Conscientious leaders recognize that our strengths won't always set us apart. Sometimes it's our ability to pivot and persevere that wins the day. We may engage in competitive arenas and not be successful at first. We may not win market shares. We may expend a lot of capital for inconclusive gains in a campaign. But there is value in the engagement. Even when we don't get an immediate return on our investment, we gain experience and brand cachet that we can later turn into victories.

It's About You

A company can sometimes lose its focus and attempt to do things that distract from its core principles. On top of every new direction or project a company takes on, it still needs to deliver on its current promises, invest in its people, pay dividends, and satisfy other competing priorities. And while some products and services or policies may have been relevant or even beloved in the past, they may not remain viable indefinitely.

Profit chasing can be a distraction that drives companies to spend, acquire, and grow until they no longer serve their customers or communities in the right ways. They may also try to reduce costs the wrong way, by slashing training, safety, and leadership programs and resources—not to mention people's jobs. Instead, leaders should strategically declutter based on the company's comparative advantages.

We must know when to divest an asset or endeavor that is no longer of value and when to declutter by moving resources or investments from under-performing segments to more high-performing ones.

Clorox, for example, has a system for figuring out when to divest or declut-ter. It designed a cross-functional management team to establish yearly reduction goals for underperforming SKUs (stock keeping unit, or product line). Before those SKUs are gradually reduced or phased out, the team reviews them with consumers to ensure they don't damage any relationships by discontinuing a product key customers care about. Thanks to this decluttering strategy, more than 90% of Clorox SKUs meet volume and profitability targets, and Clorox has more retail sales per SKU than any of its peers. Clorox opted for efficiency and was rewarded for it.

Though business consultants will say that what matters most to ascending the economic power curve is leveraging a company's business model innovation and pricing advantages, the leadership power curve demands only that leaders remain malleable to accelerate into the top quintiles of industry. This is because learning from mistakes, leveraging differentiation, collaborating across strengths, and generally leading well isn't about style, it's about you.

14 | Move 5: A Reliable Brand

In a study by Ellyn Briggs and Saleah Blancaflor the average Taylor Swift fan is generally younger, between 18 and 34, suburban, and female.[1] I am none of those things. But in August 2017, I found myself staring proudly at a freshly washed and wrapped UPS package car with the words REPUTATION emblazoned across the top, and a picture of Taylor Swift. I became a Swiftie. For months, I'd been working with Big Machine Records, a well-known record label associated with Swift, to engineer something UPS had never attempted since the company's inception in 1907. We would associate our brand with another iconic brown UPS package car.

The first UPS package cars entered service in 1916, when the company used Model T Fords for deliveries. Today, the most common package car is the P70, which was first introduced in 1990. It's a lightweight composite vehicle with a low floor for easier loading and unloading, and a modular design that allows for efficient maintenance and repair. You've undoubtedly seen them in your neighborhood. The P70 with its distinctive brown color, has become an iconic symbol of the UPS brand.

So, allowing Taylor Swift to align her brand with ours could have enormous implications.

Disney, Chipotle, Subway, Anheuser-Busch, Samsung, Pepsi, Papa Johns— the list of brands that have had to navigate major crises after association with influencers is endless. But we figured Taylor would be relatively low risk.

Taylor guards her brand just as zealously as UPS does. So, our objectives were aligned. Taylor was preparing for her inaugural *Reputation* album tour in

November 2017 and, at the same time, UPS was heading into a challenging Peak Season, and wanted to broaden its brand in the minds of the emerging and powerful demographic groups that enliven Swift's fandom.

The negotiations were intense. Taylor has very good lawyers and business people working for her, and I sparred with them regularly toward our mutual objective of protecting both brands. Both sides appreciated the historical lessons of working with social media influencers, and the careful consideration and thoughtful execution required. There were bumps along the way. Both parties, at times, were prepared to walk away from the deal over concerns about brand protection. But Taylor and I would get our parties across the finish line largely because of the strong reputation each party brought to the negotiation, making the ability to build trust easier.

The pioneering effort with Taylor Swift would lead to more opportunities for the company. The framework I established would later lay the groundwork for engagements with other major brands like Disney during the launch of the TV series *The Mandalorian*. Each cobranding campaign preceded a boost in production as increased brand awareness stoked enthusiasm for our services. Central to responding to the increase in demand was a capital program designed to strengthen our delivery capabilities.

The final move that matters for the McKinsey power curve of economic profit is productivity, which fundamentally depends on reliability. McKinsey recommends a strong productivity program that puts your organization at least in the top 30% of your industry. For our own leadership power curve, we need to look deeper than productivity. And, what lies beneath every strong productivity program is reliable performance.

Episodic and undisciplined productivity programs are seldom industry leading and often point to more fundamental concerns. Fostering a culture of reliability is antecedent to all productivity objectives. When I started my first job at 16 years old, my manager at Walmart began each day with a productivity pep talk, emphasizing production targets and other metrics. This was largely viewed as a cultural norm in large supercenters and warehouses at that time. But, often, the targets were either too high or our systems too unreliable to consistently meet said expectations. Still, we tried. I remember putting extraordinary effort in scans per hour and being the fastest in the store for months on end. But, after never receiving recognition for it, I gave it up. I was motivated and trying hard, but the fact that it was unachievable made the pep talks ring false.

Tomorrow's employees are less concerned about meeting your productivity targets, and more concerned with physical safety, job security, long-term corporate strategy, sustainability, and workplace culture. They want to be reassured that they will come home to their families, that the corporate strategy is durable for long-term growth and stability, and that the office culture accounts for their humanity above all else. Essentially, their productivity is dependent on you being reliable (to them).

As a leader, being reliable is central to building trusting relationships with your team. Not only does it create an atmosphere of respect that fuels productivity; but employees increasingly demand consistent cultural standards from their leaders too. With reliable norms as operational cornerstones, teams have the trust and consistency they need to drive work performance forward.

Janna Koretz, founder of Azimuth Psychological, a Boston-based practice focused on the mental health of people in high-pressure jobs, has spent years studying a phenomenon called the enmeshment trap, a condition where an individual ties their self-worth to career success and failure.[2] Enmeshment not only threatens the way we feel about ourselves but can turn into psychological concerns like depression and anxiety, and can even lead to substance abuse.

Close relationships can easily become enmeshed, resulting in an unhealthy level of emotional intensity and blurred boundaries between individuals. This pattern of behavior is characterized by a lack of individual autonomy, as one or both partners struggle to distinguish their own needs from those of the other person—leading them to feel trapped or controlled. In families, this issue may manifest itself through loyalty issues, whereas romantic relationships are often affected on an intimate level with feelings such as exhaustion and lack of sex. It's not easy leaving the trap behind but establishing clear boundaries and seeking professional help for underlying emotions are keys to moving forward.

In the context of a worker and employer relationship, an enmeshment trap can be formed when the employee becomes overly reliant on their employer for self-esteem and validation. This one-way reliance leads to a lack of boundaries, burnout in the employee, and high turnover rates, as well as decreased innovation within company structures; all while undermining autonomy between both parties. To escape this self-destructive cycle requires separating individual needs from those of their job and allowing employees the freedom to circumscribe work without sacrificing opportunities for professional growth and recognition in the office.

I, too, have been a victim of the enmeshment trap at points in my career. I struggled to cope with being passed over for promotion like most employees do. Largely because of this, the enmeshment of my identity and job became unhealthy. I linked extraordinary worth to my position within a company. I placed so much importance on my role that failure to achieve a promotion led me to develop severe abdominal pains, sleeplessness, and anger outbursts at home. Doctors performed MRIs, X-rays, and colonoscopies in a vain attempt to understand why a healthy 36-year-old man with no history of disease suddenly couldn't sleep, go to the bathroom, or eat anything but soup. Finally, one doctor recommended that I talk to a therapist who quickly diagnosed the enmeshment problem. And, after weeks of therapy, the symptoms went away as quickly as they arrived.

Sandra William at *Forbes* noted that COVID and its aftermath caused many people to reassess their relationships with their jobs: 38 million workers quit their jobs in 2021, and 12 million switched employers in less than fewer months in 2022, the results was lower productivity rates as 79% of employees struggled with work-related stress, and others adopted quiet quitting behaviors.[3] Many of these changes were driven by a combination of outdated corporate cultures that treated people as numbers rather than individuals, and a desire to disentangle corporate identity from personal life. This led Williams to declare that the new corporate job emerging in the post-pandemic world is "human."

Some organizations quickly understood the situation. In a push to retain talent and change pre-pandemic brand reputations often anchored in the old corporate meta, companies like Google, 3M, and even Bain quickly rolled out policies allowing employees a percentage of work time to pursue any project of interest to them within the organization. Even mindfulness norms, for example, took hold in companies like Target, General Mills, and NASA, recognizing that so many U.S. workers were struggling with work-related stress and a record 42% of the global workforce faced burnout symptoms. Today, the prevalence of flexible work to accommodate life has become standard operating procedure in virtually every company in America. Pivoting toward a more reliably humane workplace culture requires conscientious leaders with personal brands that lend credibility to the effort.

A Lesson from Cole

I once worked for a boss with an inconsistent personal brand. They were sometimes supportive and other times not, often hedging their bets to claim credit if things worked out well and to pass blame when they fell short. Sure, they often spoke with force and clarity in private meetings but melted like butter when dealing with their peers or superiors. Their indecisiveness was often revealed in moments when strength was needed and support from leadership most valuable. Nearly every time that I needed this person to lean in and have my back on an issue, they demurred and avoided conflict. Despite an ample supply of bluster and bravado to me, I came to understand there was no Wizard in Oz.

While the old meta for advancement in large organizations made this person's brand of reputational triangulation necessary for promotion, it is an ineffective strategy for the conscientious leader needed now and in the future. Leaders must have reliable brands centered on a reputation for enabling and supporting a team's bold decisions.

Building such a brand demands that conscientious leaders identify ways to become influencers in their organization, industry, and community. They engage in charitable work not only to help good causes that are personally motivating, but also because engagement with such initiatives increases visibility skill sets across wider circles. They engage in thought leadership whether by contributing articles to specific, relevant publications within their profession or writing on more general topics related to interests outside of their day-to-day employment functions. The path taken by conscientious leaders often mirrors the journey of touchstones like Chester C. Cole, who harnessed opportunities to make an indelible mark in his respective field.

Cole began building his brand as a lawyer as soon as he graduated from Harvard Law School in 1848. He launched his career in Marion, Kentucky, as a legal reporter for a local newspaper and established a law practice. Cole's business grew along with his reputation as he practiced with some of the greatest lawyers of his time in Kentucky and Illinois. Legend has it he never had a client convicted, even though he was counsel for almost every criminal case in Crittenden County, population 8,990.

After a career marked by perseverance and dedication to his ideals (which included switching political parties to support the Union when the Civil War broke out), Cole was eventually elected chief justice of the Iowa Supreme Court. He established the first two law schools in Iowa and remained deeply involved in the community, running a home for war orphans, organizing the state fire insurance company, refurbishing and expanding the library, serving as an elder at his church, and becoming a Masonic knight. He wrote and edited law publications prolifically and actively mentored other lawyers. In other words, he built a tremendously strong personal brand. This turned out to be key in helping his ruling on a landmark civil rights case impacting Iowa law. *Clark v. Board of Directors* held that racial segregation in public schools was unconstitutional under the Equality Clause of the Iowa Constitution's Bill of Rights of 1857.[4] Justice Cole wrote these magnificent words:

> Now, it is very clear, that, if the board of directors are clothed with a discretion to exclude African children . . . and require them to attend (if at all) a school composed wholly of children of that nationality, they would

have the same power and right to exclude German children . . . and so of Irish, French, English, and other nationalities, which together constitute the American . . .

For the courts to sustain . . . limiting the rights and privileges of persons by reason of their nationality, would be to sanction a plain violation of . . . our laws . . . [and] perpetuate the national differences of our people and stimulate a constant strife, if not a war of races . . .

In other words, all the youths are equal before the law.

Cole's 1868 ruling preceded the ratification of the U.S. Constitution's Fourteenth Amendment giving full citizenship to Black Americans. In fact, a few months after Cole's opinion, the Iowa legislature deleted the word "white" from four sections of the Iowa Constitution, granting Black Iowans the right to be counted in the state census, Black men the right to serve as senators in the state general assembly, and Black men the right to vote—two years before the Fifteenth Amendment was passed nationally.

Plenty of people were uncomfortable with these decisions advancing equality, but because of Justice Cole's stature—his brand—he was respected even when people disagreed with him, and he motivated them to produce results that outflanked the entire nation.

Cole's ruling had wide-ranging implications. Susan B. Clark, the very child impacted by Cole's courageous decision, went on to become the first Black graduate of an Iowa public high school. She not only graduated from Muscatine High School In 1871 with honors, but she also spoke at the commencement and remained an active community activist until she died in 1925. Our decisions as leaders have a real impact on human life.

Susan's brother, Alexander Jr., went on to become the first Black graduate of the State University of Iowa's Law School (now Drake University), which Judge Cole had founded.

Susan and Alexander's father, Alexander G. Clark Sr., became the second at the age of 58.[5]

Clark Sr. not only worked as a lawyer, but he also bought the *Chicago Conservator*, the first African American newspaper in Chicago, in which he wrote many articles about the ongoing struggle for equality. People said he "wielded a fearless pen dipped in acid." But Clark Sr. had built his personal brand long before that.

He started by making many influential relationships with Black and White leaders alike while working as a barber and then went on to buy real estate, sell timber to steamboat companies, and help organize Muscatine's African

Methodist Episcopal Church. During the Civil War, he recruited over a thousand recruits for the First Iowa Volunteers of African Descent and continued actively campaigning for civil rights for the rest of his life. He was such an effective speaker he became known as the "Colored Orator of the West."

In fact, in 1890, President Benjamin Harrison appointed Clark Sr. as the U.S. minister to Liberia, the highest presidential appointment a Black person had ever held.

Chester C. Cole and Alexander G. Clark Sr. knew their reputations differentiated them from everyone else and used that fact to encourage others to do great works. Their positive influence on Iowa and the nation is beyond measure.

That's what building a personal brand can do.

What SEALs Know About Resilience

Andrew Ledford at the U.S. Naval Academy and a team of researchers from public and private institutions set out to understand the connection between the impact of stress and resilience, hardiness, and grit.[6] To do this, the team studied the psychological and physiological growth of the Navy's Sea, Air, and Land Teams (SEALs) candidates in Basic Underwater Demolition/SEAL (BUD/S) training, commonly acknowledged as one of the most demanding trainings in the U.S. military.

BUD/S is designed to assess and select service members equipped to deal with the physical and psychological challenges that SEALs face in their careers. Ledford's research team looked to examine growth, which they refer to as "change in a beneficial direction," in both psychological characteristics and physiological markers of stress commonly associated with some psychological characteristics.

For psychological characteristics (resilience, hardiness, and grit), growth refers to an increase in the respective characteristic. Resilience, hardiness, and grit are measured using key diagnostic tools like the Connor-Davidson Resilience Scale, the 15-item Dispositional Resilience Scale, and Duckworth's Grit Scale. Answers were self-reported by the participants. For physiological characteristics they used blood tests.

For physiological markers, growth can refer to a change in biomarker concentration that leads to a favorable adaptation to stress by either increasing or decreasing the biomarker. For example, a detectable decrease in cortisol with repeated exposure to the same stressor may indicate stress habituation and thus is considered growth.

Generally, in the presence of a perceived threat, the brain secretes cortisol and dehydroepiandrosterone (DHEA). DHEA modulates the effects of cortisol by providing neuro-protective and anti-inflammatory effects, including stimulation of neural stem cells and enhancement of immune cell production. As a result, the ratio of DHEA to cortisol is often used to represent the balance between anabolic and catabolic processes. Previous research suggested that intense military training can have a negative impact on circulating biomarkers, though some studies uncovered potentially favorable neuroendocrine adaptations that indicated physiological growth (i.e., improvement) can occur during these scenarios.

Ledford's researchers found that, on average, self-reported resilience and hardiness grew throughout BUD/S despite initial declines after the start of training. On average, candidates experienced a steady growth in DHEA concentrations and in the DHEA-to-cortisol ratio, although considerable subject-to-subject variability was observed. The results demonstrate that the hardships experienced by candidates during BUD/S can elicit modest growth in self-reported resilience and hardiness, as well as some physiological adaptations to stress.

In other words, stress can be beneficial for the long-term growth of a team's tangible capabilities as well as hardiness, resilience, and grit. But the impact of stressors varies wildly from team member to team member, and are materially influenced by variables like personality, leadership skills, and the circumstances of the challenge. Even in the near term, stress may have a detrimental effect on a team's psychological and physiological well-being. But, like the SEALS who overcame the initial challenge of the BUD/S program, the challenges laid the foundation for positive growth.

The same principle that motivates Navy SEALs to develop more resilience as individuals and teams is in play in business. Stress can create near-term challenges, but resilient organizations and leaders become stronger in the end. The resilience becomes cultural, which in turn, supercharges productivity. This is why the Navy SEAL ethos includes the statement, "I am never out of the fight."

Let's return to Best Buy as a corporate case study. The company remains resilient in the face of serious market challenges. Almost a decade before the pandemic, Best Buy's sales were so sluggish that its decline had become a late-night TV punchline—a type of branding no company wants. That's when Hubert Joly took over as CEO and set out to learn what differentiated Best Buy from Amazon and other stores.

After meeting with frontline workers at various locations, he discovered one of the biggest problems: when customers found a product they liked in the store, they talked to the sales personnel about it and then left to buy it online for less.

Hubert saw the solution in the problem; it was the showroom itself—the ability to see physical products and talk to real, human tech experts—that set Best Buy apart from everyone else. To capitalize on this value, Best Buy offered price-matching so customers knew they could buy the product from the show-room at the same price as online sellers. Hubert also learned his employees felt overwhelmed by the company's 50-plus key performance indicators (KPIs), which caused confusion, stress, and underperformance. So, Hubert decluttered the KPIs to only two: (1) increase revenue and (2) increase margins. That way, every employee in the company knows what to focus on.

Those changes helped Best Buy stay afloat at a time when many other brick-and-mortar corporations were sinking. Remember Radio Shack? But Best Buy's showroom and employee morale weren't enough to rebuild the entire brand. Hubert knew they also needed purpose.

When asked what motivated them to do the company's work, most work-ers said they were motivated by their families, friends, communities, or favorite charities. That's when Hubert realized Best Buy was not actually in the business of selling phones, computers, or other gadgets—they were in the business of enriching lives through technology. So, he established dozens of Teen Tech Centers in cities around the country to provide cutting-edge technology as well as mentors and career coaching where resources were otherwise limited.

When Corie Barry took up the helm after Hubert, she continued building Best Buy's brand by committing more than $44 million over five years toward inclusive community-building efforts. That plan included goals for recruiting, hiring, and retaining employees and expanding opportunities for youth across the country.

Under Hubert's and then Corie's leadership, Best Buy bolstered productiv-ity and increased revenue and margins year after year by leaning into tried-and-true elements of its brand that customers knew they could trust. In this way, Best Buy became resilient through turbulent times.

Generational Demands for Values

A survey in 2023 found 87% of Gen Z professionals would be prepared to quit their jobs to work elsewhere if the values of the new company were more closely aligned with theirs. Millennials were not far behind. When exploring whether to move to a new job or company, 60% of Millennials and Gen Zers said values could be a dealbreaker. Josh Graff, managing director for EMEA and LATAM at LinkedIn, told CNBC that "[y]ounger generations, in particular, want to work for companies where they can, where they can evoke change where they can make a difference."[7] Graff would go on to conclude that values will be a survival issue for companies over the next decade.

A career is great, but advancement, job satisfaction, work-life balance, and making a difference in the community are part in parcel of the bargain for long-term labor. Today, reliability is a two-way street where both employee and employer are seeking loyalty from each other. This is a threshold consideration, and productivity follows thereafter. For many, even submitting an application hinges on the organization's reputation based on personal conversations and social media. The Coca-Cola Company, for example, has been around for well over a hundred years and continues to be one of the most highly selective employers in the world because it's not just a beverage company—it's a *lifestyle* company. The timeless Coca-Cola logo evokes quality, reliability, and value. The company's biggest asset is not its assorted beverages but rather its brand, which has become well-known for lived values and community investment.

Tomorrow will be more important than ever to take control of your brand. Whether climbing the corporate ladder as a professional or promoting an organization within a community, building a reputation on trustworthiness and reliability will pay dividends in the long run. It will unlock productivity and attract talent. And not only does a strong personal brand give us greater visibility and influence within our organization and community, but it also helps us to distinguish ourselves from the competition and move up the leadership power curve.

By consistently demonstrating our expertise, professionalism, and integrity, we can establish ourselves as an asset to any team we work with, and any community that we serve. So, take time to reflect on your brand. Though business consultants focus on productivity, urging executives to move up the economic power curve by improving production, the conscientious executive understands that the analogous leadership requirement to achieve that end is a quality and reliable reputation.

15

Virtuous Cycles

Trapped, John Harvey found himself in a pickle. He was sinking deeper and all attempts to surface failed. A sense of dread set in. The bulkheads permuted as water pressed against the hull with increasing force.

Engines were pushed to the limit to no avail. The weight of the sea was too much, and the craft began to sink faster. A crewman got on the radio and alerted a nearby vessel, screaming, "Have position up angle . . . Attempting to blow up."

The descent continued. The crew began feeling the increased pressure on their bodies, squeezing from all sides. The metal walls groaned and creaked in protest. Some crew members began to pray. Others frantically tried to stop the descent, but it was too late. Water breached the hull. Panic spread through the submarine as the gravity of the situation finally reached consensus.

And then, it was all over. A loud thump and violent shake were coda to a horrendous disaster.

The *USS Thresher* was a nuclear-powered attack submarine of the U.S. Navy. Commissioned in 1961, it was one of the most technologically advanced submarines, designed to be faster, quieter, and more maneuverable than any other submarine in the Navy at the time. It was designed to operate at depths of up to 1,300 feet and was capable of diving even deeper if necessary.

But in April 1963, the *Thresher*, its commander John Harvey, and 130 officers, enlisted men, and civilians, experienced a catastrophic failure and unexpectedly imploded under the titanic pressures of the ocean. There were no survivors.

So, what went wrong? How did a modern marvel of engineering suddenly sink to the bottom of the Atlantic Ocean?

The Department of Defense is unsurprisingly cagey about explaining what truly happens when disasters like this occur, but the Navy officially disclosed that improperly welded piping ruptured, causing a leak that eventually shorted out the ship's electrical systems. Additionally, the quality assurance processes during the manufacturing of the submarine failed to catch the defect.

The loss of the *Thresher* forced major improvements in the design and quality control of submarines. Twenty-five years later, in 1988, Vice Admiral Bruce DeMars, the Navy's chief submarine officer, said "[t]he loss of *Thresher* initiated fundamental changes in the way we do business—changes in design, construction, inspections, safety checks, tests, and more. We have not forgotten the lessons learned. It's a much safer submarine force today."[1]

The Subsafe program was the Navy's response to the *Thresher* catastrophe. This unique safety protocol demands robust design, testing, and documentation standards to be met for critical systems like hulls, valves, and electrical components on both new submarines as well as those undergoing maintenance or repair. There are stringent procedures requiring approval from a dedicated board before any modification can take place; it's no surprise that there has not been a similar catastrophic event involving a U.S. submarine since its inception more than six decades ago. In fact, this revolutionary standard has been adopted around the world by other industries seeking greater levels of security and resilience. The key to achieving this extraordinary record of safety is the virtuous cycle at the heart of Subsafe.

A virtuous cycle is a self-sustaining success loop, where good actions and results lead to even more positive outcomes. This creates an accelerating pattern of improvement that can drive impressive returns in the long run. It stands in contrast to a vicious cycle, which consists of negative feedback loops that produce increasingly damaging results over time.

Subsafe is a shining example of how feedback and experience can be used to continuously improve. Through the practice of collecting feedback from real operations to inform improvement efforts in tandem with strict enforcement protocols, a virtuous cycle is constructed along all points of submarine construction, operation, and refit. This ensures all Navy submarines increase in reliability over time.

During my time overseeing the airline's legal compliance with federal oversight agencies (FAA, TSA, NTSB, etc.), the deployment of virtuous cycles was fundamental to the culture of compliance that made our airline the safest cargo airline in the world from the transport of hazardous materials and dangerous goods to incident response.

The most successful organizations in the world build virtuous cycles. The Navy SEALs, for example, recognize learning as an integral part of life, a maxim exemplified by their ethos: "My training is never complete." This idea encourages SEALs to accept their mistakes and grow from them because failure can act as fuel for success if we take in stride the lessons gained from them. A culture of constant brief and debrief is established out of this virtue. In many ways, the sacrifice made by the crew of the *Thresher* is the foundation of a cycle of safety that continues to save lives to this very day. The Navy could have stopped growing its submarine fleet altogether until better fault detection technology was developed, but that would've been the slow death of many operations performed by elite units like the Navy SEALs, which often launch operations from submarines.

"When you stop growing you start dying," former UPS CEO Carol Tome was fond of saying when reinforcing the need to create virtuous cycles in all parts of our business. Public companies face the dilemma of growth or death; in this duality, success is characterized by a continuous string of good decisions resulting in better results year over year. Failure to demonstrate consistent growth can result in violent swings in share price. This swift punishment from Wall Street, which ultimately affects executive compensation, exposes the journey for every executive. We are subject to the tyranny of the growth dilemma.

Corporate life is therefore nothing more than an endless stream of opportunities and choices to either grow or die. But all too often, leaders think of their decisions solely in economic terms (from quarter to quarter). In actuality, the duality spans across an indefinite period of time. A smart, near-term economic decision could be a poor social one, and the resulting consequences a precursor to long-term failure. Similarly, decisions about who is advanced within an organization are as important as the marketing story describing "who we are" as an organization. Companies whose marketing fails to align with reality are often the most cringey to Millennials; cue the all-male executive leadership team discussing "our values support inclusion."

Conscientious executives focus on building continuous cycles of improvement; rather than saying, "We have to hit this quarterly target," they say, "We are moving in this direction," and "These milestones reflect progress because . . ."

For legal professionals, the practice of law is an ever-evolving journey. Laws change constantly, and so must one's expertise in those changes. The practice of leadership is just as challenging as the practice of law. It's a cycle, hopefully a virtuous one, that allows us to continue learning and improving skills. Each new job, company, or team member has forced me to adapt and grow as a leader—as has every setback. This journey requires constant self-reflection and

Table 15.1 Power curve comparison.

Moves That Matter	
Economic Power Curve	**Leadership Power Curve**
1 Programmatic Mergers and Acquisitions	Dynamic Omnidirectional Relationship Investment
2 Strong Capital Expenditure	Human Capital Investment
3 Dynamic Reallocation of Resources	Habitat Discordance
4 Improvements in Differentiation	The Maximization Default
5 Strong Productivity Program	A Reliable Brand

dedication to personal growth. Being a conscientious executive is not just about mastering a craft. It's about how we lead ourselves and others through change.

The moves that matter on your journey up the leadership power curve that I've described throughout this book cannot be mastered—only refined along your journey. Use these moves alongside economic strategy to achieve the best results for your business and professional journey. Table 15.1 compares the moves that matter to the strategic power curve of economic profit and the more tactical leadership power curve.

Organizational Improvement

Just like people, organizations go through developmental stages. The largest companies generally begin as a private enterprise, go through a trial-and-error period, gain experience and knowledge, and finally create a sustainable pathway as a public company. It was 92 years before UPS transitioned from private to public.

Public companies are managed very differently than private ones—and are tested by investors in unique ways. For most new companies, the transition is new terrain with a host of new regulations and relationships, not to mention heightened scrutiny and pressure. The key is to not let these obstacles define the trajectory of a company's future. The story that is written will be less about the company and more about you. It's really about you and the people you invite into leadership with you. When conscientious leaders focus on building virtuous cycles, which entails a commitment to continuous learning, growth, and perseverance, they then write the next chapter in corporate success like Best Buy and Costco. They faced their own share of challenges in their day-to-day operations, but their unwavering commitment allowed them to surpass these hurdles and ultimately achieve monumental success.

Communities and Virtuous Cycles

India struggled with depleting groundwater for decades due to deforestation, agriculture use, industrial use, and other activities. So, when the Coca-Cola Company wanted to do business there, the Indian government expressed concern about the amount of water the company would use. Rather than fight the government or go somewhere else, Coke's leaders thought about their vision, which is "to craft the brands and choice of drinks that people love, to refresh them in body & spirit," and to do it "in ways that create a more sustainable business and better shared future that makes a difference in people's lives, communities and our planet."[2] With this North Star, Coke moved forward hand in hand with local Indian leaders to do business responsibly.

The company captured rainwater and monsoon runoff, built dams, optimized water usage with technology, and reused water in secondary applications such as cleaning, gardening, and cooling towers. They collaborated with non-governmental organizations, local authorities, and communities to implement various groundwater replenishment projects, such as restoring ponds and other natural water bodies.

Thanks to those efforts in India, Coca-Cola became the first Fortune 500 company to replenish 100% of the water it uses and treat 100% of its wastewater to support aquatic life. Incredibly, it met its water neutral commitment five years ahead of schedule. And it cracked a code that so many companies were confounded by, namely, how to enter and thrive in the Indian market.

Even so, Coca-Cola leaders say achieving that goal wasn't the finish line, because they are committed to continuously supporting local communities and the environment.

The corporation is a perpetual existence in which people's ideas, processes, methods, and creativity can live on forever—and should be interconnected with the broader community's virtuous cycle of improvement.

It's a Journey

Producer and TV host Steve Harvey insightfully highlights that our mind has two hemispheres: one positive and the other negative. Steve jovially notes that when we wake up in the morning, we think, "I woke up on the wrong side of the bed. I'm tired. I wish I didn't have to go to work today." Those negative-hemispheric thoughts can cloud the rest of our day. If we instead wake up and say, "It's a nice day. I'm glad to be alive. I'm glad to have a job. I'm going to have a great day,"[3] we set our day up for exactly that. It's no secret that our mind manifests our direction with positive or negative energy—and that energy impacts those around us.

As leaders, our energy and direction have an especially profound impact on our teams and our communities. Polish American psychologist Solomon Asch, studied Nazi propaganda, and proved its correlation to anti-Semitism with the Asch Conformity Experiments he conducted throughout the 1950s.[4]

Asch had a group of people look at one line on a piece of paper and then compare it to three other lines of varying lengths on a separate paper.[5] Participants were to choose the line in the series that correctly matched the length of the first line, write down their choice, and then verbally share it with the rest of their group. Each group repeated the exercise a dozen times. Participants thought they were taking a vision test.

In truth, only one person in each group was a test subject—the others were secretly working with Dr. Asch.

For the first few exercises, all the participants chose the correct answer. After a while, however, the participants working with Dr. Asch picked different answers.

Imagine being in a group in which everyone thinks one line matches when you clearly see it doesn't. After a while you might wonder, "What's wrong with them? What's wrong with me? Am I seeing this right?"

The test subjects in each group wrote down the correct line 99% of the time. Yet after the group shared their answers aloud, 75% of them changed their answers to follow the group at least once. Because the crowd conflicted with their own views, the test subjects' bias tilted more toward the group even when they felt the group was wrong.

These and other experiments demonstrate what history has repeatedly proven: people tend to modify their thoughts and behaviors to be socially accepted and will obey leaders they admire, or feel are powerful, even against their own better judgments.

Those results add even more weight to how we practice our leadership. If we do not stay in a virtuous cycle, matters can easily deteriorate into an equally strong unprofitable or unvirtuous one.

Increasing Returns

Most people probably wouldn't think to reinvent the sock—nor would most corporate leaders think about giving away half their products for free. But after learning from the Salvation Army that socks are the most requested item at homeless shelters, Randy Goldberg and David Heath were inspired to create a company that did just that.

Following the model of TOMS shoes and Warby Parker eyeglasses—which donated one pair for every pair purchased—Randy and David spent two years researching and designing a quality sock that matched their altruism.

But when they pitched their idea on *Shark Tank* in 2014, only one investor was interested. The rest didn't think a business model that donated half its product would be profitable. They weren't willing to accept the new meta.

Six years later, Bombas Socks had donated more than 20 million pairs of socks and exceeded $100 million in yearly revenue. Advertising its philanthropy together with its new-and-improved sock design worked. Its North Star—giving socks to people in shelters—didn't take away from its founders' ultimate goal of making a profit. It enhanced it.

The core idea of a sustainable business is not to generate income. It's to increase returns for all stakeholders.

I didn't fully appreciate that when I was younger. One company I worked at produced record revenue quarter over quarter—but then our stock price would tumble, and I could not understand why.

Over time I realized the stock market saw a bigger picture. We were growing revenue, but our costs were unsustainable—we were chasing volume over profit.

But when the company later changed priorities and the stock price started going up each quarter, I was so traumatized by the previous stock dives that I behaved according to an old meta. Because I kept selling my stock after each earnings call, I missed out on that growth! Energy, be it negative or positive, can create its own cycle. In a power curve model (economic and leadership), the top and bottom quintiles accelerate steeply in either direction (upward or downward). Recall, the economic power curve is steep at the extreme ends. This is because alignment in a vicious or virtuous cycle is self-reinforcing.

Giving Back

My love for the Atlanta community is partly rooted in all the ways I see the business community here giving back to the local community. Companies like the Atlanta Falcons Football Club, Chick-fil-A, Delta Air Lines, Equifax, Georgia Power Company, Home Depot, and Waffle House give large contributions to local communities through their foundations, and the city repays them in spades by supporting their products and services and providing labor from the workforce.

While many leaders once saw charitable giving as an afterthought or a way to boost public relations, it's an important market in its own right. Atlanta is one of the fastest-growing metro areas in the United States, with a population of just over 5 million and nearly 200,000 businesses, including Fortune 500 and 1,000 companies. There's no doubt in my mind that corporate charitable contributions are a big reason why Atlanta is such an attractive place to live.

There's also no doubt that giving back can make areas like Walterboro, South Carolina, thrive as well. Your call to action as a conscientious leader is to discover ways to spread the riches and be a stabilizing influence on forgotten places and people.

Take Action Locally

Dr. Hilary King is associate professor of anthropology at my alma mater, Emory University. She inserts herself into communities all over the world to research how they create organic connections, and how those connections affect our role as community members. She also supports fair trade and farmers' markets, including the Global Growers Network (GGN).

GGN is a fascinating organization. It connects legal refugees from agrarian backgrounds to both farmland and farmers' markets in and around Atlanta. They grow much of the same produce they used to grow in their homelands, along with some local favorites, and then sell it at the weekly GGN fresh produce markets. Dr. King set up several of these markets at various public transit stations, which not only created a new market for the refugee farmers but also increased access to fresh, healthy, organic, local, and ethnic produce in some of the city's poorest neighborhoods—areas generally lacking fresh food and overall commerce. The transit stations are easily accessible for those customers, who often lack adequate transportation.

I first met Dr. King when we worked together as LEAD Atlanta fellows, and I was so impressed by GGN that I encouraged UPS to sponsor them, which it did for several years. With each investment, we made a difference for refugee farmers and low-income families in and around where I live. Other companies can support good work like what GGN does. You, too, can make a difference by merely vocalizing the opportunity to address a need.

Tomorrow Is Now

After George Floyd's death, I recognized the only way I could live a life worthy of a legacy for my daughter was to walk as the man I truly am both inside and outside of corporate America. There's no point in living inauthentically just to gain the approval of people who might not care about my family or community. America's emerging generations have clearly made the same calculation.

Today we are seeing the compounded impacts from decades of corporate decisions that didn't adequately consider community needs or concerns. A widening wealth gap further separates workers from corporate leaders and the investor class, which has galvanized social movements amid a radicalizing political divide. A watershed year for the country and the world, 2020, opened my eyes to the difficulties and challenges we have in corporate America, whether we want to face them or not. On top of a pandemic, a global supply shortage, and chaotic politics, climate change is upon us and creating more disasters and, as a result, more inequalities. All that has led many people to pessimism and the sense we're in a state of decline.

Now as a parent, however, I don't have the luxury of believing that our better days are behind us. As the old saying goes, "The best way to predict the future is to choose it." Conscientious leaders don't succumb to the fatalist. They lead others and the community to a better future. That's the legacy I hope to leave.

America is not in decline. The free market need not be supplanted wholesale. Corporations can have a tremendously positive impact on societies. We just need leaders who are bold enough to go in the direction of sustainable growth and shared prosperity. We *can* fix the problems in our communities—if we choose to do so.

As I write this, Ford Motor Company is planning two massive electric vehicle manufacturing plants in Tennessee and Kentucky, one of which will be the largest auto manufacturing site in U.S. history. It will employ approximately 11,000 people in communities struggling from the decline of the coal industry, once a major employer.

The greater business community plans to support Ford's innovation with two battery manufacturing plants and an electric vehicle fast-charging network across the region.

The path to a better future is happening—but it's a much more difficult journey to traverse than the old corporate meta is capable of making. There will be difficult quarters and lots of investment between here and there. Some Wall Street analysts will dislike the capex in labor, taxes, and infrastructure. But hiding under the guise of power and wealth won't go as far as it used to. And, eventually, balance will be restored in a market that will inspire new generations to fully embrace our free market system. We can choose this better future by choosing the right leaders. The question is, what part will you play? I hope you will join me in making the five moves that matter to move up the leadership power curve and commit to being a conscientious leader.

It's time to level up.

Notes

Introduction

1. Rivera, R. and Bean, R. (2021). Woman killed, firefighter suffers burns in Colleton County house fire. WCSC (9 February). https://www.live5news.com/2021/02/09/house-fire-kills-colleton-co/.
2. Brice Herndon Funeral Home. (2021). Wilhelmina "Meme" Young Nesbitt, Walterboro Live (15 February). https://walterborolive.com/stories/wilhelmina-meme-young-nesbitt,33663.
3. UPS. (2021). UPS surpasses one billion COVID-19 vaccine delivery milestone, continues to deliver hope around the world. Press release (14 December). https://about.ups.com/us/en/newsroom/press-releases/customer-first/vaccine-milestone-press-release.html.
4. Landier, M. (2022). U.K. heat wave, *The New York Times* (20 July). https://www.nytimes.com/live/2022/07/19/world/uk-europe-heat-fires-weather#:~:text=Britain%20recorded%20a%20temperature%20of,the%20United%20Kingdom%20if%20confirmed.
5. Acevedo, S., Mrkaic, M., Pugacheva, E., and Topalova, P. (2017). The unequal burden of rising temperatures. IMF Blog (27 September). https://blogs.imf.org/2017/09/27/the-unequal-burden-of-rising-temperatures-how-can-low-income-countries-cope/.

Chapter 1

1. Moss, T. and Pisa, M. (2021). Bitcoin mining is bad for the world: The limited options for addressing the problem. Center for Global Development (12 April).

https://www.cgdev.org/blog/bitcoin-mining-bad-world-limited-options-addressing-problem.

2. Ringquist, J., Phillips, T., Renner, B., et al. (2016). Capitalizing on the shifting consumer food value equation. Deloitte. https://www2.deloitte.com/us/en/pages/consumer-business/articles/us-food-industry-consumer-trends-report.html.

Chapter 2

1. Wilmot, M.P. and Ones, D.S. (2019). A century of research on conscientiousness at work. *Proceedings of the National Academy of Sciences of United States of America* 116 (46): 23004–23010. https://pubmed.ncbi.nlm.nih.gov/31666330/.

2. Power, R.A. and Pluess, M. (2015). Heritability estimates of the big five personality traits based on common genetic variants. *Translational Psychiatry* 5 (7). https://doi.org/10.1038/tp.2015.96.

3. Hill, P.L., Turiano, N.A., Hurd, M.D., et al. (2011). Conscientiousness and longevity: An examination of possible mediators. *Health Psychology* 30 (5): 536–41. https://doi.org/10.1037/a0023859.

4. Hoff, K.A., Einarsdóttir, S. Chu, C., et al. (2020). Personality changes predict early career outcomes: Discovery and replication in 12-year longitudinal studies. *Psychological Science* 32 (1): 64–79. https://doi.org/10.1177/0956797620957998.

5. Casserly, M. (2010). Ten archetypes of a terrible boss. *Forbes* (21 September). https://www.forbes.com/sites/meghancasserly/2010/09/21/ten-archetypes-of-a-terrible-boss/?sh=2fc358145f8a.

6. Leswing, K. (2023). CEO Tim Cook says layoffs are a "last resort" and not something Apple is considering right now. CNBC (4 May). https://www.cnbc.com/2023/05/04/apple-layoffs-are-a-last-resort-tim-cook-says.html

7. Haidt, J. (2013). *The Righteous Mind: Why Good People Are Divided by Politics and Religion.* New York: Penguin Books.

8. Edelman. (2020). 2020 Edelman trust barometer (19 January). https://www.edelman.com/trust/2022-trust-barometer.

9. James, E. (2023). Erika James on LinkedIn. https://www.linkedin.com/posts/erikajames_beyondbusiness-businessanalytics-sportsanalytics-activity-7025492759041986560-FJdB/?originalSubdomain=bn

10. CNN Transcripts. (2021, March 29). Covid war: The pandemic doctors speak out. CNN. http://www.cnn.com/TRANSCRIPTS/2103/29/nday.01.html

11. Matlin, M.W. and Stang, D.J. (1978). *The Pollyanna Principle. Selectivity in Language, Memory, and Thought.* Cambridge, MA: Schenkman.

12. Dember, W.N. and Penwell, L. (1980). Happiness, depression, and the Pollyanna principle. *Bulletin of the Psychonomic Society* 15 (5): 321–323.
13. Wooldridge, A. (2022). Young Americans aren't as woke as you think. Center for the Study of Capitalism (23 August). https://capitalism.wfu.edu/news/young-americans-arent-as-woke-as-you-think/.
14. Elson, C. and King, K. (2022). Views of democracy, egalitarianism and capitalism among millennials and gen Zs. Wake Forest University (1 April). https://capitalism.wfu.edu/wp-content/uploads/2022/05/WFU_CSC_Research-Report_Apr22.pdf.
15. U.S. Bureau of Labor Statistics. (2020). Occupational employment and wages in state and local government. https://www.bls.gov/spotlight/2021/occupational-employment-and-wages-in-state-and-local-government/home.htm.
16. Saad, L. (2023). Americans still glum about state of the union in most areas. Gallup (2 February).
17. Weise, K. and Scheiber, N. (2021). Why Amazon workers sided with the company over a union. *The New York Times* (26 October). https://www.nytimes.com/2021/04/16/technology/amazon-workers-against-union.html.
18. Amazon. (2020). Price gouging has no place in our stores (23 March). https://www.aboutamazon.com/news/company-news/price-gouging-has-no-place-in-our-stores.
19. Edelman. 2020 Edelman trust barometer.
20. *Citizens United v. Federal Election Comm'n*, 558 U.S. 310, (2010).

Chapter 3

1. Azhar, A. (2021). *The Exponential Age*. New York: Diversion Books.
2. Machado, J. (2020). What it's like to live through the Australian bushfires. Vox (24 January). https://www.vox.com/2020/1/24/21063638/australian-bushfires-2019-experience.
3. McAndrew, J. (2020). New poll: Young people energized for unprecedented 2020 election. *Tufts Now* (30 June). https://now.tufts.edu/2020/06/30/new-poll-young-people-energized-unprecedented-2020-election.
4. Taylor, C. (2022). Boycott nation: How Americans are boycotting companies now. Reuters (29 June). https://www.reuters.com/markets/us/boycott-nation-how-americans-are-boycotting-companies-now-2022-06-29/.
5. Cooper, A. (2019). Adapting for the future: 5 strategies for successfully incorporating millennials. *Longitudes* (21 November).

6. Loeb, W. (2021, May 27). Best Buy first quarter gain of 37.2% comparable sales is a winner. *Forbes*. https://www.forbes.com/sites/walterloeb/2021/05/27/best-buy-1st-quarter-gain-of-372-comparable-sales-is-a-winner/?sh=447b1cd76136.

7. Linnane, C. (2018). Nike's online sales jumped 31% after company unveiled Kaepernick campaign, data show. *MarketWatch* (17 September), https://www.marketwatch.com/story/nikes-online-sales-jumped-31-after-company-unveiled-kaepernick-campaign-2018-09-07.

8. Brizek, M.G., Partlow, C.G., and Nguyen, L. "A.". (2007). S. Truett Cathy: From young Entrepreneur to a foodservice industry leader. *Journal of Hospitality & Tourism Education* 19 (4): 7–10. https://people.umass.edu/~q4/0%200%20Profiles/Cathy_19-4.pdf.

9. Taylor, K. and Yuan, Y. (2019). How Chick-fil-A took over America, explained in charts. *Business Insider* (3 September). https://www.businessinsider.com/chick-fil-a-fast-food-domination-explained-charts-2019-8.

Chapter 4

1. Ballinger, J. (1992). The new free-trade heel: Nike's profits jump on the backs of Asian workers. *Harpers' Magazine* (August).

2. *Morgan et al. v. Board of Supervisors of Hanover County*, Va. 211021 (2023). https://www.vacourts.gov/opinions/opnscvwp/1211021.pdf.

3. Sinclair, C. (2021). CEO gets the last laugh after Fox News called him a "lunatic" for paying all employees $70K. *Boing Boing* (14 April). https://boingboing.net/2021/04/14/ceo-gets-the-last-laugh-after-fox-news-called-him-a-lunatic-for-paying-all-employees-70k.html.

4. Goldman, B. (2018). Scientists find fear, courage switches in brain. Stanford Medicine News Center (2 May). https://med.stanford.edu/news/all-news/2018/05/scientists-find-fear-courage-switches-in-brain.html.

5. Pymnts. (2022). From membership fees to $1.50 Hot dog combo, Costco holds firm on low prices (27 May). https://www.pymnts.com/news/retail/2022/from-membership-fees-to-1-50-hot-dog-combo-costco-holds-firm-on-low-prices/. Primary source earnings call available at https://investor.costco.com/news/default.aspx.

6. Payzan-Le Nestour, E. (2016). We are all gamblers at heart, but there is hope. TEDxSydney (15 June). https://www.youtube.com/watch?v=ZLvOt1zs6nM&t=1s.

7. Grant, A. (2021). *Think Again: The Power of Knowing What You Don't Know.* New York: Viking.
8. Levant, R. and Pryor, S. (2020). *The Tough Standard: The Hard Truths About Masculinity and Violence.* New York: Oxford University Press.

Chapter 5

1. Wood, W., Quinn, J.M., and Kashy, D.A. (2002). Habits in everyday life: Thought, emotion, and action. *Journal of Personality and Social Psychology* 83 (6): 1281–1297. https://doi.org/10.1037/0022-3514.83.6.1281.
2. McRaven, W. (2014). If you want to change the world, start off by making your bed. YouTube, uploaded by Motivation Inspiration, 24 June 2019, https://www.youtube.com/watch?v=NudLfyl2cXc.
3. Abraham, D. (2009). *The Price of Spring.* New York: Tor Books.
4. Pymnts. (2022). From membership fees to $1.50 Hot dog combo, Costco holds firm on low prices (27 May). https://www.pymnts.com/news/retail/2022/from-membership-fees-to-1-50-hot-dog-combo-costco-holds-firm-on-low-prices/. Primary source earnings call available at https://investor.costco.com/news/default.aspx.
5. Czarnecki, S. (2018). Delta CEO memo: We never endorsed the NRA. *PR Week* (21 May). https://www.prweek.com/article/1458500/delta-ceo-memo-endorsed-nra.
6. Isidore, C. (2021). Georgia-based companies face boycott calls over voting bill. CNN (1 April). https://www.cnn.com/2021/03/31/business/georgia-voting-law-prompts-calls-for-business-boycotts/index.html; Delta. (2021). Delta statement on SB202. Delta News Hub. Press release (26 March). https://web.archive.org/web/20230217204355/https://news.delta.com/delta-statement-sb202.
7. Hoffman, L. (2023.com/article/07/21/2023/on-the-record-with-ed-bastian.
8. Metwally, D., Ruiz-Palomino, P., Metwally, M., and Gartzia, L. (2019). How ethical leadership shapes employees' readiness to change: The mediating role of an organizational culture of effectiveness. *Frontiers in Psychology* 10. https://doi.org/10.3389/fpsyg.2019.02493.
9. Guo, K. (2022). The relationship between ethical leadership and employee job satisfaction: The mediating role of media richness and perceived organizational transparency. *Frontiers in Psychology* 13. https://doi.org/10.3389/fpsyg.2022.885515.

Chapter 6

1. U.S. Department of Commerce. (1971) Median family income up in 1970 (advance data from March 1971 current population survey). https://www.census.gov/library/publications/1971/demo/p60-78.html.

2. Candiloro, T. (2022). Housing prices vs. inflation: Why millennials can't afford homes. Anytime Estimate. https://anytimeestimate.com/research/housing-prices-vs-inflation/.

3. Horowitz, J.M., Igielnik, R., and Kochhar, R. (2020). 1. trends in income and wealth inequality. Pew Research Center (9 January). https://www.pewresearch.org/social-trends/2020/01/09/trends-in-income-and-wealth-inequality/.

4. Swaminathan, A. (2022). Average CEO pay is now 399 times more than a typical worker's wage—and one-third of that rise happened in the last three years. *MarketWatch* (4 October). https://www.marketwatch.com/story/average-ceo-pay-rose-11-in-2021-and-is-now-399-times-more-than-the-typical-workers-wages-11664895973.

5. Mishel, L. and Kandra, J. (2021). CEO pay has skyrocketed 1,322% since 1978: CEOS were paid 351 times as much as a typical worker in 2020. Economic Policy Institute (10 August). https://www.epi.org/publication/ceo-pay-in-2020/.

6. Miller, N.E. and Hart, G.L. (1948). *Motivation and reward in learning 1948 Yale University; psychology experiments.* YouTube. https://www.youtube.com/watch?v=QcbEJj-GzEU.

7. Myers, A.K. and Miller, N.E. (1954). Failure to find a learned drive based on hunger; evidence for learning motivated by "exploration." *Journal of Comparative and Physiological Psychology* 47 (6): 428–436. https://doi.org/10.1037/h0062664.

8. Reuters. (2022). U.S. productivity posts biggest ever annual drop in second quarter (9 August). https://www.reuters.com/markets/us/us-productivity-drops-second-quarter-annual-decline-largest-ever-2022-08-09/.

9. Smith, M. (2023). Workers are the unhappiest they've been in 3 years—and it can cost the global economy $8.8 trillion. CNBC (2 October). https://www.cnbc.com/2023/10/02/-employee-happiness-has-hit-a-3-year-low-new-research-shows.html.

10. Garton, E. and Mankins, M. (2015). Engaging your employees is good, but don't stop there. *Harvard Business Review* (9 December). https://hbr.org/2015/12/engaging-your-employees-is-good-but-dont-stop-there.

11. Vu, N.H., Nguyen, T.T., and Nguyen, H.T.H. (2021). Linking intrinsic motivation to employee creativity: The role of empowering leadership.

Journal of Asian Finance, Economics and Business 38 (3): 595–604, https://doi .org/10.13106/jafeb.2021.vol8.no3.0595.

Chapter 7

1. Bernheim, B., Ray, D., and Yeltekin, S. (2015). Poverty and self-control. *Econometrica* 83 (5): 1877–1911.
2. Duflo, E., Kremer, M., and Robinson, J. (2011). Nudging farmers to use fertilizer: Theory and experimental evidence from Kenya. *The American Economic Review* 101 (6): 2350–2390; Farah, M. and Hook, C. (2017). Trust and the poverty trap. *Proceedings of the National Academy of Sciences of the United States of America* 114 (21): 5327–5329.
3. Evans, G. (2016). Childhood poverty and adult psychological well-being. *Proceedings of the National Academy of Sciences of the United States of America* 113 (52): 14949–14952.
4. Haushofer, J. and Fehr, E. (2014). On the psychology of poverty. *Science* 344 (6186): 862–867.
5. Montanez, A. (2017). This is your brain on poverty. *Scientific American Mind* 28 (4): 13–16; Mani, A., Mulainathan, S., Shaifr, E., and Zhao, J. (2013). Poverty impedes cognitive function. *Science* 341 (6149): 976–980; Storrs, C., (2017). How poverty affects the brain, *Scientific American Mind* 18 (6): 19–24.
6. Appadurai, A. (2004). The capacity to aspire: Culture and the terms of recognition. In: *Culture and Public Action* (eds. V. Rao and M. Walton), pp. 59–84. Palo Alto, CA: Stanford University Press.
7. Small, M., Harding, D., and Lamont, M. (2010). Introduction: Reconsidering culture and poverty. *The Annals of the American Academy of Political and Social Science* 629: 6–27.
8. Macleod, J. (2008). *Ain't No Makin' It* (3rd ed.). New York: Routledge.
9. Congressional Budget Office. (2022). Trends in the distribution of family wealth, 1989 to 2019. https://www.cbo.gov/publication/58533.
10. Vance, J. (2018). *Hillbilly elegy: A Memoir of a Family and Culture in Crisis.* New York: Harper Paperbacks.
11. Moynihan, D. (1965). The Negro family: The case for national action. U.S. Department of Labor, Office of Policy Planning and Research.
12. Camfield, L., Masae, A., McGregor, J., and Promphaking, B. (2013). Cultures of aspiration and poverty? Aspirational inequalities in Northeast and Southern Thailand. *Social Indicators Research* 114 (3): 1049–1072.
13. Warikoo, N. (2011). *Balancing Acts: Youth Culture in the Global City.* Los Angeles: University of California Press

14. Kerner, D.A. and Thomas, J.S. (2014). Resilience attributes of social-ecological systems: Framing metrics for management. *Resources* 3 (4): 672–702. https://doi.org/10.3390/resources3040672.

15. Denchak, M. (2018). Flint water crisis: Everything you need to know. NRDC (8 November). https://www.nrdc.org/stories/flint-water-crisis-everything-you-need-know; Masten, S.J., Davies, S.H., and Mcelmurry, S.P. (2016). Flint water crisis: What happened and why? *Journal of American Water Works Association* 108 (12):22–34.https://www.ncbi.nlm.nih.gov/pmc/articles/PMC5353852/; Felton, R. (2016). How Flint traded safe drinking water for cost. *The Guardian* (23 January). https://www.theguardian.com/us-news/2016/jan/23/flint-water-crisis-cost-cutting-switch-water-supply; The Center for Michigan. (2016). Michigan truth squad: Who approved switch to Flint River? State's answers draw fouls. *Bridge Magazine* (21 January). https://www.mlive.com/politics/2016/01/michigan_truth_squad_who_appro.html.

Chapter 8

1. Farrugia, C. and Sanger J. (2017). *Gaining an employment edge: The impact of study abroad on 21st century skills & career prospects in the United States.* IIE Center for Academic Mobility Research and Impact (October). https://www.iie.org/wp-content/uploads/2022/12/Gaining-an-Employment-Edge-The-Impact-of-Study-Abroad.pdf.

2. Thurman, R.A.F. (1998). *Inner Revolution: Life, Liberty, and the Pursuit of Real Happiness.* New York: Riverhead Books.

3. Taft Comms. (2022). New poll: Attitudes on diversity in US workplaces show significant divisions by race, gender, political affiliation (15 March). https://www.taftcommunications.com/new-poll-attitudes-on-diversity-in-us-workplaces-show-significant-divisions-by-race-gender-political-affiliation/.

4. Centers for Disease Control and Prevention. (2020). Disability inclusion (16 September). https://www.cdc.gov/ncbddd/disabilityandhealth/disability-inclusion.html.

5. Ogushi, F., Kertesz, J., Kaski, K., and Shimada, T. (2017). Enhanced robustness of evolving open systems by the bidirectionality of interactions between elements. *Scientific Reports* 7: 6978. https://doi.org/10.1038/s41598-017-07283-9.

Chapter 9

1. Taft Comms. (2022). New poll: Attitudes on diversity in US workplaces show significant divisions by race, gender, political affiliation. (15 March).

https://www.taftcommunications.com/new-poll-attitudes-on-diversity-in-us-workplaces-show-significant-divisions-by-race-gender-political-affiliation/.

2. Treisman, P.M. (1985). *A study of the mathematics performance of Black students at University of California, Berkeley.* University of California, Berkeley.

3. Smit, S. (2019). How to make the bold strategy moves that matter. McKinsey & Company (6 December). https://www.mckinsey.com/capabilities/strategy-and-corporate-finance/our-insights/how-to-make-the-bold-strategy-moves-that-matter.

Chapter 10

1. Lovelace, B. (2018a, June 13). Steve Case to AT&T: Learn from my AOL-Time Warner failures. CNBC. https://www.cnbc.com/2018/06/13/steve-case-to-att-learn-from-my-aol-time-warner-failures.html.

2. Smit, S. (2019). How to make the bold strategy moves that matter. McKinsey & Company (6 December). https://www.mckinsey.com/capabilities/strategy-and-corporate-finance/our-insights/how-to-make-the-bold-strategy-moves-that-matter.

3. Cai, J. and Lian, R. (2022). Social support and a sense of purpose: The role of personal growth initiative and academic self-efficacy. *Frontiers in Psychology* 12: 788841. https://doi.org/10.3389/fpsyg.2021.788841.

4. CNN Transcripts. (2023, February 22). Outgoing Starbucks CEO talks nationwide unionization campaign. CNN (22 February). https://transcripts.cnn.com/show/ctmo/date/2023-02-22/segment/02.

Chapter 11

1. Hartnett, C.S. and Gemmill, A. (2020). Recent trends in U.S. childbearing intentions. *Demography* 57 (6): 2035–2045. https://doi.org/10.1007/s13524-020-00929-w.

2. Shameek Rakshit, McGough, M., Winger, A., et al. (2023). How has U.S. spending on healthcare changed over time? Peterson-KFF Health System Tracker (15 December). https://www.healthsystemtracker.org/chart-collection/u-s-spending-healthcare-changed-time/.

3. Smialek, J. and Casselman, B. (2022). In an unequal economy, the poor face inflation now and job loss later. *New York Times* (8 August). https://www.nytimes.com/2022/08/08/business/economy/inflation-jobs-economy.html.

4. Huler, S. and Bethune, G. (1999). *From Worst to First Behind the Scenes of Continental's Remarkable Comeback*. New York: Wiley.

5. Baer, J. (2021). The breakout cities on the forefront of America's economic recovery. *Wall Street Journal* (9 May). https://www.wsj.com/articles/the-breakout-cities-on-the-forefront-of-americas-economic-recovery-11620584178.

6. Dobis, E.A., Krumel, T.P., Cromartie, J., et al. (2021). *Rural America at a glance*. Economic Research Service. https://www.ers.usda.gov/webdocs/publications/102576/eib-230.pdf.

7. Kerlin, M., O'Farrell, N., Riley, R., and Schaff, R. (2022). Rural rising: Economic development strategies for America's heartland. McKinsey & Company (30 March). https://www.mckinsey.com/industries/public-sector/our-insights/rural-rising-economic-development-strategies-for-americas-heartland.

8. Tax Cuts and Jobs Act of 2017, Public Law 115-97.

9. Inflation Reduction Act of 2023, Public Law 117-169.

10. Carey, N. (2017). China regulator oks joint venture of UPS, SF holding. Reuters (28 September). https://www.reuters.com/article/us-united-parcel-sfholding-china/china-regulator-oks-joint-venture-of-ups-sf-holding-idUSKCN1C31TB.

11. Fonrougegab, G. (2022). Rising thefts at Walmart could lead to price jumps, store closures, CEO says. CNBC (6 December). https://www.cnbc.com/2022/12/06/walmart-ceo-says-shoplifting-could-lead-to-price-jumps-store-closures.html.

12. Nassauer, S. (2023). Walmart closing four stores in Chicago, citing years of losses. *Wall Street Journal* (12 April). https://www.wsj.com/articles/walmart-closing-four-stores-in-chicago-citing-years-of-losses-c302d730.

13. Bennett, N., Hays, D., and Sullivan, B. (2022, August 1). 2019 Data Show Baby Boomers nearly 9 times wealthier than millennials. U.S. Census Bureau. https://www.census.gov/library/stories/2022/08/wealth-inequality-by-household-type.html.

14. The Coca-Cola Company. (2022). For every drop of water we use, we give one back (23 August). https://www.coca-cola.com/ph/en/media-center/for-every-drop-of-water-we-use-we-give-one-back.

15. Daniel, W. (2023). 'We may be looking at the end of capitalism': One of the world's oldest and largest investment banks warns 'greedflation' has gone too far. *Fortune* (6 April). https://fortune.com/2023/04/05/end-of-capitalism-inflation-greedflation-societe-generale-corporate-profits/.

16. Harter, J.K., Schmidt, F., Agrawal, S., et al. (2022). Gallup Q12® meta-analysis. Gallup (7 June). https://www.gallup.com/workplace/321725/gallup-q12-meta-analysis-report.aspx.
17. Gesel, S.A., LeJeune, L.M., Chow, J.C., et al. (2020). A meta-analysis of the impact of professional development on teachers' knowledge, skill, and self-efficacy in data-based decision-making. *Journal of Learning Disabilities* 54 (4): 269–283. https://doi.org/10.1177/0022219420970196.

Chapter 12

1. Porter, M.E. and Nohria, N. (2021). How CEOS manage time. *Harvard Business Review* (8 July). https://hbr.org/2018/07/how-ceos-manage-time.; Bandiera, O., Hansen, S., Prat, A., and Sadun, R. (2017). *CEO behavior and firm performance*. NBER working paper. https://doi.org/10.3386/w23248.
2. Iyer, K.V. and V.S. Dole. (2021). Impact of advertising on educational apps used by children. *International Journal of Web-Based Learning and Teaching Technologies* 16 (6): 1–13. https://doi.org/10.4018/ijwltt.287097.
3. Ioannidis, J.P.A. (2015). Stealth research: Is biomedical innovation happening outside the peer-reviewed literature? *Journal of the American Medical Association* 313 (7): 663–664. doi:10.1001/jama.2014.17662.

Chapter 13

1. Reisinger, S. (2011). Blood brothers. *Corporate Counsel* (October). https://www.alston.com/files/docs/Blood%20Brothers.pdf.

Chapter 14

1. Blancaflor, S. and Briggs, E. (2023). The Taylor Swift fandom is white, suburban and leans Democratic. *Morning Consult Pro* (14 March). https://pro.morningconsult.com/instant-intel/taylor-swift-fandom-demographic.
2. Koretz, J. (2019). What happens when your career becomes your whole identity. *Harvard Business Review* (26 December). https://hbr.org/2019/12/what-happens-when-your-career-becomes-your-whole-identity.
3. William, S. (2023). The new corporate job is human. *Forbes* (26 April). https://www.forbes.com/sites/columbiabusinessschool/2023/04/26/the-new-corporate-job-is-human/?sh=5a548e5534dd.
4. *Clark v. Board of Directors* 24 Iowa 266 (1868), https://libguides.law.drake.edu/ld.php?content_id=39814115.

5. Frese, S.J. (2009). Clark, Alexander G. *The Biographical Dictionary of Iowa*. Iowa City, IA: University of Iowa Press. https://perma.cc/679A-BHHG.

6. Ledford, A.K., Beckner, M.E., Conkright, W.R., et al. (2022). Psychological and physiological changes during basic, underwater, demolition/SEAL training. *Physiology & Behavior* 257: 113970. https://doi.org/10.1016/j.physbeh.2022.113970.

7. Kiderlin, S. (2023). Overwhelming majority of gen Z workers would quit their jobs over company values, LinkedIn data says. CNBC (20 April). https://www.cnbc.com/2023/04/20/majority-of-gen-z-would-quit-their-jobs-over-company-values-linkedin.html.

Chapter 15

1. History.com Editors. (2024). Atomic submarine USS Thresher sinks in the Atlantic, killing all on board. History.com (9 April). https://www.history.com/this-day-in-history/atomic-submarine-sinks-in-atlantic.

2. The Coca-Cola Company. (n.d.). Purpose & Vision. https://www.coca-colacompany.com/about-us/purpose-and-vision.

3. Harvey, S. (2022). Wake up on the wrong side of the bed? *Motivational talks with Steve Harvey*. YouTube (6 October). https://www.youtube.com/watch?v=ZmnNi7SgSGc.

4. Cherry, K. (2021). Biography of psychologist Solomon Asch. Verywell Mind (24 April). https://www.verywellmind.com/solomon-asch-biography-2795519.

5. Mcleod, S. (2023). Solomon Asch conformity line experiment study. *Simply Psychology* (24 October). https://www.simplypsychology.org/asch-conformity.html.

Acknowledgments

There's an old saying that two are better than one because if one falls then the other can help them up. Three, they say, is even better than two because a three-fold cord is not easily broken. So clear is this truth that Helen Keller herself proclaimed "alone we can do so little; [t]ogether we can do so much." I therefore extend my gratitude to those whose influence, guidance, and mentorship have sculpted my perspective on business and leadership. Because of you, we are influencing millions and accomplishing much.

The seeds of this book took root nearly three decades ago, along a dusty South Carolina road, where my father, a lifelong marine and minister, instilled in me a wellspring of love for people. Our debates and discussions in that old Ford F150 are the foundation of my understanding of leadership, and for his enduring influence, I am grateful.

That old Ford stopped one day at an airport. I hopped out and onto a plane to test the principles we developed in the real world for myself. The plane landed in Washington DC. There, I wandered between Senator Ken Salazar's office on Capitol Hill and GW classrooms without a firm direction, as most youngsters do, but never without a firm foundation. One semester I stumbled upon transformative teachers who, like my father, fostered deep discussions about people and our responsibilities to them. Donna Minnich, my sociology professor, taught me the importance of applying scientific rigor to their stories, while Dr. Wally Mullin, my economics professor, taught me to discern patterns in the world through numbers. Together, these two intellectual giants helped to construct a framework for the leadership structure I would build. Thank you.

With the frame set on a solid foundation, I sought materials to build my career. And so, I flew south. While I played the role of graduate student during the day and dutiful employee at night, I searched for opportunities among

231

Atlanta's many companies. A chance encounter with Jennifer Manning at Coca-Cola, who fished my résumé from the bottom of a trash bin, and the guidance of the late Dinisa Folmar infused wisdom and love into my professional journey. These remarkable women equipped me with the words, tools, and customs of the world's greatest corporations. Their mentorship quite literally put a roof over my head and for that I am eternally grateful.

No edifice is complete without investing time and hard work to make what could just be walls and windows into a place with character and comfort. Professionally, that does not happen without context and experience gained from an invitation to learn and grow. I am grateful for the invitation to understand the character of so many corporations that have been my clients over the years like Microsoft, Cerner, Sprint, Coca-Cola, UPS, and Meta. To them, I am grateful. I am mindful, however, that the invitation was only given because of the willingness of so many partners at Shook, Hardy & Bacon to bring me along the way. I must acknowledge the indelible contributions of Chairman John Murphy, Leonard Searcy, Pat Lujin, Bill Sampson, Ryan Dykal, Clint Newton, and Bart Eppenauer to my leadership journey.

The true test of my theories came when I had the opportunity to lead at UPS Airlines. My heartfelt thanks go to colleagues Brendan Canavan, Houston Mills, Bill Moore, and Tracy Roberts, who entrusted me with responsibilities, shared the challenges of leadership, and weathered the storm of pandemic crisis management together.

Corporate leadership is a weighty responsibility, often fraught with challenges and politics. But, the effort to be a conscientious leader is made indefatigable with the love and support of a true partner. And so, to my partner, Amy, who picked me off the floor many nights while I pained over this or that, and to my daughter, Claudia, whose smile always enlivens my spirit, thank you. You are my rocks. Together, we will strive to inspire others in our small business and in corporate America to build a more ethical house, knowing that though the workers are few, the harvest is abundant.

About the Author

Andrew Cooper is an internationally recognized executive leader and apologist for compassionate business practices. He led as a history-making first Millennial and Black executive to serve as general counsel of UPS Airlines, the world's largest logistics airline with over 20,000 employees operating in 220 countries. Cooper's team was essential to the success of Operation Warp Speed, the United States's pandemic vaccine relief effort. Cooper helps organizations regain and retain high performance through leadership transformation. The *Ethical Imperative* is Cooper's first book.

To learn more about his work, visit andrew–cooper.com.

Index

238

Index